DAPAA

IPSITA CHAKRAVARTY

Dapaan

Tales from Kashmir's Conflict

HURST & COMPANY, LONDON

First published in the United Kingdom in 2025 by
C. Hurst & Co. (Publishers) Ltd.,
New Wing, Somerset House, Strand, London, WC2R 1LA
© Ipsita Chakravarty, 2025
All rights reserved.

Distributed in the United States, Canada and Latin America by
Oxford University Press, 198 Madison Avenue, New York,
NY 10016, United States of America.

The right of Ipsita Chakravarty to be identified as the author
of this publication is asserted by her in accordance with the
Copyright, Designs and Patents Act, 1988.

A Cataloguing-in-Publication data record for this book
is available from the British Library.

This book is printed using paper from registered sustainable
and managed sources.

ISBN: 9781805262916

www.hurstpublishers.com

CONTENTS

Introduction: The Storyteller's Tale   1

PART I
LAUGHING AT THE KING

1. *Zulm*   33
2. Crackdown *Paether*   51
3. You May Be Turned Into a Cat   79
4. The Buffoon King   89

PART II
POSSESSION

5. *Raantas*   109
6. The Steel *Daen*   117
7. The Braid Choppers   137
8. Ghosts in the Ground   151

PART III
LOSS

9. Singing Bodies   171
10. Melancholia   185

PART IV
BLOOD MAPS

11.	The Trials of Majnun	211
12.	Blood Towns	221
13.	Firdous Cinema	241
14.	Light and Dark	249
15.	The Afterlives of Land	255
	Conclusion: Dismemberment	273
	Acknowledgements	289
	Glossary & Abbreviations	293
	Notes	297
	Select Bibliography	313
	Index	317

INTRODUCTION

THE STORYTELLER'S TALE

His brother recorded the play when it was aired on Radio Kashmir, and they listened to it over and over again, so he knows it by heart. It was a Kashmiri play called *Myean Jigraki Daade Wath*, 'Let My Heart's Ache Lift'.

Two children grow up together. A boy who goes by the nickname Nika and an orphaned girl, a Kashmiri Pandit called Sahaba. As they grow older, they fall in love, but it will not do. Nika is sent away to study law and Sahaba is married off. Years pass. Nika also marries and has a daughter.

Then the story goes where all stories go in South Asian dramas. A fairground, so large, so teeming with people, so full of pleasure that nothing good can come of it. Both Nika and Sahaba end up at the same fair. Both are so careless as to lose their children in the crowd. The two children end up together while their parents draw nearer, calling out their names.

Here the storyteller stops, a catch in his voice. And what is the little girl's name? Sahaba. Nika has named her after his long lost love. 'Sahaba, Sahaba,' he calls out, looking for his daughter. And a different Sahaba turns around. The years fall away.

The years have fallen away, too, for the storyteller. He has not heard the radio play since the eighties. In his mind, the story of

DAPAAN

Sahaba and Nika is tangled with the jaunty notes of *Hawa Hawa*. The Pakistani singer Hasan Jahangir had come out with the hit number in 1987, and they had the audio cassette. They were still listening to it when everything changed. '*Haalaat kharaab hua*,' explained the storyteller, who is now a businessman in Srinagar, the summer capital of Indian-administered Jammu and Kashmir. *Haalaat kharaab hua*, conditions got bad. The police and the military started searches. You did not want to be caught with songs by Pakistani singers. So they buried the tapes. And with that, the other tape also disappeared, the story of heartache.

What else was lost? In houses across Kashmir, families were sorting through their things. Photographs of sons who had crossed over for arms training. Those had to be buried deep underground. Family photos of picnics and weddings where the sons were part of the group. Those had to go too, so that when the search parties came they could pretend the sons did not exist, had never existed. What else? Photographs of trekking in the mountains, because knowledge of mountain routes was suddenly suspect, proof of intention to go to the other side. What else? Pictures of Pakistani cricketers collected over the years. An Urdu sports magazine called *Akbar-e-Noujawan*, which often had pictures of Pakistani cricketers. A Pakistani novel about Partition. A collection of speeches by a religious preacher. What else? A pair of decorative swords. What else? Jokes, romances, tall tales told on winter nights.

All these were driven underground and, in the darkness, went through a reconfiguration in their elements, a derangement that could only have been worked by the '*haalaat*'. This is the word used in Kashmir to describe the time after 1989. *Haalaat*, conditions, which is to say militancy, militarisation, a geopolitical dispute, a freedom movement, but also something more. Something approaching atmospheric conditions, like the work of earth and water as they seep into buried photographs, twisting

INTRODUCTION

hands and faces. It is said, two things can change at any time in Kashmir, the weather and the *haalaat*.

The word '*haalaat*' is plural. This is how it is used when referring to the time after 1989. '*Haalat*', the singular form, does not quite cover the whole range of meanings and experiences required of the word. Long ago, it passed from Arabic into Hindi, Urdu and Kashmiri, where it acquired new lives. Over time, the *haalaat* have almost become a unit in Kashmir, a collective noun for all that cannot be named.

The *haalaat* may also be the story that Kashmiris tell of their lives since 1989. Sometimes, it seems to be just another one of the stories that Kashmiris have told for centuries. This is because *haalaat* stories often bear the storyteller's signature—the Kashmiri word '*dapaan*': it is said.

Folktales in Kashmir usually start with the word *dapaan*. It is said, a *djinn* once turned itself into a seven-legged beast that could not be killed, because if its blood fell to the ground, new *djinns* would sprout from each drop. It is said, the serpent prince turned himself human to be with a princess of the earthly realm. It is said, you must not answer the call of women whose feet are turned backward. These are stories of counsel, how to act or not to act when faced with the world.[1]

Oral histories in Kashmir, telling the story of an event, an individual or society in the distant past, also begin with '*dapaan*'.[2] The word makes a story sound authentic, even as it folds in myth with historical memory. Don't take it from me, the storyteller suggests; these are not my observations. This is what countless others have said before me, therefore it must be the truth.[3] There are advantages to the word *dapaan*, says an elderly history writer in Srinagar, because the storyteller refuses to take responsibility.

It is wise to put in caveats when talking about the *haalaat* because one word here or there could be the difference between life and death. It is said, there is a curfew so don't go out today.

DAPAAN

It is said, soldiers stormed the village last night and took away all the boys they could find. It is said, the taps of Srinagar are running with poisoned water—drink at your own peril. Stories of the *haalaat* are part fact, part rumour, part fever dream. That does not mean they cannot be true.

Stories are a way of knowing the world. A community is often defined by its shared stories. They start with 'experience which is passed on from mouth to mouth,' writes Walter Benjamin.[4] When a story is told, it becomes part of the listener's experience. To Benjamin, writing in the desolation of interwar Europe, it was a way of knowing that had lost value because people were no longer able to communicate their experiences.

The *haalaat* worked the opposite effect in Kashmir. Everyone was furiously telling stories of the strange conditions that had descended on their lives. Old stories were buried and then resurrected, somehow disfigured by the *haalaat*. New stories were found everywhere. These stories of experience knitted together the Kashmiri public, constituting its knowledge of the *haalaat*. This is a story about stories told in Kashmir.

Such stories could rarely travel outside because the fellowship of experiences passed on from mouth to mouth did not exist, certainly not in the mainstream Indian public. To this public, sealed off by its own mythologies, the experiences contained in *haalaat* stories were incommunicable.

Having lived and worked within this public, I doubt I understood them either. I had been a journalist in the national media, where Kashmir was mostly a security problem. While television channels played out lurid fantasies about Kashmir, the more dignified legacy media operated in the sphere of national interest. Even independent outlets, which tried to lend a sympathetic ear, had to keep to certain frameworks laid down by the state if they were to stay alive. Besides, some stories just weren't news.

So this was what brought me to the businessman's shop on a cold Srinagar afternoon, a heater blowing energetically at me

INTRODUCTION

while I drank sweet, milky tea. I was trying to listen better, to absorb his stories into my experience.

* * *

Where to begin? I could start with 1989. While *Hawa Hawa* was growing its fan club, armed rebellion was spreading in Kashmir. Hundreds of Kashmiri men were crossing the western frontier to learn how to shoot a gun and plant a bomb. They would return to use their new skills against the Indian state. In the next few years, their numbers would swell to thousands.

But that's not when it began. Official histories in India and Pakistan will tell you it started in 1947, when the two became separate nation states. Both claimed the entire region of Jammu and Kashmir, which sits astride the northern Himalayas as well as parts of the Karakoram mountain range. The two countries speak the language of a territorial dispute, deploying a series of anatomical metaphors perfected over the course of three border wars in the region—Kashmir is an 'integral part' of India and Pakistan's 'jugular vein'. Official histories of both nation states echo these working assumptions, which have filtered into their textbooks, media and respective public spheres.

Along with land, Indian and Pakistani histories were also partitioned after 1947. So, they offer rival stories about the roots of Kashmir's rebellion, how it may be defined, what its aims are. These official histories could also start with the caveat *'dapaan'*. It would gesture to a certain fluidity in the facts the two sides intend to marshal for their arguments, to the myths that surround their horizons, to the silences they cannot breach. But almost every official history is entrenched in its own certainties. Perhaps that is where war begins.

But that is not where it began, either. There is another strand of history writing, not official because it is not connected to any state. It traces the life of a *tehreek*, or movement, against political occupation. The aim of the *tehreek* is *azadi*, freedom, no matter what shape that takes. These are works by Kashmiris whom anthropologist Mohamad Junaid calls '*tehreek* history writers', not always professional historians but journalists, activists, politicians and former bureaucrats engaged in resisting official accounts.[5]

In these histories, the *tehreek* did not start in 1947 but in 1931 as Kashmiri Muslims rebelled against Maharaja Hari Singh, the Dogra ruler of the princely state of Jammu and Kashmir. It continued even after Hari Singh signed over his kingdom to the newly formed Indian Union. The original crime was the 'sale deed' of 1846, the Treaty of Amritsar, under which the British colonial administration had parcelled off Kashmir to the Dogra king of Jammu for seven and a half million rupees. The treaty granted the Hindu Dogras internal autonomy so long as they acknowledged British paramountcy.[6] They would spend the next century trying to ward off colonial interference.

Tehreek histories emphasise the plight of Muslim subjects under Dogra rule.[7] They speak of decades of discontent about land, faith, taxes, famines. This came to a head on 13 July 1931, when Dogra forces shot down Muslim protesters in Srinagar. The *tehreek* in these years was not so much anti-colonial as an anti-feudal movement directed at the maharaja. In 1942, crowds marching in the plains of India asked the British to 'Quit India'. In 1946, crowds in Kashmir asked Hari Singh to 'Quit Kashmir'.

According to Junaid, '1947 is thus traumatic not because any fundamental change in Kashmir's condition took place; it is traumatic because a singular possibility of freedom was forcibly taken as well as naively lost.'[8] In official Indian accounts, the border war of 1947 started because tribal raiders backed by the Pakistan Army rolled down the mountains of Kashmir, forcing the Indian Army to intervene. *Tehreek* history writers argue the conflict had started earlier, with armed rebellions within the Dogra state. In

INTRODUCTION

these histories, the Indian Army is not seen as a liberator. Instead, 'Indian forces invaded and annexed Kashmir', providing cover for the large-scale massacre of Muslims in Jammu.[9] Many sources suggest Dogra forces and Hindu nationalist militias were behind the killing spree.

The famously dithering Hari Singh was jolted into action as the raiders entered Kashmir's Baramulla district. He signed the Instrument of Accession in October 1947, attaching the princely state to the Indian Union. This was considered the legal imprimatur for Indian forces landing in Srinagar. But the legalities of this document are hotly contested: whether it was signed under duress; whether it was signed before Indian troops landed in Srinagar or after; whether it was predicated on the massacres and subsequent migrations that would turn Muslim-majority Jammu into a Hindu-majority province.

Either way, the border war of 1947–48 laid a ceasefire line through the former princely state of Jammu and Kashmir, dividing it into Indian-controlled and Pakistan-controlled sectors. *Tehreek* histories often dwell on a promise made by Jawaharlal Nehru, the first prime minister of independent India. Didn't Nehru stand in Lal Chowk, Srinagar's very own Red Square, and tell Kashmiris they could choose their political future in a plebiscite? And wasn't this exercise in self-determination to be monitored, not by India or Pakistan, but by a neutral authority, the United Nations? Political leaders of the *tehreek* have made the eternally deferred plebiscite part of their charter of demands.

The *tehreek*'s history writers have also puzzled at length about the calculations of Sher-e-Kashmir, the Lion of Kashmir, Sheikh Abdullah.[10] He had led the Kashmiri agitations since 1931. By the late thirties, however, he had drifted closer to Nehru and the Indian National Congress, and farther away from party colleagues who were drawn to the two-nation theory proposing a Muslim homeland in Pakistan. Abdullah soon claimed to be fighting for Naya Kashmir, a secular Kashmiri homeland run on socialist principles. But in 1947, after years of agitation and doing time in Dogra prisons, Abdullah seemed to change tack. He took charge of an emergency administration in Jammu and Kashmir, with the maharaja as titular head of a state that had joined the Indian Union. Later, he became the first prime minister of the state.

Tehreek histories put this down variously to 'opportunism' and 'naïveté', with the Sheikh betting on a plebiscite in the near future.[11] They are also sceptical of the fledgling Indian state's claim to secularism, which was supposed to make the country a safe harbour for religious minorities and set it apart from Muslim Pakistan. Whatever the Sheikh's calculations, they went badly wrong in 1953, when the Nehru government had him imprisoned for questioning the accession. Over the next few decades, Abdullah's Jammu and Kashmir National Conference would be bludgeoned into obedience by Delhi while the demand for self-determination was kept alive by other groups and parties.

History writers of the *tehreek* emphasise the continuities between the anti-colonial movements of the early twentieth century and the armed movement for *azadi* that gained momentum in 1989. They draw attention to repressive laws of the Indian state which take inspiration directly from colonial laws.[12] They bristle at official Indian histories which cast the armed rebellion as a proxy war by Pakistan, as the disaffection of a Kashmiri public 'alienated' from their natural government and the assertion of Islamic fundamentalism.[13]

The killing of Kashmiri Pandits, a Hindu minority, in the early years of the armed movement and the mass migration of the community are often held up, in officially sanctioned Indian histories, as proof of the *tehreek*'s Islamist tendencies. *Tehreek* history writers point out that, in some instances, Pandits were targeted by militant groups not because of their religious identity but because

INTRODUCTION

they worked for the Indian government, with whom Kashmir was at war. They echo a belief, widely held in Kashmir, that the mass migration of Pandits was encouraged by the Indian government to tar the *tehreek* as a communal or religious movement and to pave the way for counterinsurgency operations.[14] In response to allegations that Pandits were driven out by a suddenly hostile Muslim populace, these history writers point to deep ties between the two communities and to Muslims protecting their Pandit neighbours even as the *tehreek* raged around them.

Some histories of the *tehreek* were written by leaders of the All Parties Hurriyat Conference, a conglomeration of parties demanding *azadi*, formed in 1993. The Hurriyat, whose leaders claimed to stand for non-violent agitation, reflected the many strands of the movement for *azadi* and their diverse ambitions. It would later split into factions over these differences, including whether to enter into talks with the Indian government, whether to merge with Pakistan, and whether to participate in Indian elections.

But the factions banded together again in the decade of mass protests that swept Kashmir from 2008. Three faces represented the 'joint resistance leadership', as they were called in the Kashmiri press: Syed Ali Shah Geelani, whose faction of the Hurriyat favoured merging Kashmir with Pakistan and rejected talks with the Indian government; Mirwaiz Umar Farooq, often called a 'moderate', who favoured talks with the Indian government; and Yasin Malik, who steered the Jammu and Kashmir Liberation Front (JKLF) away from militancy into political negotiation as it fought for a secular Kashmiri state. These leaders marshalled the currents of protest, which pitted civilians directly against government forces.

Junaid points out they used the vocabulary of the Indian freedom movement, including '*hartal*', strikes, and '*chalo*', marches.[15] Yet their politics were outlawed by the Indian state, which insists they worked in tandem with armed groups. The JKLF and several

Hurriyat groups are now banned. Geelani died under house arrest in 2021. The Mirwaiz has spent years in a political fiction, ostensibly a free man but frequently detained when he tries to leave his house. Malik is serving a life sentence after being convicted of 'funding terrorism' during mass protests in 2010 and 2016 and, at the time of writing, faces an appeal by India's National Investigation Agency to bring the death penalty against him.

Tehreek histories, for their part, are deeply engaged in recording the toll of militarisation in Kashmir. According to Indian home ministry figures, 44,729 people died in 'terrorist violence' from 1988 to March 2019.[16] A report published by a human rights group in 2008 found at least 70,000 people had been killed, 8,000–10,000 subjected to enforced disappearance and 60,000 tortured in detention.[17] Hundreds more have been killed and thousands detained since then. Government figures suggest about a third of the casualties were civilians. Most other sources suggest the share of civilian deaths was much higher.

Questions may be asked of the different figures. For instance, which deaths were counted? Who was a terrorist and who was a civilian? Does a silent wave of state violence hide in the higher death toll?

* * *

Official histories, which speak in terms of territory, carry cartographic fantasies.

The Dogra state of Jammu and Kashmir was an illusion to begin with. For it was really Jammu, Kashmir, Ladakh and Gilgit-Baltistan—a patchwork of provinces that pulled in different directions. Post Partition, the map grew even more fragmented, each province coloured by its own politics.

The ceasefire line was turned into the Line of Control in 1972, soon after the Bangladesh War of Independence raised India–Pakistan tensions once more. The LoC starts in the foothills of

INTRODUCTION

the Himalayas in Jammu province. About 740 kilometres long, it flows north and then takes a sharp turn east before disappearing into the snows of the Karakoram near the disputed Siachen glacier. The temporary boundary has turned into an implacable frontier, with thousands of soldiers massed on either side.

Areas west of the LoC are controlled by Pakistan. This includes parts of Jammu and Kashmir, often called Azad Kashmir, and Gilgit-Baltistan. Pakistan ceded control of the Shaksgam Valley, originally part of Baltistan, to China in 1963.

India controls areas east of the LoC. This includes Jammu division, which became a Hindu-majority region after Partition. Then there is the Buddhist-majority Ladakh division, which also includes the Shia-majority district of Kargil. Indo-Chinese border skirmishes laid the Line of Actual Control across Ladakh, so that the vast tracts of the Aksai Chin plateau in eastern Ladakh are now controlled by China. That leaves the Kashmir division, the seat of the armed rebellion against the Indian state, sharp mountains arranged around an oval valley just a hundred and thirty-five kilometres long and thirty-two kilometres wide.

The name Kashmir is often used as shorthand for the entire region. That is one cartographic fantasy.

Recent political maps of Pakistan cover all of Jammu, Kashmir and western Ladakh. That is another.

This was in response to yet another fantastic map handed out by the Indian government in 2019. The state of Jammu and Kashmir had vanished. In its place were two Union Territories controlled directly by Delhi. An azure blue terrier that was the Union Territory of Ladakh. A yellow egg under its belly that was the Union Territory of Jammu and Kashmir.

Much of the terrier and the egg was out of the Indian government's control. But the government did not rely on maps alone to support its claim. The Indian meteorological department now listed temperatures in Gilgit, Baltistan and Muzaffarabad, all west of the LoC, as part of its weather bulletin.[18] As if knowing the temperature of a place, when the sun will rise, when the rain will fall, were a measure of territorial control.

This cartographic sleight of hand came with new legislative fictions. By 2019, Nehru's promise of a plebiscite was ancient history. Over the decades, the Indian position had travelled from 'bilateral dispute' to 'internal matter' to be solved within the country's borders and the terms of its constitution. Now, the government declared the dispute solved. No matter if the compact between the Indian government and the state of Jammu and Kashmir was completely undone.

Unlike other states, Jammu and Kashmir had negotiated the terms of its accession to the Indian Union.[19] Its special status was defined in Article 370 of the Indian Constitution, which recognised the former subjects of the princely state of Jammu and Kashmir as politically and culturally distinct. India's only Muslim-majority state would have sovereignty on all matters except defence, foreign affairs and communication. Where other states had a chief minister, Jammu and Kashmir was to have a prime minister who shared sovereign power with the Indian government. It was also to have its own flag and its own laws, written in a separate constitution drafted by a constituent assembly elected by the people of the state.

Other provisions flowed from this recognition of a distinct political identity. Article 35A of the Indian Constitution, created by a presidential order in May 1954, granted the state legislature of Jammu and Kashmir the power to determine and confer privileges on its own 'permanent residents', irrespective of the laws of India. This provision was absorbed into the Jammu and Kashmir Constitution, adopted in 1956. It limited permanent residency to subjects of the former Dogra state and their descendants, as well as Indian citizens who had lawfully acquired property and lived in the state for at least ten years as of May 1954. The state constitution drew a protective circle around permanent residents, reserving for them the right to own land and hold state government jobs in Jammu and Kashmir. For decades, this bureaucratic structure was the crucible that contained Kashmiri public life and defined much of its politics. The Kashmiri politicians who stood for Indian elections curried votes by promising to preserve special status and the rights that came along with it.

Reams have been written on whether Article 370 was supposed to be a lasting or temporary arrangement. According to legal scholar AG Noorani, both Nehru and Abdullah sought finality but in different directions.[20] Abdullah thought the arrangement would come to an end once India and Pakistan came to an agreement on Kashmir. Nehru saw Article 370 dissolving into greater integration with India. As it engineered the Sheikh's dismissal in 1953, Delhi showed it was not shy to interfere, special status or not.

By 1965, the prime minister of Jammu and Kashmir had been demoted to chief minister. Other autonomies guaranteed under Article 370 were also whittled down over the decades. Delhi accomplished this through instruments of dubious legitimacy. It passed presidential orders extending central laws to Jammu and Kashmir and bullied state governments into accepting them. If the state government was not sufficiently compliant, it suddenly suffered a collapse. According to one former governor of Jammu and Kashmir, those who headed the state between 1953 and 1975 were little more than nominees of the central government.[21] In 1975, Abdullah signed an accord with Delhi giving up the Kashmiri demand for self-determination.

Decades of debate were extinguished on 5 August 2019, when Prime Minister Narendra Modi's Hindu nationalist government gutted the autonomy guaranteed by Article 370 and did away with Article 35A. The government also passed the Jammu and Kashmir Reorganisation Act, which carved up the state into two

Union Territories. It repealed a slew of state laws, imposed over a hundred Union laws on the region and weakened the old land regime. There would be no more permanent residents, only domiciles, a loose category that included central government employees, and anyone who had lived in the region for a certain number of years. Some state laws were retained, such as the Jammu and Kashmir Public Safety Act (PSA), a preventive detention law used to sweep up dissidents.

The legality of these legislative changes was debated, especially when they were enacted after placing the people of Jammu and Kashmir under lockdown and a communications blackout. The government passed off the deathly quiet as 'normalcy', even as hundreds were arrested under the PSA, including former chief ministers, legislators, Hurriyat leaders, activists and lawyers. Then, in 2023, the Indian Supreme Court ruled the changes were legal, so they were.

As far as Delhi was concerned, the Kashmir dispute was solved. But quiet panic spread among the residents of Jammu, Kashmir and Ladakh. The floodgates, it was feared, had been opened. People from other states would buy land and move in, overtaking fragile local populations. Demographic change would alter political outcomes. Local identities would be decimated. All regions of the former state felt growing disquiet. But it was Muslim-majority Kashmir that felt most under siege.

To the people of Kashmir, 5 August 2019 has become a date much like 1931, 1947 and 1989. It has become a date that will shape future cartographies. For it is here, in the oval valley ringed with mountains, that the most fraught questions of identity and territoriality are decided. So this is where I went looking for stories.

* * *

Where to begin? The 'life of the state'—kings, prime ministers, armies, territories—felt very far away as I sat in the businessman's

INTRODUCTION

shop that cold afternoon.[22] He was as cautious as he was kind, insisting I keep the heater to myself, urging me to pick up another biscuit. He was open to talking about his favourite television shows but wasn't about to get too political.

We were sitting under the watchful eye of his son, who had asked a few piercing questions of me before the interview began. What were my intentions? What kind of story was I looking for exactly? These were questions I was also asking myself.

The events and actions that flow from the life of states are considered historic.[23] But what can be known about a time, how life was lived in that time, through such histories?

The historian Ranajit Guha recommends listening to the 'small voice of history' drowned out by the imperatives of the state. He draws attention to voices from civil society, people who have little to do with the working of state power and are cut off from dominant narratives. Listening to these voices disorders and complicates statist historiography in fertile ways; it makes 'a mess of its plot'.[24]

I am no professional historian, only a journalist, and I have a simpler project. The stories I collected have little to do with the 'biography of a nation' and are not concerned with the fate of Indian nationalism.[25] I wanted to hear about Kashmir as Kashmir, how people living here experienced the *haalaat*, how they spoke of their experiences and how these stories helped form a certain political subjectivity.

Consider, for instance, the taste of fear. Consider the businessman back in the early nineties, out walking his dog in downtown Srinagar one day. His hands and clothes are coated with dust and cement because they are building a new house. Some time later he tethers his dog and stops to have a smoke with a friend. The dog disappears from the story after this.

While they are talking, a man with a long beard rushes past them. That one came here to throw a grenade yesterday, says the friend. The businessman is still laughing at the idea—the man can't be a militant, he's as thin as a stick—when they hear the explosion. Suddenly everywhere is smoke and everyone is running, the businessman in one direction, his friend in the other. He runs so hard, he leaves his slippers behind at the shop where they were smoking.

The businessman reaches home to tell his sister that there has been a grenade blast, and if there has been a blast then boots will follow. They take refuge in a neighbour's house. It does not save them. Soldiers enter the house and start beating them up. The businessman and an elderly neighbour are taken away, strung up by their ankles and beaten again. They might have died that day had an officer not intervened. He asks why they are being beaten. The businessman replies that he saw a man run past him seconds before the blast but he doesn't know anything else about him. Somehow, his smoking partner is found. He corroborates the story. The slipper left behind in panic is also found. They are released. It is only when the businessman goes to the river to wash the blood off that he sees his wounds in the clean flesh.

Three decades later, he has filed it away as another instance of *zulm*, oppression, that Kashmiris have had to bear during the *haalaat*. This story comes towards the end of our meeting, when I have run out of questions to ask and the interview has turned into a chat. The conversation that started with comedy shows from the eighties and the tragic romance of Sahaba and Nika has flowed into this memory of a quiet day turning into terror. It has become a story among other lost stories.

Over the last two decades, several Kashmiri writers have recorded their experience. In Basharat Peer's *Curfewed Night* (2008), cousins leave for arms training across the LoC and villages scatter in fright as gunfights break out. *Of Occupation and Resistance* (2013), a collection of essays edited by Fahad Shah, has

INTRODUCTION

a number of first-person accounts: a gravedigger told to bury unidentified bodies; a boy caught in a military crackdown; a photojournalist who cannot help a dying child. In *Rumours of Spring: A Girlhood in Kashmir* (2021), Farah Bashir describes twisting out strands of her hair as she waits, unsleeping, for night curfews to end. In *Do You Remember Kunan Poshpora?* (2016), five Kashmiri women excavate the details of an alleged mass rape that occurred during an army raid in 1991 and was suppressed in official records. In *Before I Forget* (2024), MK Raina remembers a childhood in the fifties and returning, decades later, to a ravaged valley to direct plays performed by folk actors and musicians.

Some stories are fiction, but only just, from *The Collaborator* (2011) by Mirza Waheed to *Life in the Clocktower Valley* (2021) by Shakoor Rather. These are only some of the stories that have been written down in English. And only some stories have been written down in English. There are more stories written in Urdu and Kashmiri. There are many more stories that were never written down at all.

When I first visited the Kashmir Valley as a journalist in 2016, I found the *haalaat* was continually being turned into story. There were always two stories about any news event, one from state authorities and one from local residents. By the time I reached the Valley, it had become a truism that there were no facts in Kashmir, only versions. A police officer in South Kashmir complained bitterly about the 'subaltern' school of journalists who insisted on talking to local residents.

But there were stories that lay beyond the economies of news gathering. A journalist collects and verifies stories as best they can, explains why they are important, turns them into information. A storyteller does something else. To Benjamin, information 'does not survive the moment in which it was new'.[26] It must be digested as soon as possible. A story preserves its psychological power precisely because it does not explain itself. Something about a story turns a moment to the light in a way that a news report never can.

A river of stories swirled around me in Kashmir. They were told in kitchens, in cafes, on the street and online; they were personal memories, inherited histories, urban legends, rumours, myths that never made it to any news report. Friends in Kashmir gave me many reasons why it was necessary to tell stories. For relief. To make sense of what was happening to you. To assert some sort of agency over what was happening to you. There were old habits of storytelling in Kashmir.

* * *

It is said, if you want to start a rumour, you spit into the Jhelum river at Zainakadal in downtown Srinagar. The waters will carry it around the city in no time.[27]

Srinagar spreads out on either side of the Jhelum like a rich alluvium. It was once known as the city of seven bridges. There are now at least eleven bridges across the Jhelum, but that is another story. Between the third and seventh historic bridges lies downtown Srinagar, the oldest, thickest part of the city. Zainakadal is the fourth bridge, originally built in the fifteenth century, destroyed and rebuilt several times since. There was always something in the air in Zainakadal.

It was a business hub, says a former resident of the area. Large markets were clustered around Zainakadal, the smell of fish mingling with the clang of copper vessels, all of it carried up in clouds of smoke blown out through hookahs in rows and rows of shops. For centuries, Zainakadal had drawn merchants from all over Kashmir and Ladakh. They traded in goods but also in news. Since news from official sources was scarce, rumours filled the gaps. If it was *khabr-i-Zainakadal*, news from Zainakadal, it was bound to be false.[28] But it is said the rumours were always true even if the news was not.[29]

INTRODUCTION

Rumours started from Zainakadal, says the former resident, and so did politics. Traders pulling on their hookahs discussed prices, political scandals in the Valley, the latest outrage by Delhi. It helped that Zainakadal was close to the seat of religious power in the Valley. The papier-mâché brilliance of the Khanqah-e-Moula mosque lay in one direction and the solemn pillared halls of the Jamia Masjid in another, their clergies aligned with rival political camps. Talk from the mosques flowed into the markets. Even the houses of Zainakadal were in conversation, built close together and fitted with a *daeb*, a latticed wooden balcony jutting out into the street, so that the difference between inside and outside became thin.

Such was the power of the Zainakadal streets that journalists also went looking for material there. For years, Sanaullah Bhat, the editor of *Daily Aftab*, an Urdu newspaper run from Srinagar, wrote a satirical column called 'Khizar Sochta Hai Wular Ke Kinare', Khizar Thinks On the Banks of the Wular. It is said, he sat with traders at Zainakadal, sharing their hookah and picking up political gossip. The area in its glory days was perhaps a microcosm of the Kashmiri public sphere: a mix of rumours, gossip and news; a chaos that always threatened to tip over into rebellion.

Historian Chitralekha Zutshi theorises the existence of a Kashmiri narrative public, a community formed by a shared pool of common talk.[30] The Valley's historical imagination, she writes, has always moved between textual and oral narratives, between fantastic and factual registers, between myth and lived experience.[31] Chroniclers of Kashmiri history depended on oral accounts, often slipping the word *dapaan* into their texts. It is telling that Walter Roper Lawrence, the whiskered British settlement officer sent to Kashmir in the late nineteenth century, was writing a treatise on the Valley largely based on conversations with 'uneducated villagers' around the same time that the missionary J. Hinton Knowles was collecting folk tales from a similar pool of interlocutors.[32]

Written texts were also disseminated beyond the reading public, which was not large until the middle of the twentieth century. In the countryside, *dastaangoh*, professional storytellers, sat up nights recounting epic tales from Arabic, Persian and Kashmiri traditions, as well as stories of heroic battles fought in the past. Much of this was passed on orally, without written text. But some remember the story of Gulrez, a Persian narrative poem that was adapted in Kashmiri in the nineteenth century, being read out on winter nights. A young man in Ganderbal district said his grandfather, who had been a part-time *dastaangoh*, read stories of historic battles and recounted them on demand.

The Kashmiri narrative public, Zutshi notes, was intensely engaged with history keeping. Often, these were histories of dissent that were to be guarded from the state even as they circulated within the community. Disguises had to be found. *Ladi shah*, or travelling minstrels, went from village to village singing satirical verses about the latest calamity. The past was constantly resurrected in the light of the present. The repertoire of *bhand paether*, or folk theatre, included stock plays about the tyrants of history. But they changed shape every time they were performed, laced with jokes and references that spoke of the present. Meanwhile, historical memory was buried in folk tales and adages, swear words and everyday idioms, a hidden ore of meaning only available to those who lived within the narrative public.

These were habits of silence cultivated through long years of subjugation, writes historian Farooq Fayaz.[33] For centuries, Kashmiris had felt themselves to be living in a surveillance state, where secret agents would carry information back to the authorities and dissent would be punished. Such conditions bred 'silent societies' where the 'metaphors of rebellion' would have to be used in secret.[34] Silence was so valued that it found its way into a popular saying. *Tshopt chey ropt stu[n]z, karakh tey sont stu[n]z.*[35] Silence is silver; if you keep your silence, it turns golden.

INTRODUCTION

The armed conflict was a time of noise. Dissent burst into the open with gunshots and protest marches cutting across the Valley. The air was thick with rumours. Traffic between oral and printed narratives persisted. The local press grew exponentially in these decades, reporting popular sentiments. New histories of the *tehreek* were also written, drawing on popular memory. This was a way of 'reclaiming a subjugated knowledge and shaping Kashmiri political subjectivity,' argues Junaid.[36] When a second generation joined the armed conflict, the public sphere crept online. Social media platforms were flooded with messages of rebellion.

It was also a time of silence. As the Valley grew militarised, the government intensified crackdowns on free speech, often citing national security. With every season of protest, there were long internet blockades. A surveillance state, spreading its tentacles into every neighbourhood, was now hopped up on technology. You had to watch your words.

By 1989, many of the old metaphors had fallen out of use. Folk traditions of storytelling and theatre had been losing popularity for a while. As the armed conflict broke out, they went underground for a decade. But for centuries they had been so deeply entwined with the rhythms of everyday life that they left their traces in ways of remembering, in patterns of storytelling. To my outsider's ear, it seemed these traces also carried a distinctly Kashmiri political subjectivity. So I went looking for these traces. I wanted to hear what was remembered but also how it was remembered.

* * *

Where to begin? Four kinds of stories floated up in conversation. Stories of loss and laughter. Stories of haunting and stories concerned with place-making. Like discerning words in birdsong, I thought I heard the inflections of older oral traditions in these stories.

DAPAAN

The businessman, after telling the story of the day he nearly died, had said heavily, '*Yahan pe bahut zulm hua*, madam.' There has been a lot of oppression here, madam. And so that is where I begin Part I of this book, 'Laughing at the King', by exploring the idea of *zulm*, which forms the horizon of Kashmiri political life. It is the idea that Kashmiris have been subjugated by five centuries of outside rule, linking past oppressions to the present. Memories of *zulm* have left their residue in everyday language, in popular myths and the songs of the *ladi shah*. I find that political constructions of *zulm* in the twentieth century continue to drive modern rebellions.

Dark humour flowed from *zulm*, which was the main subject of *bhand paether*. Folk players performing to rural audiences perfected the art of using coded language to mock state power. It was the language of people used to being watched. *Bhand paether* lost its sting once it was drawn into circuits of government patronage, but patterns of humour found in folk theatre surfaced in the most unlikely place: military crackdowns in Kashmir. Trapped in the panopticon of military cordons, Kashmiris learnt to speak in coded language.

During crackdowns, your fate depended on the watching eyes of 'cats', informers who were either paid or tortured by government forces until they gave up names of militants and their supporters. They became the refracted eyes of the state. The folklore of military crackdowns is rich with jokes and stories about cats.

As they retreated from the village square, *bhand paether* and other folk arts were turned into programmes on state channels. This was tame fare but dissent escaped sometimes. The idiom of folk theatre was used in *Hazaar Dastaan*, a wildly popular serial in the eighties which lampooned political events and personalities. In the laughter of the audience, there was growing anger against the government. This would explode in armed rebellion by the end of the decade.

INTRODUCTION

In Part II, 'Possession', the militarisation of the Valley becomes a haunting. Folktales about the *raantas* and the *daen*, demonic women who roam at night, become a metaphor for military presence. Panic spread across Kashmir in 1993, when it was rumoured that *daens* were prowling neighbourhoods, attacking anyone they encountered. Stories on the street and in the local press soon pointed to curious affinities between *daens* and military vehicles. The mass panic of 1993 died out in a few months but ghost stories kept cropping up in pockets of Kashmir.

There is more than one kind of haunting. For instance, stories may haunt stories. In 2017, Kashmir was gripped by rumours that shadowy creatures were attacking women and shearing their hair. While the braid chopping rumour had started in the plains of North India, it gathered new force in Kashmir. In many accounts, the braid choppers sounded remarkably like the *daen* who had roamed the Valley a quarter of a century earlier.

Finally, there are places haunted by an unresolved past. In the spring of 2000, a triad of killings in South Kashmir's Anantnag district left nearly fifty people dead, but no one was ever brought to justice. To the families of the dead, justice is spectral, constantly out of reach. The unquiet past surfaces in the stories they tell. For instance, they remember the ghosts that invaded their villages before the killings that spring.

'Loss', Part III, explores how militant bodies are mourned and how this mourning becomes a form of defiance against the state. As the *haalaat* claimed lives, militants were memorialised in traditional wedding songs often composed, improvised and sung by women. For centuries, wedding songs have done the work of history keeping, especially when such histories will not be admitted in official records. Personal grief entered the public through these occasions. Wedding songs were also sung at militant funerals, where an ecstatic grief led many young mourners to take up arms. The funeral of Burhan Wani, the Hizbul Mujahideen mili-

23

tant whose death triggered mass protests in 2016, was one of the largest Kashmir had ever seen.

Mourning gives way to Freudian melancholia, which keeps the past alive by refusing to let go of loss. This melancholia may be found in stories about Burhan Wani. The young militant had passed into legend in Kashmir, and not just because of stories passed on from mouth to mouth. Posters and videos of Burhan and his band of militants circulated online, creating a cloud of Facebook folklore. When Burhan Wani died, these online traces became objects of grief in the Kashmiri public sphere. Now even these traces have been driven underground by a government crackdown, but the memory of them keeps the past alive.

The final section, Part IV, 'Blood Maps', starts with the tales of the *dastaangoh* and the mythic geographies they hold. For instance, Majnun, the famously tormented lover of Laila, wanders through different realms in a fugue state. The *dastaan*, or story, inhabits the fevered psychoscapes of Majnun, its plot driven by his wandering mind. The *haalaat* was its own fever dream, which took hold of each person differently. Familiar geographies dissolved. Cities were remade in each person's mind, drawn by their experience. Everyone now possessed their own memory map of their hometown or village. I call this a 'blood map'. The landmarks on this map are places freighted with emotional significance.

Majnun also moved seamlessly between worlds. There were moral universes such as Jannat, paradise, and Jahannam, hell. There were other worlds in between, the land of the *djinns*, the home of the *peris*, or fairies. As the conflict broke out, different places in the Valley stood for such different registers of experience, they no longer seemed to belong to the same reality. Underworlds opened up in the form of camps and detention centres which swallowed people. Movie halls crossed worlds. Many remember them in a paradisal past before the *haalaat*. Then they were shut down and turned into camps.

INTRODUCTION

Finally, land—owning it, protecting it—was always important to the politics of the *tehreek*. But stories told about certain kinds of land gave them an afterlife beyond their legal and material existence. The grave of a Sufi mystic cast a protective spell around the village where he was buried. New graveyards reserved for those killed in the *tehreek*, considered martyrs, possessed miraculous properties. The LoC became a frontier where all laws, natural and manmade, stopped working. Such fantastic geographies were ideal for hiding inconvenient bodies.

* * *

After thirty-five years, an armed conflict does not stay in the streets. It enters homes and minds; it enters language. A friend in Srinagar once said the conflict made itself felt not just in actual violence but also as an electric charge that crackled through everyday life. It became a madness that injected a sense of fictionality into everything.

This was what I tried to listen for when I started gathering stories for this book in 2022. The public furies of the earlier decade seemed to have gone missing. Instead, I found a time of complete silence. It was not just the state of Jammu and Kashmir that had been dismembered in 2019; it was the entire Kashmiri public sphere that had thrived for decades.

Lal Chowk, the clock tower square where this public sphere had been performed for the outside world, was being dug up. Protest sites were being replaced by selfie points for tourists. The local press and human rights groups were decimated. Journalists and activists were in prison. So were hundreds of others. You could go to jail for just looking like trouble; the police had the Public Safety Act for that. You could go to jail hundreds of miles outside the Valley, in the sweltering plains of Delhi, Rajasthan, Uttar Pradesh, and not be tried for years. For other offences there was the Unlawful Activities (Prevention) Act, an anti-terror law that may be liberally interpreted. Celebrating the defeat of the Indian cricket team?[37] UAPA. Cheering Pakistan in social media posts? UAPA. Protesting because you want the body of your sixteen-year-old son, who was killed and labelled a militant? UAPA, UAPA, UAPA.[38]

Quite naturally, few people wanted to be interviewed. Most of those who agreed to speak did not want to be quoted or even recorded while they were interviewed. So I cannot tell you their names. In place of names, I have used letters, which do not even stand for their real initials. Nor can I tell you where exactly they live. In many instances, I cannot even tell you what they look like or what they do for work. But I can convey to you some of the words they used.

Certain words have mythic weight. '*Haalaat*', of course, a deadpan generality humming with subversive undertones. Also, '*azadi*', '*tehreek*', '*hartal*'. Then there is the word '*markaz*', or power centre, most often used for Delhi but sometimes also a veiled reference to Islamabad.

The *markaz* works through 'agencies', a word uttered darkly. It refers to the intelligence and security agencies of this side and that. Pakistan's Inter-Services Intelligence lurks in the shadows, along with India's Intelligence Bureau, Research and Analysis Wing, military intelligence, National Investigation Agency and local police intelligence networks. The *haalaat* is often a shadow war between agencies, a game of feint and advance that causes strange phenomena in the Valley.

Government troops are 'forces', as though they are forces of nature whose furies cannot be stopped. But the word is also used because it is not always clear which troops were involved in a particular incident. So many military and paramilitary forces set up camp in the Valley after 1990. There were various battalions of the army, including its counterinsurgency wing, the Rashtriya Rifles. There were paramilitaries such as the Border Security

INTRODUCTION

Force and the Indo-Tibetan Border Police, whose duties had been expanded from patrolling borders to counterinsurgency, as well as the thinly stretched Central Reserve Police Force. Then there was the Territorial Army, a military reserve force which took in many renegade militants in the nineties.

The local Jammu and Kashmir Police has also acquired counter-insurgency units which have absorbed renegade militants. There was the special task force, also called the special operations group, SOG. In the early 2000s, this force was apparently disbanded. Yet the term 'special operations group' still floats up in press releases and news reports, used to describe the police's counterinsurgency wing. It remains in a bureaucratic twilight zone, passed off as part of the regular police force. But it is common knowledge that there is an SOG camp in every major town and village. Smoke and mirrors that contribute to the fictionality of everyday life in Kashmir.

There are some notes and cadences I cannot quite convey. The habit of telling a story through a series of questions, as if the listener is being tested in comprehension—after a brief pause, the storyteller will answer the question themselves. The very dry humour of having seen very bad times and lived to tell the tale. The quiet sorrow of living with loss. No written words can match the power and beauty of the stories I heard.

In this silent time, much of the public I encountered were in Sumos. These are ten-seater SUVs used for public transport in Kashmir. Often, it seemed to me, everyone travelling in the Sumo must know one another. They would jab the next person to pass on the fare or hold each other's babies. Heated discussions would start or the whole car would suddenly burst into laughter. I got sidelong glances at first, as my fellow passengers tried to place me. Definitely *nebrim*, outsider. Possibly agencies. Then curiosity would overtake caution. Where was I from? What was I doing here? Was I alone? Where were my parents? Was I married? Why not?

DAPAAN

By the end of the Sumo ride, my suitcase was being unloaded from the rooftop trailer and I was getting instructions on how to reach where I was going. I may be *nebrim*. I may or may not be agencies. But they were Kashmiri and they were going to make sure I reached my destination safely. Also along the way, some stories. The woman who had just lost her father and was feeling strange on her first day back at the school where she taught. The student who was waiting for her graduation results. The shawl trader who knew my hometown, Kolkata. The young man whose grandfather turned out to be a part-time *dastaangoh*.

This book does not cover every story. Nor does it claim to be the definitive story of the *haalaat*. There are experiences that remain closed off to me and groups of people whose views might not fit the dominant political subjectivity of the Valley. Kashmiri Pandits, for instance, figure in most stories as an absence, deeply mourned by their friends and neighbours. Some of the people I interviewed belong to the Gujjar community, who have traditionally been nomadic herders living in the mountains, but our conversations did not have much to do with their identity as Gujjars, a minority whose politics and experiences do not always match those of ethnic Kashmiris. The same is true of people from the Pahari community, another ethnic minority in Kashmir, whose specific experiences also have not been recorded in this book.

Finally, fear was not the only reason many people in Kashmir did not want to speak to me when I started my research in 2022. Earlier, residents of the Valley had told their stories to visiting journalists with some hope of breaching the wide gulf between the Kashmiri and mainstream Indian publics. After 2019, hope died. The citizens of a Hindu-majoritarian India were seen celebrating what Kashmiris regarded as a humiliation. As panic about demographic change grew in the Valley, Kashmiri militant groups targeted migrant workers. These attacks did not meet with public approval. But a certain anger pulsed through many conversations.

INTRODUCTION

To some people, I was an outsider whose government had taken away their rights. There was no reason to trust me. But it was not just a matter of trust. Once, a young man in Anantnag district said he did have stories but he would not tell me because who was I to tell his stories? This question is right and fair.

I have this to say. First, I would like to think of myself as a listener, writing down the stories I have heard. I do not claim to speak for Kashmiris. Second, I write because I will never have complete knowledge. I have never been there, listening to the drip-drip of a tap while waiting for news of a brother taken away to a camp. I have never held myself stiff as strangers with guns entered my house and kicked a flower pot on the way out just because they could. I have never had a gun pressed to my throat while my children buried their heads in my lap and said I didn't know anything, *Bhagwan ke kasam*, swear on God, I didn't, and had the gun removed because I said Bhagwan, not Allah. There will always be a gap in my knowledge because I was never there. I write to close this gap, knowing that it will never be closed, that I will never fully know.

PART I

LAUGHING AT THE KING

1

ZULM

It is said, two brothers went up the mountains of Tral for a picnic one day. Burhan and Khalid. Men in uniform stopped them on the way and asked them to fetch cigarettes. The brothers obeyed. It did not matter. The men in uniform still made them do sit-ups and beat them. Afterwards, they were allowed to go, red-faced and bruised.

Some say it wasn't a picnic and it wasn't in the woods. The brothers were sent to the market around the bus stand in Tral town. On the way, they were stopped by men in uniform and asked to show ID. It did not matter. The story ends the same way. The brothers were beaten up before they were allowed to go, red-faced and bruised.

Khalid, the older one, could be reasoned with, said their father, Muzaffar Wani. Burhan was just fifteen. He did not listen. He kept repeating, why did they beat me? I was minding my own business, why did they beat me? Not long afterwards, he left home and did not return. He had joined the Hizbul Mujahideen, the largest Kashmiri militant group.

That was in 2010. A few years later, Khalid's torn body was returned by forces. They said he too worked for the Hizbul

Mujahideen, even if he had not gone underground. By the time Burhan Wani was killed in 2016, he was the divisional commander of the Hizb and a household name in the Kashmir Valley. Everyone knew the story of how he had been beaten by men in uniform before he took up arms.

Muzaffar Wani told my colleague and me the story when we visited his house in Tral, a bright house with large windows and a garden. Burhan Wani was still alive. None of us knew then that he only had a few weeks of life left. Several other visiting journalists were also told the story, so it travelled widely outside Kashmir. Already, Burhan Wani had passed into legend for having survived the forces for so long.

There was a lot of talk about the Hizb commander in those days. A few pointed to uncles and cousins of Burhan who had also become militants. They said that his family was 'Jama'ati'—linked to the Jama'at-e-Islami Jammu and Kashmir, a socio-religious group long accused of contraband political sympathies. They said the Valley was already angry in 2010, when over a hundred people had been killed in mass protests. They said the beating, in the mountains or in the market, never happened.

It did not matter. Mass protests started as soon as Burhan was killed in a gunfight with forces on 8 July 2016. As far as thousands of Kashmiri teenagers were concerned, he had taken up arms to fight *zulm*, oppression, by the Indian state. Now they too rose up in rebellion. '*Burhan, tere khoon se inqilab ayega,*' they chanted. Burhan, revolution will flow from your blood. Some were shot as they surged against police and paramilitary forces. Many were sprayed with metal pellets that got into their eyes, their lungs, their gut. Still the crowds kept surging.

For this was no ordinary *zulm*. It carried the weight of five hundred years. It had become an element in Kashmir. It flowed in the waters of the Jhelum; it descended to the earth in *chinar* tree leaves; it crackled in concertina wires; it circled the skies in drones. *Zulm* was killings, disappearances, crackdowns, curfews. *Zulm* was also more everyday humiliations. When you were frisked at checkpoints; when you waited for hours on the highway because a convoy was passing through; when the electricity went off in deep winter; when you could not get a passport because a distant cousin had been a militant long ago so his family was forever held suspect, deemed liable to mutiny.

Binding together these oppressions, big and small, was the conviction that Kashmir was not free, had not been free in five hundred years. Not since the Mughal emperor Akbar sent his generals to Srinagar and added Kashmir to his list of conquests. From that day, this blighted Valley had been under the baleful eye of a *markaz*, a centre of power, far away. First the Mughals, ruling from the plains of North India, then the Afghans from their seat in Kabul, then the Sikhs with their headquarters in Lahore, then the Dogra kings, who preferred Jammu and were really under the thumb of the British. And now this. *Zulm* is the heaviest word in Kashmir.

Zulm is buried in language itself. Generations forced to live and die in silence, leaving no trace but in words. Hold up that old saying. Hold it close to your ear. You will hear them, countless voices surging up as briefly as leaves in the wind. '*Drag salih tai dag tsalih na*. The famine will disappear but the stains will not disappear.'[1] This hunger has not just hollowed out our stomachs; it has made us mean. Now hold that other saying to your ear. '*Koli khog kol che sardy*. Each stream is icier than the last.'[2] Each reign is more cruel than the one before.

* * *

In the summer of 2016, novelist Shabir Ahmed Mir is laid up in bed in South Kashmir's Pulwama district, recovering from knee surgery. Every day from his window, he sees the same scene play out. A bridge arcs across the square of the window. Teenagers swarm the bridge and chant slogans. When forces arrive, they throw stones. Forces reply with shelling. They could be tear-gas shells, releasing clouds of pungent vapour, or a burst of metal pellets fired from 12-gauge pump-action guns. By evening, there are hospitalisations, injuries, casualties.

The scene at the window is his daily bulletin. For weeks, there has been a blockade on mobile networks and most internet connections. Shabir has not heard from friends who live in other parts of the Valley. Sometimes, visitors arrive bearing rumours. Someone is in jail, and their father is haunting police stations to free them. Someone else has been wounded. Bullets have been fired in some distant neighbourhood.

With little news, his mind begins to fill in the blanks with pictures from the past. That time he escaped certain death. Earlier losses, long buried or barely acknowledged. So many faces from his childhood, disappearing like confetti in a blue sky. He did not think about it then. Only a vague sadness remained with him. Now, it is as if the dead have died again.

To look at suffering directly is unbearable. Shabir needs to find words to veil his grief. But which words? He writes in English, but the good-taste, MFA-style writing he has encountered in books and movies so far does not feel adequate to the moment. He remembers an old rhythm he has known since childhood. He turns to satire.

The verse he writes will appear under the title 'Ladi Shah' in *Kashmir Life*, a Srinagar-based magazine, in February 2017:

> Ladi Shah Ladi Shah at your door
> Knot your tongue and talk no more.
>
> ...
>
> Hundreds dead and thousands blind,
> Untold-PSA Quarantined:
> Yet everything is fit and fine,
> The expert says on news at nine[3]

Shabir's grief has turned to anger. Beneath the singsong words, he is raging at the government, at the national media, at laws that sweep people into jail without charges and give soldiers the power to shoot with impunity. He is raging at floods that recently swept the Valley, water climbing up houses because the streams and canals that would have carried it away have been paved over by the government. But the refrain of a song about protest shuts down the possibility of protest. Knot your tongue, talk no more, finally culminating, in the last couplet of the poem, in the command to 'close the door'. Dissent, Shabir says, means danger.

The song is written, not sung as it should be. It is in English, although the refrain carries the cadences of the original Kashmiri. '*Ladi shah, ladi shah*, at your door,' echoing a well-known line that has summoned listeners for centuries. '*Assalam alaykum, ladi shah aw.*' Peace be upon you, the *ladi shah* is here.

Repeat the line once more—*assalam alaykum, ladi shah aw*—and a figure takes shape in the words.

He draws near ripening fields of paddy and it is revealed that he wears a turban and a loose robe. He carries a *dhukar*, an instrument made of two metal rods fitted with metal rings, which he strikes as he sings. Both the singer and the song are called by the same name. *Ladi shah*.

* * *

For centuries, the *ladi shah* has been the poet of *zulm*, arriving at harvest time, singing as people worked in the fields, paid in grain. His song changed from year to year, explains Ghulam Mohi-ud-din Aajiz, a folk actor who used to perform *ladi shah*. When there were fires, he sang of fires. When there was famine, he sang of famines. But always in a light vein, mocking the folly of kings and governors. Always in a light vein so that if officials came for him, he could say it was only a joke, it did not mean anything. Always in the same rhythm, one-two-three, one-two-three, one-two-three, one. The *ladi shah* inhabited the Kashmiri public sphere by tapping into cultural memory as he spoke of the present, and setting off ripples of dissent that would travel far into the future.

In 1831, the *ladi shah* sang of a flood called Sehlaab Singh, named after the Sikh governors of Kashmir.[4] *Sehlaab* means flood in both Urdu and Kashmiri. Singh is a common last name for Sikhs. Sikh rule had become an idiom for disaster, so pervasive and devastating in its effects that it could hardly be distinguished from natural calamities. In 1832, the *ladi shah* sang of the famine that followed the floods. It was nicknamed '*Sher Singhun Draag*', the famine wrought by Sher Singh, the governor of Kashmir at the time.[5] When the Dogras arrived, the *ladi shah* sang of taxes that wrung the countryside dry.[6]

In 1949, the *ladi shah* sang of the *nuun draag*, or salt shortage. 'How many good people were wasted for salt?' his song went, flirting with dangerous sympathies. Ever since the borders were drawn between India and Pakistan, salt had become a sore point in Kashmir. The heavily guarded ceasefire line meant the Valley was cut off from the supply of pink salt that came from Khewra, in what was now Pakistan.

Decades later, this vanished pink salt has acquired the glow of legend. There was a mountain made of salt, the stones all pink, says Khaleeq Parvez, a writer in North Kashmir's Baramulla district. After Partition, everyone had to eat salt from the sea, and they forgot the taste of salt from the mountains. Another young man had heard his forefathers would go to Lahore through Baramulla town and Rawalpindi before 1947. Yes, they were taken for *begaar*, forced labour, but they brought back Pakistani salt. Of course, it wasn't Pakistan yet.

In the early years after Partition, there was hardly any salt, not from the mountains and not even from the sea. A historian in

Srinagar remembers his parents telling him about those times. Roads to the Valley were so bad the government dropped salt from planes. Once, a government plane flew into Khanabal in South Kashmir's Anantnag district and the sacks broke as they fell to the ground. People standing around the airfield gathered salt in their fists.

So, how many good people were wasted for salt, the *ladi shah* asks.[7] He goes on to tell the sad history of salt. How salt disappeared after the first border war. How aeroplanes full of salt came to Kashmir but corrupt bureaucrats ran off with it before it could reach the public. How committees of village leaders refused to distribute salt from the Indian mainland. How a merchant from Baramulla made a fortune hoarding salt. The *nuun draag*, it seems, was the first failure of Sheikh Abdullah's new administration.

You did not mess with salt in South Asia. If you 'ate someone's salt', you owed them your loyalty. Everyone in Kashmir had heard the Lear-esque folk tale about the king and his three daughters. When the king asked his daughters how much they loved him, one replied he was like a god to her, another said she loved him as much as honey, and the third said he was as dear as salt. This last comparison proved too prosaic for the king so he cast off his third daughter. After many twists in the tale, she invited him and his ministers for dinner, serving them food without salt. When the guests spat out the food, the king finally realised the importance of salt. The exiled daughter was welcomed back, and it was she who inherited the kingdom.

After Partition, salt was political, a declaration of fealty to this side or that. The ration shops set up locally were often run by Sheikh Abdullah's National Conference workers. Since Abdullah had parted ways with party colleagues who favoured Jinnah and linked his lot to Nehru, there had been muttering. Among his detractors in downtown Srinagar, many of whom still longed for Pakistan, this muttering was quite pronounced. Some of these dissensions crystallised in salt.

DAPAAN

As it entered common talk, songs and doggerel verses eddied out of the *nuun draag*. Ghulam Ahmad Mahjoor, often called Kashmir's 'national poet', versified the political anxieties set off by salt. The poet Zareef Ahmad Zareef, who lives in downtown Srinagar, rattles off Mahjoor's verse from memory:

Nuun-daed gayos, National waanas,
Dopam godi rul Hindustanas saet.
Buzith ye wachem thar thar panas,
Kari kya, dil chu Pakistanas saet.

I went to get salt, National [Conference] told me,
Become Hindustani first.
Hearing this, I started shaking,
What to do, my heart was Pakistan's.[8]

Pink salt, the lack of it, the secret possession of it, kept alive the question of fealty in the decades that followed. Waving rocks of pink salt became a sign of dissent against National Conference governments widely believed to be propped up by Delhi.

Even today, recollections of the salt shortage may partly be shaped by political belief. To Parvez, pink salt stands for loss. He had been a dissident in the fifties, marching in the rallies of the Political Conference, an opposition party. These exertions got him exiled to Pakistan for seven years. When he returned to Kashmir, he stayed away from politics but still missed the taste of pink salt.

Others suggest stories of the National Conference's venality might have been exaggerated by the opposing camp. There were myths, sniffed a bureaucrat in Srinagar. In downtown neighbourhoods, for instance, it was said that ration cards were issued in two colours, one for National Conference supporters and one for the party's detractors. Pure myth.

The salt shortage would be forgotten amid new calamities. So would the *ladi shah*'s salt song, which had been such a hit for a while. But the energies released by such songs have lingered in common talk. Pink salt has become a memento of oppression.

* * *

In 1895, Walter Roper Lawrence, British India's settlement commissioner for Jammu and Kashmir, observed that ordinary Kashmiris were made to believe they were 'serfs without any rights' whose many deficiencies made them '*Zulm parast*, or worshippers of tyranny'.[9] Lawrence, as the emissary of a British government trying to nose its way into greater control of Kashmir, might not have been completely disinterested—the more tyrannical the Dogra, the stronger the case for imperial control of the administration. But his observations are still held up as evidence in Kashmir. It is not just said that Kashmiris suffered oppression, it is written, that too by an outsider.

Colonial chroniclers, on the whole, were not shy of recording a history of tyranny in Kashmir. The English missionary J. Hinton Knowles found Kashmiris using a particular phrase for oppression: '*Ata Muhammad Khanin gadih begari.*'[10] Forced labour for Ata Muhammad Khan's fort.

The fort crowns a hill in the heart of Srinagar. Ata Mohammad Khan, an Afghan governor of Kashmir, finished building it in the early nineteenth century. It is said, Khan was in a hurry. He decreed that on Fridays, a day of prayer for Muslims, every single person in the city, man, woman, child, had to carry a rock up the hill to the burgeoning fort. Along with other kinds of forced labour, this was compulsory, says Zareef, who lives in the shadow of the fort.

But even Ata Mohammad Khan's villainy pales beside that of Kakar Khan, another Afghan governor. It is said, Kakar Khan made his way to Srinagar through the northern town of Baramulla. There he crossed paths with a funeral procession. The governor stopped and asked his men to cut off the ears of the corpse. Why, everyone asked, horrified. Even the kingdom of the dead should know that Kakar Khan has arrived in Kashmir, the governor announced, before proceeding to unleash a reign of terror.

It is also said the governor concerned was Chiragh Beg and not Kakar Khan. Either way, both became names for mad, bad behaviour.

Each regime perfected its own form of tyranny. The Mughals had an eye for beauty. They turned forests into precise squares of green. These became pleasure gardens. Then they bisected the gardens with water channels and placed pavilions over wild springs. They had an eye for beauty but they were blind to the suffering of the people, pronounces Zareef. The Afghans were worse, prone to addictions, working their subjects to the bone, proscribing Shia rituals of public mourning so that *marsiyas*, poems on the martyrdom of Hussain, were read in secret cellars underground. The Sikhs went further, banning the *azan*, the Muslim call to prayer, and using the Jamia Masjid as a stable for military horses. As for the Dogras, they turned Kashmiri peasants into mediaeval subjects, stripped of rights to land or livelihood, left to die in floods and famines.

The popular history of *zulm* has supplied tyrants who are resurrected again and again in everyday life. If you are bad news, you are a *pog mogul*. A Sumo driver swerving to avoid a truant cyclist will stick his head out the window and shout, 'Oi, Chiragh Bega!'

There were other bad news men who spread across the Valley with the *haalaat*. A police officer who was liberal with PSAs, an army officer who was known for being trigger-happy, a renegade militant who dreamt up new and creative torments, a governor from Delhi with cold eyes behind thick glasses. *Pog mogul, shikas mogul*, Kakar Khan, Chiragh Beg, people muttered as they were dragged off to jail, as strangers broke down their door at night, as bullets found bone. The tyrants of history walked again in everyday speech. Freedom belonged to the distant past and an ever-receding future.

* * *

It is said, Yusuf Shah Chak, the last Kashmiri king, was betrayed by his nobles, who invited the Mughals to invade. Yusuf Shah was a romantic. Riding through the fields of South Kashmir one day, he heard the sad songs of Habba Khatoon, a poet trapped in a cruel marriage. The king fell in love immediately, swept her off to his palace and lived in a state of rapture for the next few years. Some historians are sceptical about whether they met at all. But it does not matter. From that day on, their names were joined in history.

In 1586, the dashing Yusuf was forced into exile, never to return to Kashmir. Habba Khatoon spent the rest of her life writing songs of longing for him, although there is some debate about the authorship of her songs, whether she wrote all of the verses attributed to her, whether they accrued more lines as they were passed on from mouth to mouth. Either way, as the centuries passed, her songs became a lament for freedom, which had disappeared over the Pir Panjal mountains as Yusuf Shah left the Valley.

It is another matter that the Chaks were not originally from the Kashmir Valley. They were a clan from the borderlands of Kashmir who rose to power in the court of the Shahmiri sultans in Srinagar.[11] The Shahmiri sultans were not from the Valley, either. They had travelled to Kashmir from the west. And it is another matter that Yusuf Shah Chak wasn't the last of the Chaks to rule Kashmir. His son, Yaqub Shah, had briefly tried to hold his own against the Mughal advance.[12] But it was not to be.

In some written accounts, Yusuf Shah Chak wasn't even a very good king, so lost in songs and pleasure that he neglected his kingdom and was deposed two months after coming to power.[13]

He would become king again, but by then the Mughals had smelt blood. A section of the Sunni elite believed themselves oppressed by the Shia Chaks and invited the Mughals to Kashmir. With good reason, wrote many Sunni historians through the centuries.[14] Yusuf Shah himself might have seen Mughal rule in Kashmir as inevitable and gone into exile with some relief. The Mughals, who tried to arrive at land and revenue settlements, might not have been such bad news after all.[15]

But then again, maybe the dreamy Yusuf Shah was a good enough king in his own way. The Chaks' conversion to Shi'ism was a tactical move to gain influence in court, so maybe they weren't too particular about matters of faith.[16] Far from being the bigoted tyrant of so many histories, Yusuf Shah tried to seal truces with diverse groups and abolished the *jizya* tax imposed on Kashmiri Pandits by his ancestors.[17]

The ambivalences of historical record are largely lost to public memory. In the pool of common talk where songs, myths and gossip are dissolved, Yusuf Shah Chak was the last free Kashmiri king. When he left, Kashmir became a *subah*, or province, tethered to a distant *markaz* and descended into five hundred years of darkness.

He returned as a political idea in the twentieth century, as Kashmiris marched against Dogra rule. The Reading Room Party, a band of newly educated men from Srinagar, had started meeting in 1930, their thoughts often turning towards revolution.[18] What had started with Kashmiri Muslims trying to win more rights from an autocratic Hindu king turned into something more after 13 July 1931, when the maharaja's forces shot down protesters in Srinagar. Anger at the shooting would eventually contribute to a movement to dismantle the Dogra state. In 1932, the Reading Room Party dovetailed into the Muslim Conference, a channel for public mobilisation headed by a lanky young postgraduate called Sheikh Abdullah.

But then Abdullah gravitated towards Nehru and the Congress, acquiring the energies of an anti-colonial moment in South Asia. In 1939, the Muslim Conference was renamed the National Conference, its membership consisting of both Kashmiri Muslims and Pandits. The party's Naya Kashmir manifesto, published in 1944, borrowed heavily from the Soviet constitution and proposed a secular, socialist state in place of the Dogra autocracy.

This new political moment required new mythologies, which would shift emphasis from religious identity to ethnic identity, explains historian Hakim Sameer Hamdani. In the National Conference's mythos, it was no longer enough to be Kashmiri Muslims fighting Hindu Dogras. Now they were ethnic Kashmiris, natives of the Valley, resisting a longer history of outside rule. This philosophical approach also came in handy as National Conference members were put on trial for sedition in Dogra courts. But Your Royal Highness, they could argue, it is not just you we are fighting—it is a political condition.

Yusuf Shah Chak was pressed into service. Though he might not have been the ideal monarch, he would do. 'He might have been a bit oppressive but the Chaks before him were worse,' says Mohammad Yusuf Taing, a writer who was Abdullah's amanuensis for his autobiography, *Aatish-e-Chinar*. According to Taing, who has also been a National Conference legislator, the ill-fated Yusuf was Kashmiri enough. He came from Gurez, which falls within the political frontiers of Kashmir, and he spoke Kashmiri.

The idea of five hundred years of *zulm* would be welded even more firmly to Kashmiri politics after 1947. The National Conference kept its Naya Kashmir promise, abolished large landholdings and redistributed land to tillers, ensuring the party a solid electoral base for decades. Yusuf Shah's place in history was also solidified. For years, it had been rumoured that the exiled Chak was buried in Biswak, a village in Bihar. In 1978, Taing suggested to Abdullah that they make a pilgrimage to the burial site. 'I told Sheikh *saab*, he was the last indigenous ruler of Kashmir, we should go see,' recalls Taing. So they went. By the time they made the journey, he says, there were no Muslims left in Biswak; they had all fled during Partition. But they met an ancient farmer who confirmed to them that not only was Yusuf Shah Chak buried there but also Habba Khatoon.

In this telling of history, the doomed lovers had not been separated forever. Yusuf Shah had sent for Habba Khatoon after he reached Bihar and she travelled six months to be with him. She has a tomb, just south of Srinagar, but that edifice, according to Taing, is more sentiment than history. Habba Khatoon died in Bihar and was buried next to Yusuf Shah Chak, he insists. There was nothing to mark the spot in Bihar so two new tombs had to be built. For Yusuf Shah Chak's memorial tablet, the National Conference leaders took *devri* stone from Kashmir. The soapy grey stone prised out of the mountains is found in walls, steps and hammams across the Valley. Finally, the last free king of Kashmir had a grave from his homeland.

But the National Conference was no longer the party of *azadi*, having given up its demand for Kashmiri self-determination. Over the next few decades, it would drift farther away from *azadi* politics, ceding ground to other parties and strands of political belief. Still, the idea of an ancient and implacable *zulm* cut across ideological fault lines.

You didn't need myths to believe in five hundred years of oppression. You didn't even need songs and stories. By the time Abdullah launched his agitation in the thirties, Hamdani points out, more than two generations of Kashmiris had been starved, enslaved and stripped of land rights by the Dogra regime. They would have needed little persuasion to believe that it had always been so—Kashmiris had always suffered under outside rule.

Seven decades after Partition, the ravages of Dogra rule were still within living memory. In August 2019, I met a ninety-year-

ZULM

old man in Baramulla district who remembered working in the fields of the Dogra king. As they worked, overseers would check their teeth to see they had not eaten any of the grain, said the ninety-year-old, tapping his teeth in the memory of phantom grain. Younger men sitting around him remembered stories they had heard from their parents and grandparents, how they would eat one meal a day, how on some days there was nothing to eat but grass. After Dogra rule ended, they had gone from scarcity to subsistence to relative plenty.

These memories had returned powerfully now that Kashmir was stripped of autonomy and statehood. Abdullah's land reforms, which had changed the fortunes of so many rural Kashmiris, were under threat. In the terror and confusion of the weeks that followed, many were calling it the 'comeback of Dogra rule'.[19]

* * *

Back in Shabir's home, it is 2016 again. *Zulm* has claimed a new harvest over the summer. Fourteen-year-old Insha Mushtaq, who was watching protests from her window when she caught a burst of pellets in her face and eyes. She will never see again. Eleven-year-old Nasir Qazi, found face down by the water, his body perforated with pellets, his right arm twisted behind his back.[20] Irfan Maqsood Dar, who had not finished tenth grade when he was killed, hit on the head with a brick as he tried to save his younger brother.[21]

All summer, the government and national media close to the government have been claiming that the protesters, chanting slogans and throwing stones at forces, have been paid five hundred rupees apiece by Pakistan. It has enraged the Valley even further and now reporters from the national press are no longer welcome. As if anyone would give up their life and liberty for five hundred rupees.

DAPAAN

Years later, a former protester in Srinagar will reflect that the chaos of that time was made up of many elements. There were *jazbaati* boys, sentimental boys, like himself, those who were moved by Burhan Wani's death and his cause. There were people who joined protests out of frustration. They had nothing to do; months of curfews and shutdowns meant they were losing income. And yes, there were some boys who had been paid, not by Pakistan but by local opposition parties interested in destabilising the state government. In his experience, the paid boys would start chanting slogans, which would draw out the crowds. By the time forces arrived, they would quietly recede to the background, leaving the *jazbaati* boys to take the pellets and bullets.

But that is neither here nor there. By the time the protests peter out in the winter of 2016, about a hundred civilians have been killed. Many have been arrested or detained and will never return to the lives they had once planned. This, too, is evidence of *zulm*, recorded by Shabir in his 'Ladi Shah'.

The staccato rhythms of the poem match his grief and fury. But he regrets that he cannot write it in Kashmiri, that he has no audience to sing it to. *Ladi shah* is not the same as it once was. By the time Shabir was born in 1986, the *ladi shah* no longer went to fields at harvest time, singing songs that mocked the king. He sang for the radio or appeared in agricultural talk shows on Doordarshan, the public broadcaster. This was more watery fare. He sang of price rises, water shortages, the bitterness of winter, the effects of modernity on rural life—reproaches that could be indulged in a country that claimed to be a democracy. In the rational calm of a Doordarshan studio, the *ladi shah*'s song no longer spoke of *zulm*. It did not object to the government itself.

Shabir knows the songs of harvest time because he has heard stories from his parents, and they had heard stories from their parents. Maybe even the memory of a memory leaves its trace in the mind, so that when he writes, the words follow a familiar pattern—*assalam alaykum, ladi shah aw—ladi shah, ladi shah*, at your door.

The summer of protest has produced a fresh crop of Kashmiri rap songs by boys who grew up listening to Tupac Shakur and 50 Cent. But many are proud of declaring that Kashmiris are the original rappers. They know how to sing their rage because they have been doing it for hundreds of years.

As Shabir writes, the boys are still chanting on the streets. '*Yeh goli-sholi, na bhai na. Yeh pellet-vellet, na bhai na. Yeh shelling-velling, na bhai na. Yeh naukri-shaukri, na bhai na,*' they are telling the government. No to your bullets, no to your pellets, no to your shelling, no to your jobs. For centuries, they have been called *zulm parast*, tyranny worshippers. They will no longer be called *zulm parast*.

2

CRACKDOWN *PAETHER*

It is said, when the *haalaat* first turned bad, people in villages did not know what guns were.

One day, during a crackdown, an army man turns up at a village home and demands, '*Gun kidhar hai?*' Where is the gun?

The man who answers the door thinks he is asking for his brother, Gani. They call him 'Gun' for short. 'Gun is inside,' he says, politely.

The army man storms into the house and hollers for Gun. 'Who, Gun Kak?' someone in the house asks him. For that is what young people call Gani. Gun Kak, Gun Uncle.

By now, the army man is sputtering with rage. 'Gun cock?' he roars. 'Gun cocked?' The hapless Gani is found and beaten up. Chaos ensues.

Where did the story come from? The *bhands*, or folk artistes, of Wathora, a village in central Kashmir's Budgam district, said they wrote the bit in the nineties and slipped it into their plays. An audience getting acquainted with crackdowns in real life would laugh. But the joke is also told by people who lived through crackdowns in Kashmir. This happened, in some hamlet in some corner of the Valley. When, where is not important. It happened, before it passed into *bhand paether*, folk theatre.

Village to stage, stage to village. No one is very sure where the story comes from anymore. But then, once upon a time, the village was the stage.

Picture a *chinar* tree, very broad, branches sweeping low towards the ground. Sunlight drips through its five-fingered leaves and makes a pool of light and shade.

Now picture a group of *bhands*, dressed in bright robes and pointed caps. The *bhands* are drawing a circle with their sound. First the sharp notes of the *swarnai*, rising like flares into the glimmering air. Then the beat of the *dhol*, raising a shiver through the ground.

The *chinar* is next to a shrine, perhaps. A green shrine with a pagoda roof. Afternoon prayers are done. Men streaming out look towards the sound.

Now the *maskhara*, the jester, has joined the musicians. 'My mother died, and the whole village came to me and said, don't worry, we are all your mothers,' he begins.[1] 'My sister died and they came and said we are all your sisters. My grandmother died and they said we are all your grandmothers. Then my wife died.'

He raises his eyebrows and looks around.

'Nobody came.'

The men have drawn near. It is late June and the paddy has been sown. The days have acquired a pleasant languor. Women have joined the crowd; they will sweep the kitchen floors later. They form a circle with their bodies. The stage is set. The play can begin.

Let's say the *bhands* have chosen *Shikargah Paether* for today. A thrill goes through the crowd as the deer enter the circle, followed by the lion. They are actors in costume; everybody knows that. But the lion's mask is almost demonic and the deer very tall.

CRACKDOWN *PAETHER*

Now the animals have flitted away and another *maskhara* enters the stage, this time dressed as a cowherd. He squabbles with his wife about the lunch she has packed for him, then settles down for a nap.

The cowherd is rudely awakened by a hunter from the imperial court who enters the Shikargah looking for the deer. The Shikargah is a patch of forest in South Kashmir that has been turned into a hunting retreat. Later, the hunter is joined by two soldiers.

The soldiers from the imperial court speak in Persian, the peasants and forest dwellers they encounter in Kashmiri. They talk at cross purposes. Laughter and lashings ensue, for when the soldiers cannot understand the poor Kashmiris, they draw their whips on their backs.

Halfway through, it is discovered that the lion has been killed and an inquest is held to find out who did it. In the end, the lion is resurrected and asked to name his killer. 'The soldiers killed me,' the lion says. 'But really you all killed me, soldiers, hunters, guards and peasants. You, who were meant to be preservers of the forest, conspired to kill me.'[2]

Laughter has disappeared in the silence that follows. But then the *swarnai* players strike up a tune and all the actors on the stage dance together. The tension evaporates into the cool evening air.

There is no script. All the parts are played by men, as *bhand paether* does not admit women. The actors and the *maskhara* have salted the old story of *zulm* with a few sly jokes that only people from the village will understand. Which stream is running dry, who is fighting whom over land, how the tax officials have been especially eager this year.

Should a government official enter the laughing crowd, the actors will signal to each other in '*phir kath*', upside-down words. *Phir kath* is the coded language of *bhands*, used to send a number of messages. You missed a cue there. Change tune here. Watch your words, the officials have arrived.

Maybe the play has continued late into the evening and the shadows have deepened under the *chinar*. The actors rig up lanterns and keep going in the deep gold light. Everyone is drunk on laughter, on the faint danger of laughing at the king.

Later on, there will be feasting. Maybe the audience will treat the *bhands* to a curry made from chickens slaughtered for the occasion with piles of *haak*, collard greens, on the side. Maybe, as a special extravagance, some *aab gosht*, mutton cooked in milk. When the *bhands* return later in the year, they will be given *shaali*, freshly harvested paddy, and bushels of rice. This is payment. This is how it has been for centuries.

* * *

Ask how long *bhand paether* has existed in Kashmir and *bhands* grow dreamy.

There was a time when the Valley was filled to the brim with water, begins Ghulam Mohammad Bhagat of the Alamdar Bhagat Theatre. Then the sage Kashyapa drained the water and people started streaming in. There was nothing to eat here, only boulders. There was nothing to wear. Then they started cultivating fruit; they learnt how to weave cotton; they fashioned slippers out of grass. *Bhands* have been here since then.

Gul Mohammad Bhagat of the Kashmir Bhagat Theatre tries to be more precise. There have been *bhands* in Akingam, a village in South Kashmir's Anantnag district, since the eleventh century at least.

This much is certain. The roots of *bhand paether* lie beyond recorded history in Kashmir. *Bhands* have always been here, travelling from village to village, witnessing the rise and fall of empires, the cycles of suffering and rebellion, the seasons of flood and drought.

CRACKDOWN *PAETHER*

They lived on food and grain from audiences, claimed as a right, not charity. For they spoke about people's troubles. *Bhand paether* was a free press, a people's theatre, says Ghulam Mohi-ud-din Aajiz, who is patron of the National Bhand Theatre. It was how a public knew itself.

A handful of stock plays have survived the centuries, passed down from mouth to mouth. Their subject is *zulm*, their language, laughter. In play after play, it is the same pattern. A foreign ruler who does not speak Kashmiri but wants the spoils of the land—fruit, grain, honey, animals and women, who are hardly seen as distinct from chattel. Poor Kashmiri peasants who are flogged for not understanding the king and his men. Jesters who try to outsmart the king.

In *Shikargah Paether*, forests have been turned into a pleasure garden to meet the appetites of a distant king. In *Raaze Paether*, a government official tries to extract honey and chickens from peasants who have nothing to give but dirt.[3] In *Darze Paether*, the Afghan ruler preys on Kashmiri women and demands tributes. In *Angrez Paether*, it is the British; in *Chakdar Paether*, the corrupt revenue collectors of the Dogra king. Other plays explore how different communities, barbers, boatmen, farmers, negotiate power. In *Armeen Paether*, vegetable growers have found a way around official demands of *begaar*.[4] Farmers with means marry their daughters to poor men and take them into their households. When the king's men arrive to ask for their sons, they send their sons-in-law instead. Audiences in Dogra times would have known a thing or two about *begaar*, as their sons were taken away to help fight wars and build roads in Gilgit, dying in hundreds.

The plot is fluid, changing over time, threaded with the here and now. Before *bhands* performed in a village, says Gul Bhagat, they would sit down with the elders, learning of local grievances, picking up snippets of gossip. Sometimes they carried news from other villages. These made their way into the performance as jokes.

The secrets of language are the weapons of a joyous rebellion in *bhand paether*. In the world of the play, the oppressors do not understand the oppressed. In the village audience, only those who are part of a shared network of lives and relations will understand certain jokes. In the charmed circle of performance, the players often talk in *phir kath*, the upside-down language of reality.

Bhands insist *phir kath* is the coded language of the craft, a means of communication between players in front of other people. Every trade has a language like this, they say, from weavers to the famous *wazas*, or chefs, of Kashmir. But *phir kath* is more than the internal language of a trade, says Arshad Mushtaq, a playwright based in Srinagar. It is a form of communication carried into everyday life—words freighted with symbolic meaning that may only be decoded by people within the community. Translated literally into other languages, these words become nonsense. *Phir kath* is a habit of language acquired by people used to being watched.

Village audiences were not the only ones watching *bhand paether*. The hawk-eyed Settlement Commissioner Lawrence noted the Dogra king often had his officials spy on performances. The maharaja learnt much about his subjects from the chatter of the *bhands*. Lawrence confessed he too had learnt about Kashmir from *bhand paether*. He noticed that *bhands* had quite a hold on people and often used the 'peculiar argot' of *phir kath* for stage directions.[5]

Maybe the intentions of the king were not always malign. Gul Bhagat recounts a story from the reign of Maharaja Gulab Singh, the first Dogra king. Kashmir had been saddled with a governor who was particularly trying. One day, when the king was passing through the Valley, *bhands* danced in the royal pageant, weaving their way close to his palanquin. They carried a note, slipped into

CRACKDOWN *PAETHER*

the crack of a bamboo rod used as a prop, detailing the governor's iniquities. The bamboo rod brushed the curtains of the palanquin and the note fell inside. The governor was dismissed soon afterwards.

When the *haalaat* arrived in 1989, such communication between the public and the government was no longer possible. Kashmir was watched more intently than ever before, but now it was the logic of war. There were, as the newspapers liked to put it, boots on the ground. You did not talk to boots, not if you could help it.

There were other reasons why *bhands* found themselves out of work for about a decade. '*Bhand paether* is about joy,' says Manzoor Saaz, a performer with the National Bhand Theatre. 'There was no village where someone had not died. My father said, how can we go to a place of sorrow and play the *swarnai*?'

And then there were the crowds. After 1989, the crowd became suspect, says JB, who lives in Anantnag district. You did not know who was standing next to you, militant, army man in plain clothes, government informer. Crowds could turn into a body of protest demanding *azadi*. Crowds could become bodies; all it took was one grenade.

Besides, the *tehreek* was serious business. When your life was at stake, when you had this fire in your belly, there was no room for the jokes of gentler times, explains JB.

The charmed circles of *bhand paether* vanished from Kashmir. But there were other circles. Crackdown circles. Cordon and search operations which drew rings around localities, defining a theatre of conflict. If *zulm* had a shape in those years, it was a circle filled with eyes. Those who had once watched plays were now the main actors. They performed to a terrifying audience.

Picture a column of soldiers advancing down a street. The column stretches out and curves right. Then it stretches out still more, taking another right, and another, until it has found its tail. It has girded several blocks of houses, a school building, a park with new graves, the local bakery, startling the man behind the cooling breads. Soldiers are webbed across the high streets and back alleys. No one can go in or come out. This is the cordon, circling a zone of interest. Everything within is under a bright scrutiny. Every house will be searched and every resident numbered. The stage is set for the crackdown.

The head of the *mohalla* committee, or neighbourhood committee, is summoned just as he is dipping his bread into a cup of salted pink tea. Go to the mosque, the soldiers instruct him. Tell all the men to go to the park. This is not just a search; this is a crackdown.

Now picture the park filling up with men. Some are barely men, teenagers still trying to grow out their moustaches. Back home, women are watching as soldiers enter, turning out cupboards, knocking over barrels of rice. They try not to flinch as the soldiers open drawers in the bedroom, fingering their underwear.

In the park, the men are told to squat in rows, hands behind their heads. They lower themselves to the ground, drawing their knees up to their chin, sack-like under their *pherans*, loose woollen robes. Before them, a row of Maruti Gypsies, cars favoured by the military for such operations, reinforced with dark bulletproof glass and wire mesh. Behind the armoured glass, eyes.

Informers have led the soldiers here in the first place. Militants are hiding in that house, they have told soldiers, guns were seen in the back of a car. Now, the men in the park are paraded in front of the Gypsies and asked to look straight into the darkness behind the armoured glass. Suddenly, a horn goes off. Yes, that's the one, the informer says. It's him I saw in the car with guns.

The man is picked off the parade, a bag pressed over his head. Soldiers beat him as they bear him towards a Gypsy. He may never be seen again.

All day this continues. This tense parade in the park that follows a familiar script by now. Sit, walk, turn, look, walk. If you are lucky, you go home in the evening to your wife and parents still shivering in the kitchen, a house turned inside out and little left to eat. If your luck is out that day, a bag over your head and then lights out.

In the stage-lit world of the cordon, habits of *phir kath* come in handy. Like all the troubles that have gone before, this terror too will be turned into laughter. But it will not come from the *bhands*. For *bhand paether* is facing a crackdown of its own, had been facing a crackdown, in fact, decades before the *haalaat* arrived.

* * *

It is said, Akingam takes its name from a story about song. According to Gul Bhagat, the village was once home to a singer called Gannak. She was a favourite of the king, even if he was just a local king who ruled over a few villages.

Every evening, Gannak would go to the palace gardens to sing. It's still there, says Gul Bhagat, an empty length of land known as Gannak ki Bagh, Gannak's garden. But then the king's subjects started whispering about her, giving her a bad name. Even today, women who sing are given a bad name, adds Gul Bhagat, forgetting his story for a moment as he remembers more recent grievances.

Gannak was so hurt, she decided she would no longer sing for the king, only for her god. It was late, past midnight. Gannak ki Bagh was deserted when she reached there. She started singing, and as she sang, she wept, asking God to take her. Suddenly, she heard a voice speak to her. 'Ei, Gannak, take the chain in front of you and come up.'

Gannak opened her eyes to find quite a sturdy chain dangling in front of her. She was open to the idea, but then she thought of her musicians. She could not leave them behind. God said she could bring them along. Then it struck Gannak that her village had got a bad name because of her and she could not abandon them. So God asked her to bring the whole village. In the morning, the king's subjects woke up to see the village had disappeared in the wind.

And that is how Akingam got its name. *Akh* (one)—*niu* (taken)—*gam* (village), the village taken by one.

But long after Gannak left, itinerant performers who took the last name of Bhagat continued to live in Akingam and surrounding villages. According to actor Bhawani Bashir Yasir, who started his career in Anantnag district, the Bhagats get their name from the Sanskrit word *bhakt*, or devotee. The goddess in Akingam's Shiva Bhagwati temple had commanded her devotees to make music for her into eternity. It was only later that the Bhagats of Akingam turned to Islam. Mohripora, the next village, was still home to Hindu *bhands* when the *haalaat* arrived.

Akingam also had Sufi shrines where *bhands* sang and played music to pray for rain and crops or to convey other requests for divine intervention. Then there were weddings, festivals, harvests, all the punctuation marks of life, attended by *bhand paether*.

Hindu or Muslim, it did not matter very much, not to the travelling performers, who were as devoted to their art as they were to their god. And certainly not to Mohammad Subhan Bhagat, Gul Bhagat's father, who started his own *bhand* troupe. Subhan Bhagat, with his flaming white hair and his vast sympathy, his habit of speaking about people's concerns that led some to mutter under their breath, 'communist'.

He played the *swarnai*, composed songs and knew all the ragas of Kashmiri folk music. He did not just perform the old classics; he wrote and directed plays using the idiom of folk theatre. He could play emperor and clown and sage. Subhan Bhagat was a *magun*, a person of many talents. It was not just about having many skills. It was a certain alchemy that combined them all into greatness. The title of *magun* had to be earned, Bhawani explains, and Subhan Bhagat was among the last of the *maguns*.

CRACKDOWN *PAETHER*

Starting from the fifties, Subhan Bhagat went from village to village collecting plays. Already, *bhand paether* was dying out as audiences turned to new forms of entertainment. The plays, passed on from mouth to mouth through so many generations, were fading from public memory. Subhan Bhagat committed them to paper. Plays that once ran for five hours were cut down to a pithy hour and a half. Then he put them in books, such as *Kashur Loki Theatre* and *Bhand Jashen*.

But new diversions were not the only reason village audiences were turning away from *bhand paether*. From the fifties, the state government of Jammu and Kashmir started drawing *bhand* troupes into its fold. Under the ministrations of the new state cultural academy, art forms were made to speak of the National Conference's Naya Kashmir, which was now a blueprint for governance rather than a manifesto for revolution.[6] The party had been impatient of dissent ever since Sheikh Abdullah took charge of the administration in 1947, jailing political rivals or sending them into exile in Pakistan. When Abdullah himself was jailed and replaced by Bakshi Ghulam Mohammad in 1953, the state administration grew even more steely, pairing a fetish for surveillance with a keen interest in taking culture into its own hands.[7] Performances moved from the *chinar* to the stage, often at Tagore Hall, the tip-top auditorium built in Srinagar in 1958. Public offerings of food and grain dried up. 'We adopted *bhand paether*,' says Mohammad Yousuf Taing, who was secretary of the state cultural academy almost continuously from 1973 to 1993.

Now there were official recognitions, registrations, orchestrations, awards, rewards. Mohammad Subhan Bhagat and Party became the Kashmir Bhagat Theatre in 1961 and registered with the state cultural academy in 1969, which made them eligible for a monthly stipend of fifty rupees. They were expected to put on two plays a month, performing live in villages across Kashmir. In addition, there were annual theatre festivals organised by the cultural academy. In the seventies, Doordarshan cameras followed them around and the Srinagar station reserved one hour a week for *bhand paether*. A few years later, the Sangeet Natak Akademi, run from Delhi, started sponsoring folk theatre and giving out awards. Subhan Bhagat registered his troupe with the Akademi and won an award in 1983. Other *bhand* troupes soon followed the government route. It was felt to be their best chance of survival.

Those were days of plenty. Village audiences were disappearing, replaced by ministers, bureaucrats and other luminaries. *Bhands* performed for India's Republic Day, Independence Day, assorted government functions and political rallies. Networks of government patronage also sent *bhands* outside the Valley to Jammu and Kerala and Delhi. Gul Bhagat remembers they were eating backstage after a show in Delhi in 1986 and who should turn up but Rajiv Gandhi, then prime minister of India. In 1983, when Gul landed a coveted government job with the irrigation department, his father had waved it away. What did they need jobs for? They had *bhand paether*. It was a choice, Gul says, that would come back to haunt him.

Nowadays there are only *sarkari bhands*, performers carrying the government's message, says Bhawani with some disdain. According to both Bhawani and Mushtaq, the moment *bhands* were separated from their audiences by the curtain of a proscenium theatre, something was lost. Since *bhand paether* was no longer sustained by the largesse of ordinary people, their anger and grievances did not seep into the world of the play. Also missing were the acrid political jokes that referred to the world outside and suddenly made audiences realise the *zulm* of kings and emperors was not confined to the past.

Even if the government's adoption of *bhand paether* was not deliberately aimed at neutralising a traditional form of dissent, it might have been a welcome side effect. Taing protests that the government only wanted to preserve Kashmir's cultural heritage. But yes, he concedes, human beings are intelligent and very good at adapting. When *bhands* were invited to perform in the Dogra court, Taing points out, they would tone down the satire. Likewise, when the state cultural academy financed them, the plays wouldn't be the same.

Certainly, the plays were changing, because you could not laugh at the king if the king was watching. When Subhan Bhagat was collecting plays in the fifties and sixties, the lion still died in *Shikargah Paether*. But in most later versions it was kept alive. Many speculated it was because Abdullah, the Lion of Kashmir, was still a hot favourite. After spending most of the fifties and sixties locked up, the Sheikh came back to power in 1975. It would not do to have lions dying on stage.

Instead, the virtues of the government were performed. State conservation policies kicked in and the Shikargah in Tral was converted from a hunting retreat to a sanctuary. The *bhands* might have been nudged to do a small rewrite. In older versions of *Shikargah Paether*, natural resources as well as bonds between local people and their environment are ravaged by power. In modern iterations of the play, it is power that saves them. The king decrees that nobody will hunt lions because the lion is a symbol of himself.

Other *sarkari*—governmental—projects also infiltrate the play. For instance, the government's preoccupation with timber smuggling. In 1978, the Sheikh's government passed the Public Safety Act, ostensibly to curb timber smuggling. Since then, some versions of *Shikargah Paether* have been dutifully rewritten. The villain of the piece is no longer the hunter but a timber smuggler. He enters the forest to steal wood but is then put through a quick tutorial in conservation.

As the *haalaat* spread across the Valley, of course, it was not timber smugglers who were put away under the PSA. Hundreds disappeared into preventive detention because they were deemed a threat to public safety, because they objected to the Indian state. To talk of such things, *bhands* would need a whole new play. But which *akademi* would sponsor a play called 'Crackdown *Paether*'?

* * *

The *haalaat* came to Wathora in *bhand* fashion. A high street binds together the hamlets of Wathora. Ghulam Mohi-ud-din Aajiz lives here, in the hamlet of Balapora. His home doubles up as the offices of the National Bhand Theatre. Manzoor Saaz, his nephew, lives across the main road in Hanjigund. Almost everyone in Hanjigund and Balapora belongs to a *bhand* family.

Manzoor's father, Ghulam Ali Majboor, who died in 2009, was generally acknowledged as a *magun*. Aajiz's face lights up at Majboor's name. As young men, they had always performed together. Neither had the freedom to be a *bhand* all the time. Majboor had worked in the education department. Aajiz worked with the police as a wireless operator, tied to a desk all day, taking down messages sent from various districts.

Then again, according to Aajiz, the wireless was rather like *phir kath*. Both worked in code. At the police control room, important places and people were given codenames. A series of beeps made up each codename. Aajiz memorised them as tunes. Ta-ta-ta, ta-tat, Location 1, Srinagar. Ta-ta-ta-ta-ta-ta, Location 11, the airport.

Late one night, sometime in the nineties, Aajiz turned up at Majboor's house in Hanjigund and sat down, looking worried. He had a drink of water before he spoke.

There had been a letter, delivered to his house in Balapora. It seemed to be from a militant group and it was not friendly. *Bhands* got money from the Indian government, the letter said; they had to pay up or face death.

Two days later, there was another frantic visitor at Majboor's house. It was Aajiz's brother-in-law. A group of militants had turned up at Balapora. They had been looking for Aajiz but got the name wrong, asking for Ghulam Nabi Aajiz instead of Ghulam Mohi-ud-din Aajiz. Aajiz, who had answered the door, told them quite truthfully that Ghulam Nabi wasn't home. But the ruse would not last long. What was to be done?

Fear crashed over Hanjigund. Everyone was thinking about the letter. Many counselled Majboor to stay away. The men had guns after all. Eventually, he set out with a few others.

Something did not seem right. Militants had been known to extract money, but they rarely turned up fully armed at your doorstep in broad daylight. Did they really have guns?

Back at Aajiz's house, matters had taken a convivial turn. The gunmen had declared they were bona fide members of a militant group. Do not mess with us, they insisted rather nervously. But then they were persuaded to have a cup of tea, to stay for a bit of lunch. A boy was sent to the market to buy some chicken.

The visitors must be tired, press their feet, Aajiz told a couple of the boys gathered in his living room. It was *phir kath*. What he was really telling them was, check their weapons.

The boys obeyed, letting their hands travel up the visitors' *pherans* and feeling the weapons hidden in the folds. Instead of gunmetal, they found wood. These were toy guns. The visitors were thieves, cashing in on the current fad of militant extortions.

It became a bit in a play after that—the thieves who would be militants.

But the *bhands* of Wathora were soon to learn tragedy. Majboor's son, Manzoor, remembers waiting outside Tagore Hall in Srinagar for a bus that was two hours late. When it finally arrived, the driver had grim news. Batpora, a village on the way home, was burning. There was a pitched battle between militants and forces. The bus couldn't take the group home. For days, they took shelter in another village as blasts and fighting continued in Batpora. Manzoor remembers a child was killed.

DAPAAN

In 1998, Tagore Hall itself was damaged in a fire. The *haalaat* turned the hall into a Central Reserve Police Force camp, making it the object of militant attacks.

In 2005, militants had taken cover in a house in Balapora. A gunfight followed and the house was burned down by soldiers. Aajiz was on duty that day. As the wireless sprang to life, he took down the code words. Halfway through the message, it struck him they were talking about his house. It was his house in Balapora that had been burnt down.

Aajiz rushed home but could save nothing except his *saaz-e-Kashmir*, a stringed instrument that had belonged to his grandfather. For six months, he did not return to Balapora. There were people in the village who had told the army that he had sheltered militants. Then they told militants that he had betrayed their colleagues to the army. It was only after the militant group had conducted its own investigations and decided that he was not the informer that Aajiz felt it safe to return.

* * *

Everywhere, there were eyes. The relentless organising gaze of the *markaz*, which had come to regard Kashmir as a zone of interest, fragmented into thousands and thousands of eyes. Cordons, checkpoints, bunkers, agencies, informers, collaborators. Even if you were not actually being watched, you constantly felt the prickle of a gaze on your back.[8]

In the cold light of surveillance, words and gestures were suddenly thrown into sharp relief, rendered almost theatrical. Nowhere more so than during a crackdown, with the military cordon marking out the area under scrutiny. It was like living in a panopticon but also in Dante's circles of hell, says GP, who grew up in Baramulla district. You were disciplined and you were punished.

The Wathora *bhands* had pushed their luck when they worked the Gun Kak joke into their plays. Maybe they hoped the government heavies in the audience would not understand. Officials from Delhi did not know much Kashmiri. Officials from Kashmir would suppress a smile and not explain to their colleagues.

Across Kashmir, there were now thousands of Gun Saebs, gentlemen with guns. If you wanted to inquire about the fate of a local militant, you asked politely if Gun Saeb was keeping well. *Bhand paether* might have vanished from the public square, but *phir kath* was thriving in the towns and villages of the Valley. Certain information had to be conveyed so that soldiers watching nearby would not understand.

While people under crackdown were being watched, they were also making their own observations. As crackdowns spread, so did crackdown jokes. It is said, *maskharas* were the life of *bhand paether* because they kept the laughs coming. An old Kashmiri saying goes, 'if we do not laugh, how can we live'.[9] So now Kashmiris were telling jokes as if their lives depended on it. They were telling them after the cordon lifted, as families recovered in kitchens, as men gathered on the *pe'end*, or shop front. Over time, some of these became stock jokes. Nobody was sure where they had happened or to whom. But they were proof of life.

In *Shikargah Paether*, comedy had arisen from soldiers speaking in Persian and peasants speaking in Kashmiri. Now, the gap between languages birthed laughter once again.

The *haalaat* had disgorged into the Valley thousands of soldiers who did not speak or understand Kashmiri. In the early years, many Kashmiris, especially in the rural areas, did not know much Hindi or Urdu either. They quickly picked up what words they could. If you were to be punished, GP explained, you needed to know the language you were being punished in. But these linguistic skills were often imperfect. Words travelled from Kashmiri to Hindi as bombs.

Take the fireman who had to go to work, but there was a crackdown in Nowhatta in downtown Srinagar. Soldiers had circled the area around the Jamia Masjid but were nervous about entering the narrow lanes behind the mosque that seethed with rebellion.

The fireman, or *bam wol*, as they say in Kashmiri, emerged from the alleys and peered out from one end of the boundary wall guarding the mosque. He ducked back in. Too many soldiers. He peered out from the other end of the boundary wall and ducked back in again. Too many soldiers. The third time he tried to slip out, the soldiers caught him—what did he think he was doing? The fireman tried to explain in Hindi that he had to go to work. '*Mai bam hu,*' he said, quite reasonably. I am a bomb.

Other words also became weapons. YA remembers soldiers entering their workshop in downtown Srinagar during a search operation. It had a loom where they spun coarse woollen cloth, called *raffal* in Kashmiri. When the soldiers asked what the workshop was used for, YA replied that they made *raffal*. The soldiers jumped. You make rifles?

Everyone knew of the carpenter who told soldiers he was carrying '*samaan*'. In both Kashmiri and Hindi, the word means 'things'. Except, in an exquisitely bland Kashmiri euphemism, *samaan* had come to mean weapons. The soldiers had picked up on this euphemism. They frogmarched the carpenter to a camp and asked him to empty his bag. He did so, producing nothing more deadly than a trowel.

Needing to use the facilities during a crackdown could also be explosive. Consider, for instance, the old man who had to take a leak during a long crackdown in North Kashmir. '*Me aav chaar,*' he thought in Kashmiri, I'm bursting. He decided to convey the urgency of the matter in his newfound Hindi.

The old man walked up to the patrolling soldiers and politely said, '*Hum chaar.*' We are four.

'Oh? Where?' the soldiers asked, suddenly alert.

The old man repeated patiently, '*Hum chaar.*'

'Yes? Where are the other three?'

CRACKDOWN *PAETHER*

This went on forever. It is possible there is still a park in North Kashmir where an old man tries to explain he is bursting and soldiers ask him, yes, where are the other three?

Someone in downtown Srinagar who wanted to take a shit also ended up sounding seditious. The Kashmiri phrase indicating imminent bowel movement is *'meyo gus'*. After sweating quietly for hours, the man had said in his best Hindi, *'Hummay gussa aya.'* We are angry.

Once, a crackdown started very early in the morning and the gathering soldiers bumped into the village milkman, *gour* in Kashmiri. The milkman tried to explain why he was out at that hour. *'Mai gaon ke gouri hun,'* he said in Hindi. I am the village belle.

It is not clear which village this happened in or when. Maybe it happened over and over again, in many villages to many milkmen. Another story seems to have happened twice, once to a former Border Security Force man and once to a militant.

It is said, when a search operation was announced in a village in Baramulla district, the retired BSF man panicked. He had carried out searches before but had never been searched himself. Many of his neighbours were making a run for it, hoping to escape before the cordon closed. The BSF man decided to dive into a barrel of rice. Almost every Kashmiri household has them, large tin drums filled with supplies for the winter months.

Soldiers barged into the house, turning out the drawers, poking at the barrels, hollering, 'Who's there?'

The terrified BSF man thought he had better come clean. 'Sir, *mai chawal hu*,' he answered in a quavering voice. Sir, I am rice.

He never lived that down. Everywhere he went in the village, people called after him, *'mai chawal hu'*.

But GP is certain it was a militant who dove into a barrel of rice in another village in Baramulla district. The stories are identical apart from the ending. The BSF man was taunted by his neighbours. The militant went to jail.

* * *

Meanwhile, in Akingam, laughter was running out. The militants who turned up at Subhan Bhagat's house on 17 July 1990 carried real guns. Trouble had started six months earlier, when his troupe had performed for Republic Day functions in Delhi. Eyebrows had been raised in Akingam, where the *tehreek* was gathering force. When the *bhands* returned to the village, Subhan Bhagat was advised to stay in and lie low. The gentlemen with guns showed up anyway.

Subhan's son, Gul, remembers it was ten at night. They had eaten dinner and most of the family had retired to their rooms. While Gul's wife washed up in the kitchen, Gul and his father sat in one of the rooms on the ground floor. When they heard a knock on the door and saw the outlines of eight to ten people outside, Gul unplugged the lights. They waited in tense silence.

Three militants entered the room and placed a gun on Subhan Bhagat's chest. They had two demands. First, from now on he should cut out mention of Hindus in his plays and follow Islamic principles. Second, he should offer one of his children to the jihad.

But what would happen to the plays he had already written, where Hindus and Muslims mixed freely, the *magun* asked. This problem was easily solved. The militants searched the house for scripts and set fire to what they could find. Out of fifty-four plays written by Subhan Bhagat, only twenty-nine survive. The rest burned that night.

As for giving one of his children to the *tehreek*, Subhan Bhagat said he would think about it and asked if the militants could please come back a few days later. The next day, he told his sons to leave home. When the militants returned, the ageing *magun* shrugged and said his children had left but they could take him, an offer so ludicrous they would obviously turn it down. As punishment, Subhan Bhagat had to pay a fine of two hundred thousand rupees. He was also placed under house arrest.

Suddenly, the family was plunged into debt. Work had dried up because of the *haalaat*. I had to beg, said Gul Bhagat, his face crumpling. Gul, with his soft voice and his delicate face, had played women for thirty years. As his face and voice grew heavy, he started to play men. As his hair grew white, he started to play aged men. There was no other work he was cut out for. But when they came for his father, he had no choice. He began going from door to door selling clothes he had scrounged from his uncle's garment business.

Subhan Bhagat was allowed to leave the house just once a week for Friday prayers. Every few days, militants would check that the terms of the house arrest were being observed. When they visited, they expected to be fed well, with meat and milk and vegetables that the family could no longer afford.

They did not have to visit all the time. It seemed as if the whole village had turned jailer. Many families had sons who had become militants. Public sympathies for the *tehreek* ran high. Next door to Akingam, the Hindu *bhands* of Mohripora were fleeing the Valley. No one was going to openly defy the decree of militants.

Even now, there are conflicting theories about why they came for Subhan Bhagat. His family believes it was because *bhand paether* did not sit well with militant groups that followed a more puritanical strand of Islam which forbade music and revelry. Others object. There were militants and there were militants. Local Kashmiri boys who quite enjoyed an evening of *bhand paether* would not interfere because of religion or because of religion alone. Most believe it was because Subhan Bhagat had thrived on government patronage; all famous *bhands* became suspect overnight for their affiliations to the culture ministry and state broadcasters. Then there are murmurs of a financial dispute between the *magun* and other performers, who might have encouraged the late night visit and the hefty fine.

Whatever it was, this much is certain: Subhan Bhagat went into decline under house arrest. He grew heavy and ill. In 1993, Gul got permission from the militants to take his father to Delhi for treatment. Doctors testing him at the All India Institute of Medical Sciences asked if he had trouble with his wife or his children, any sort of grief or worry that had tripped up the workings of his heart. But no, the only grief Subhan Bhagat had to bear had been brought on by the *haalaat*. The doctors suggested he move to Jammu but he refused. Kashmir was his home.

In May, Subhan Bhagat did a play for Radio Kashmir called *Awuzan*, Strung Up. It was, Gul says, their family's story told through drama. That would be Subhan Bhagat's last play.

And then, how to put it? The stage offers many metaphors for death. Lights out, curtains, exit left. This was the last act, the final scene, the swansong. But all metaphors fail for the *magun* of Akingam. Maybe all play had run out by the end, or maybe the end brooks no metaphor. Suffice it to say that in June 1993, shortly after consigning his life to drama, Mohammad Subhan Bhagat died.

* * *

Elsewhere, a kind of exaggerated theatricality was flourishing. Militants caught in a crackdown had to develop their own charades and fictions. For the play, as they say, is the thing. That was how you survived. Take GP's uncle, a militant commander who had lived through many crackdowns.

Once, GP's uncle played a teacher. The whole village, men, women, children, had been turned out and herded into a field outside a local school. In the early nineties, GP says, women had been allowed to stay indoors as searches began, but by the end of that decade, no one was spared in those parts of Baramulla district. Men and women, young and old, all out in the field as the crackdown was announced.

GP's uncle had streamed out with the rest of the village. Since he said he was a teacher, the soldiers treated him with some deference, even giving him a chair to sit on while the others squatted on the ground. Everyone in the village knew he was a militant commander but went along with the story. An elderly woman, who was known for being fidgety, grew restless with the secret. Suddenly professorial, GP's uncle barked at her to sit still and not disrupt the crackdown.

It turned out the soldiers were looking specifically for GP's uncle. They knew his name but not much else. Did anyone know a militant by this name? The question was thrown to the crowd in general, not to anybody in particular. No one gave him away. After the crackdown, GP's uncle fled the village. The soldiers came back a few days later, better informed this time. They beat up the man's brother, GP's father—why didn't you tell us it was him? But you never asked me, he replied.

GP's uncle had a flowing beard, so another time he told searching soldiers that he was a maulvi. Unconvinced, they were going to arrest him anyway. But then women from the village started protesting. How dare they lay a finger on their maulvi? The soldiers backed away.

Very often, militants tried to hide when a crackdown began, ambitious disappearing acts that were doomed to fail. One fighter crouched in a hayrick but neatly arranged his slippers outside.

Another fighter told his friends to tie him up inside a bale of hay stored in the attic. When soldiers arrived, they asked his friends to toss the bales down to the courtyard below. They obeyed, until they got to that one heavy bale. When they said they couldn't lift it, the soldiers replied with blows. So they heaved it up and threw it down.

DAPAAN

Oh, I'm dead, I'm dead, said a voice from the hay as it hit the ground. The hiding militant had broken his back. To add insult to injury, he was then jailed for several years.

* * *

Bhand paether made a tenuous return to Akingam years after Subhan Bhagat's death. Once the massive crackdowns that marked the first decade of the *haalaat* had eased. Once most of the gentlemen with guns had been killed off. Once the other gentlemen with guns, the RR, BSF, CRPF, JKP, SOG, TA, SSB and various other acronyms of state, had firmly taken over.

As the number of militants fell, the *markaz* started making plans to launch a tourist villages project in Kashmir. This brainwave of the Union culture ministry would be implemented by the Jammu and Kashmir Tourism Department, along with the regional branch of the INTACH, the Indian National Trust for Art and Cultural Heritage. Certain villages of cultural, historic or scenic interest were to be improved so as to attract tourists. Akingam was one of them.

After several rounds of discussion, it was decided that the village would get a brand-new, tip-top cultural centre, complete with an auditorium. Construction started around 2006. It was still under construction when *bhand* troupes started holding workshops in 2009, says Gul Bhagat, who was involved with the centre in the early years. But programmes and workshops trickled out and the centre grew deserted. The tourists never came. Gul Bhagat abandoned theatre and took up work as a school bus driver.

After 2016, Gul says, only God knows what happened. As mass protests spread across the Valley, all government buildings became suspect. Elsewhere, government schools and *panchayat* or village council buildings were being burnt down before they could be turned into camps. It is said, sometime around 2018, the army did eye the empty cultural centre for a new camp but did not move in permanently. But now the building was doubly suspect. It is said, local boys vandalised the centre, setting fire to the equipment inside.

Nowadays, the centre is locked up. It is only opened when a tourist department or cultural academy official visits. Ghulam Mohammad Bhagat of the Alamdar Bhagat Theatre complains there are no lights, no chairs, no equipment and layers of dust—how are they supposed to perform there? The older haunts of the *bhands* in Akingam are also deserted. Nothing remains of the old Shiva Bhagwati temple where the goddess ordered *bhands* to perform. A new brick temple has been built, topped with a saffron flag and laced with concertina wiring. A security guard dozing in the courtyard wakes up to tell visitors they can't go in. Some of the Sufi shrines where the *bhands* once performed are also locked. A new generation of Kashmiri Muslims consider the veneration of saints idolatrous and have stopped going. Occasionally, the Sangeet Natak Akademi sponsors an old-fashioned show, such as *Shikargah Paether*, performed by the Alamdar Bhagat Theatre in a nearby village in August 2024. Village audiences look intrigued, crowding around the players as they record the performance on their phones. Most of the time, *bhand paether* is put to more official uses.

Nowadays, *bhands* are deployed in polio vaccination and AIDS awareness campaigns. Around Independence Day, there's the central government's campaign for Har Ghar Tiranga, meaning a flag in every house. In the run-up to the general elections of 2024, *bhands* were asked to submit plays on Viksit Bharat, a mystical scheme for economic prosperity, and other subjects close to the prime minister's heart.

Nowadays, anyone prone to histrionics is called a *bhand*. Not a serious person, not genuine. Maybe it is because *bhands* have forgotten the upside-down words of a people being watched. Or because in *bhand paether*, *zulm* has become a thing of the past and not part of the urgent, living present.

DAPAAN

Picture, for instance, early autumn in Wathora in 2022. The National Bhand Theatre is rehearsing *Chakdar Paether* in a small room while the *chinars* are turning scarlet outside. The peasants harvest their paddy. They must give up most of it to the *chakdar*, who has appeared to collect taxes. The peasants will starve if they forfeit so much of their grain. But when they protest, they are beaten. Then it is 1947 and *azadi* has arrived. The peasants dance, free of the *chakdar*'s tyranny at last. The *bhands* will perform *Chakdar Paether* at a government college where, to most students, perhaps, *azadi* did not arrive in 1947. Only the British left.

Now picture a blustery spring day at the brand-new Chadoora Government Degree College just a few kilometres from Wathora. It is the only building amid acres of open land. The stage is a badminton court that is still under construction. The wind carries the dense smell of sheep flitting through the fields. The cultural academy has organised a day of folk entertainment for the students of the college. Many of the students who turn up have never seen *bhand paether*. Everyone shivers in the cold as they wait for the programme to start. Finally, a bureaucrat arrives. The programme may start.

Early in the programme is *Angrez Paether*. The *Angrez*, the English, are still allowed to be old-school villains, as if to say, are we not glad they left? They enter the stage in bright wigs, red and blond, and what must be an English accent. They are pleasure seekers who want to taste the bounties of Kashmir. A local official enters, whipping two Kashmiri peasants. They have been brought in for *begaar* and must serve the whims of the *Angrez*.

The foreigners demand apples, and the peasant is whipped because he takes a bite of the apple first. No one laughs. Then they demand nuts, which the local official hears as '*laath*', kicks. The peasants are duly kicked around. No one laughs. Some of the students have melted away. One girl has burst into tears; it is not clear if the play is responsible or her own romantic troubles.

CRACKDOWN *PAETHER*

Not like the crowd at Tagore Hall, which was restored in 2015 and is tip-top once more. It is now late autumn in 2022, and the lieutenant governor himself has been invited for the folk arts festival, which begins under a heavy blanket of security. Men in black suits stand with their backs to the stage, watching the watchers. Everyone is nervous. A bamboo gateway plastered with the lieutenant governor's picture collapses before he can arrive.

The lieutenant governor arrives, descending from the maw of his massive black car in his signature costume of bright-orange kurta, hot-pink waistcoat and golden Covid-19 mask. When he takes the stage to speak, the audience turns itself into a durbar, now clapping, now exclaiming, 'Wah! Wah!'

The lieutenant governor is presented with an award for suggesting the festival be organised (the organiser is almost in tears as he speaks of the governor's magnanimity). The local leader of the ruling party is presented with an award for being the local leader of the ruling party. The organisers present themselves with an award for organising the festival. Then they remember the *bhand* performers and present one of them with an award as well.

Sometime in between the awards, the speeches and the pageant of security officers, dancers are allowed on stage, Dogri, Pahari, Kashmiri, colourful cultural artefacts of the brand-new, tip-top Union Territory of Jammu and Kashmir. They beam at the audience as they dance. A government official sitting next to me, who says she was once a television actress, starts singing along to a folk song.

Now something else is emerging from the crowd of swirling women, something that does not quite belong there. Two deer, a tiger and a *maskhara*. The characters of *Shikargah Paether*. But the tiger does not die today; the *maskhara* has no jokes. There is no sparring between Kashmiri peasants and soldiers who do not understand their language. No lines, they seem to have been

DAPAAN

told—it will only slow down the programme. Not too much time in the spotlight, either, for audiences would prefer to look at amiable young women. So the deer, the tiger and the *maskhara* take centre stage for a couple of minutes, bobbing wordlessly to the music. Then they fade back into the heaving mass of dancers.

3

YOU MAY BE TURNED INTO A CAT

SK woke up one morning to the announcement, 'Sisterfuckers are saying get out of the house.' It was Arif Moet, using the loudspeakers of the local mosque.[1] This was downtown Srinagar in the nineties.

SK pieced together what must have happened. The army must have cordoned off the area for a search operation. They were following the usual drill: get someone to announce the crackdown from the local mosque and have all the men in the neighbourhood out in the street before the search begins. Evidently, they had not been able to find the imam or the head of the *mohalla* committee, someone trusted in the neighbourhood. Instead, they had chosen Arif Moet for the job.

True to his name, Arif Moet had not minced words. For centuries, every village and town in Kashmir has had a *moet*, a version of the holy fool who is touched with divine madness, who speaks his mind because he cannot tell the difference between truth and civility. Arif Moet was perfectly amiable but could not tell the difference either. His brother Ahmad was the same.[2] The third brother was a serious man. He had joined the Jammu and Kashmir Liberation Front early on in the *tehreek*.

DAPAAN

SK remembers one of the first crackdowns in downtown Srinagar, sometime in 1990. Men had been forced out of their homes in the morning and ordered to crawl for part of the way. Then they were told to walk with their hands behind their heads and taken to a narrow alley where they were made to line up, facing the wall.

SK and the others stood in silence, wondering what was going to happen next. The silence was broken by Ahmad, who suddenly decided to burst into song. For this impromptu performance, he had chosen *'Jaago Jaago Subhu Hoi'*, Wake Up, Wake Up, It Is Morning. It was a popular anthem of the *tehreek*, often sung during protests or played on mosque speakers. Ahmad, however, was not singing in defiance. He was singing because he felt like it.

The men in the line-up were convinced they were going to die that day. One old man turned to Ahmad's brother, the JKLF militant, and asked him sorrowfully, 'What was your mother eating when she had him?'

When the soldiers had forced men out of the house that morning, the JKLF man had taken his chances and joined the line-up. Those were early days and not many people knew he had become a militant. He survived that day but later on he would be arrested and tortured so badly that he lost his manhood, as SK puts it. A cat must have given him away.

* * *

In the dramatis personae of crackdowns—the soldiers who circled the neighbourhood; the officer who barked out orders; the militants trying to blend into the crowd; the men in the parade worrying about wives and children at home; the OGWs, overground workers who secretly helped militants, trying to arrange their facial expressions to look neutral—'cats' played the most pivotal role. They were the ones who did the watching.

YOU MAY BE TURNED INTO A CAT

Informers were called cats. The word probably came from a security term imported from counterinsurgency operations in Punjab in the eighties. According to a former police officer in Kashmir, it might have been short for 'concealed anti-terrorism squad'. Or it might not have been a short form at all. In Punjab, writes one security analyst, counterinsurgency was a 'cat and mouse game'. Small-time criminals, former militants and militant sympathisers were forced or induced to become police informers and embedded in militant groups; set loose the cat to catch the mice.[3]

The word caught on quickly in Kashmir, entering the new argot of conflict along with crackdown and curfew. In 1993, *Greater Kashmir*, a local daily, ran a series of articles with the headline, 'Kashmir—Victim of C', a potted dictionary of words brought in by the *haalaat*, all beginning with C, as though that particular letter had malign powers.

The word 'cats' may or may not have been handed down by forces, but once it entered the Kashmiri public, it became a potent *phir kath* of the time, loaded with meanings that would make no sense to anyone outside. Cats had heritage; cats had history in Kashmir. The spies of the Dogra king might have been decommissioned after 1947, but the continuing battle between this *markaz* and that, the insurrections within, had made the government watch closely for signs of disaffection.

It is said, Bakshi Ghulam Muhammad consolidated an army of vigilantes who patrolled the streets at night. Having ousted Sheikh Abdullah with some help from Delhi, Bakshi was particularly nervous of dissidents. Apart from old political rivals, the National Conference itself was drained of members who did not approve of the direction taken by the party and who now formed the Plebiscite Front to keep alive the demand for self-determination.[4]

The vigilantes were mostly unemployed boys from the towns who had time on their hands and no money. Officially, they were called the Peace Brigade. Most people called them Kuntrih Pandah, Twenty-Nine Fifteen, because of the salary they got. This was supposed to be thirty rupees a month, but even spies were not exempt from bureaucracy. In those days, the rupee had not been decimalised, and it was sixteen annas to a rupee. The government clerks dispensing the salary took off one anna for stamp duty. So the spies got twenty-nine rupees and fifteen annas.

They were also called '*khoftan fakir*', vagabonds who wander after evening prayers. In Kashmir, travellers a long way from home would often shelter in the local mosque at night. But these travellers were not asking for shelter. They were out to spread fear. Houses were pelted with a sudden hail of stones. It was rumoured that anyone caught listening to Radio Pakistan would be beaten up and reported for treason. After eight o'clock in the evening, many households turned off Radio Pakistan and switched dutifully to All India Radio and Radio Kashmir, which was set up during the first border war to counter propaganda from the other side.[5] You never knew who was watching at the window.

Cats were recognised as descendants of *khoftan fakirs*. Only the *fakirs* had been deployed by the state government, even if it was a government installed by Delhi. Cats, more often than not, were the refracted eyes of the *markaz*. Every central force and agency had them. As the local police got involved in counterinsurgency, they too acquired cats. Mention cats in Kashmir and eyes still light up in recognition.

* * *

There were two kinds of cats in Kashmir. There were personal cats, regular informers on the payrolls of agencies. They carried on with their daily lives or joined militant groups but secretly passed on intelligence to forces. The second kind of cat was a cat under duress, people who had been captured and tortured until they gave up names. Trouble was, anyone could be turned into this sort of a cat anytime.

YOU MAY BE TURNED INTO A CAT

YA remembers praying for deliverance as he walked in the parade during crackdowns in Srinagar. It was like crossing the *siraat*, he says, the bridge over hell that is thinner than a strand of hair and sharper than a sword. Ten Maruti Gypsies would be lined up but only one or two of them contained a cat; you did not know which at first. But after a while, you identified the Gypsy where the horn was being pressed. The sound was like a bullet. You never knew whom it came for. The boy identified by the cat and dragged out of the parade would be turned into a temporary cat. If ten boys were caught this way, all ten would be turned into cats for the rest of the crackdown.

You could be taken even if you had nothing to do with militants. Cats were not too particular about whom they named. They could take names to settle old scores. There were times when cats, forced to name someone, named their friends, hoping they would understand. It was like calling in a favour.

YA was seized by the Border Security Force in 1996, locked up for three days and beaten. His friend, a temporary cat, had given him up. YA confronted him about it later. You are my friend, the temporary cat replied—who else would I name?

Sometimes it ended well. After they were released, cats would laugh about how they saw you during the crackdown that day, wearing that yellow shirt, but they did not take your name.

Sometimes it did not. Quite often, militants would shoot cats, even temporary cats who had cracked under interrogation. In their book, it was only reasonable. If militants were ready to die for the *tehreek*, why couldn't the cats take a few blows or electric shocks?

* * *

Militants could turn into cats too. Some were personal cats who had quietly infiltrated the ranks, passing on information to agencies or encouraging defections. Some militants, like AB, were forced to become cats.

DAPAAN

When the *haalaat* came, AB was still in school and curious. He wanted to see what militants were like. He noticed how everyone was delighted when they visited, as if receiving a new groom for the first time. In the mid-nineties, he joined the Hizbul Mujahideen and crossed the Line of Control to learn how to use a gun. Eighty-five boys went over; a hundred and five boys came back three months later. Back home in downtown Srinagar, AB kept a low profile. He moved from house to house and stayed away from the main roads, where the cats roamed.

But one day, AB's father and brother asked him to go home for dinner and he could not refuse. He went, along with four other local commanders of the Hizb. They had dinner and slept by ten. The next morning, his father knocked on their door and said there was a cordon around their house. A personal cat had informed forces they were visiting home.

The five militants tried to escape, first this way, then that. Both routes were closed. They tried a third alley, which led to a mosque where they took shelter. But the army arrived. They had been informed. The militants would have surrendered but for the one Pakistani commander among them. He had a taste for martyrdom, recalls AB, his voice very dry. This man threw a grenade at the forces and a gunfight started. The army must have had instructions to take them alive, AB says, because when they were finally captured, they were badly injured but not dead. For seven days, they were treated for their wounds at a Srinagar hospital. On the eighth day, the torture started.

There was beating, but sticks were like flowers compared to the electricity, says AB. They cut his fingernails and toenails and wound copper wires around them. Then they passed electricity through the wires. This was a different order of pain, so sharp you remembered everything, you remembered drinking your mother's milk. The electric shocks caused such a pain in his stomach that he could not take it anymore. He cracked. This is

YOU MAY BE TURNED INTO A CAT

my rank, this is the number of boys under our command, this is where we operate. And then the catting started.

Every day, AB would be driven around downtown in a car and would tell the army men what he knew—there are weapons in that house, there's a militant in there. The moment he gave them information, they would cordon off the area. If they didn't find anything, they would beat him.

After about three weeks, all five commanders were transferred to Papa 2, the interrogation centre that would later have the distinction of being converted into the chief minister's residence. They were now in the custody of the Border Security Force. The army, said AB, followed rules when they tortured prisoners. The BSF did not know what those rules were. The three BSF torture specialists assigned to him were *zaalim*, tyrants. They nearly killed him once because they mistook him for another militant who had the same first and middle names.

Catting started again from Papa 2. If he didn't give them boys, the torture would be worse that day. There would be less food to eat or meals would be served at odd hours. It would be about three months before he was transferred to Kot Bhalwal Jail in Jammu and three years before cats would get him again.

* * *

So there were many ways to be turned into a cat. For instance, militants, with their Kalashnikov swagger, had given others a taste for play-acting. This could lead to trouble or, more specifically, crackdowns, which led to the making of cats. Take the story of the cat from Qammarwari.

Crackdowns were genteel in Qammarwari. In the nineties, it was a quiet, marshy area on the outskirts of Srinagar that was just being built up. There were hardly any militants here. Not like Chhattabal and Batamaloo nearby, so hot with the *tehreek* that people called them liberated zones. For a few years, forces would not dare enter these places.

DAPAAN

KF, who lived in the boring respectability of Qammarwari, longed to see militants. When a friend offered to take him to a hideout in Chhattabal, he was overjoyed. They went. KF was impressed. He took pictures posing with guns. Back in Qammarwari, he went to the local photo studio to get the reel developed.

The studio owner said he could do it at three rupees, twenty-five paise per photograph. This struck KF as injustice. Taj Studio in Lal Chowk would do it for three rupees per photograph. The Qammarwari studio owner refused to bargain. His was a small business; this was the best they could offer. KF took his reel to Taj Studio.

Lal Chowk, the nerve centre of Srinagar, a town square arranged around a clock tower, is always bristling with forces. A one-tonne, as the olive-green military trucks are known in Kashmir, is usually parked outside Taj Studio. As KF went to collect the pictures, soldiers decided to search the shop. Not surprisingly, he was arrested. Pictures with guns are prone to getting you arrested.

KF was now a cat, all his taste for adventure gone. He agreed to take them to the hideout in Chhattabal. A cordon was laid around the area. So many bullets flew that day, says KF's neighbour, who is telling the story, suddenly quiet.

* * *

Militants, however, grew skilled in the art of *phir kath*, secret codes to warn one another. If there was danger, they would brush their hair back with one hand, much like Shah Rukh Khan in the romantic films of the nineties. If they rubbed their face with both hands, it meant no danger, all clear. AB would come to know the codes well.

By the late nineties, he was back in Kashmir after three years in Jammu prisons. Jail time did nothing to reform militants, he says; it only turned them into hardened militants. Those had

YOU MAY BE TURNED INTO A CAT

been eventful years. He had met famous Hurriyat leaders, witnessed prison riots and conspiracies. Secret messages were passed out of prison in the piping of blankets. The guards checked everything but missed the piping. They were often deadly messages: blow up a tower, recruit this one, bump that one off.

When AB was released, he also carried a message in his blanket; he did not know what it said. He found out a few days later, at a rendezvous with a Hizb commander so famous he had a million-rupee reward on his head. It turned out AB had carried his own summons in his blanket. He was to join the Hizb again. The commander handed him a gun and asked him to lie low while he waited for instructions. A few weeks later, AB got his first task: to blow up a certain special task force officer.

AB set out with a small band of militants. The police must have got wind of it, for they followed them to Peer Bagh, an affluent part of Srinagar, where they were planning to carry out the assassination. The militants opened fire and managed to fob off the police for a while. But AB thought it would be wise to hand over his weapon to one of the other boys. He was the one they were looking for and he couldn't be caught with weapons on him. What AB didn't know was that the militant he handed the gun to was a personal cat of the BSF. The next day, the inevitable cordon around his house. AB found himself at Shiraz Cinema, a movie theatre turned into a camp in downtown Srinagar, and face to face with his old tormentors, the three BSF torture specialists from Papa 2.

This time, he tried to hold out. He denied everything because he knew they would beat him either way. But the BSF's personal cat gave away half the story so AB was forced to fill in the other half. Yes, that was the name of the Hizb commander who had drawn him back into militancy. Yes, he was supposed to meet the commander at the Jamia Masjid that Friday. It was back to catting again.

DAPAAN

When Friday came, AB was taken to the Jamia Masjid compound by a contingent of BSF men, all disguised in 'khan dress', the long shirt and pyjamas that are everyday clothing for many men in South Asia but which forces insist are the favoured garb of 'terrorists'. Soon enough, AB saw the Hizb commander walking down the steps of the compound, coming towards him with a smile on his face. It was the smile that stopped him. AB had got a lot of men caught in his life but he could not bring himself to give this man away. He lifted one hand and brushed his hair back. The Hizb commander ran.

AB's second stint in custody was shorter. His brother paid a local legislator two hundred thousand rupees to get him out and sent him away from Kashmir for some years. Two years after he left Kashmir, AB was on the phone with his mother when she told him that the Hizb commander had been sent to his *sasural*, his in-laws' house. AB understood that he had finally been killed.

4

THE BUFFOON KING

So this is how it begins. A group of actors gets together and decides to put up a show. It will be one of the greats, the classics. A masterful exposition of kings and ministers, power and folly.

The actors start pulling on their robes. They start painting their faces. They slip rings over their knuckles and chains around their necks. What historical period does their drama belong to? They are not too particular. They dress as *badshahs* and *begums* and *wazirs* dress in the movies. They dress the way you imagine a *badshah* when you close your eyes.

Roles are decided on the spot. You will be the first *wazir*, they say, pointing to one actor, and he becomes the first *wazir*. You will be the second *wazir*, they say to another, and he becomes the second *wazir*. You will be king, they say to another actor, very thin, with a pencil moustache and eyebrows raised in perpetual surprise.

And that is how Ahad Raaz becomes king. They say he is, so he is.

Bhand musicians play the *swarnai* to announce his arrival. The freshly crowned *badshah* enters his kingdom, followed by a retinue of ministers and a procession of impressive length. But this fine display of omniscience is interrupted by a moneylender who appears before the *badshah*. Ahad Raaz, it turns out, is a great believer in debt financing. When he fails to return the money he had borrowed, he must forfeit his robe and crown to the moneylender. Enter chaos.

Alas, Ahad Raaz, the crown never did rest easy on his head.

* * *

That was the first episode of the Kashmiri serial *Hazaar Dastaan*. Or at least how Nazir Josh, the actor who played Ahad Raaz, remembers it. The show was first aired on Doordarshan Srinagar, the regional iteration of India's public broadcaster, in 1985.

Hazaar Dastaan made Josh a star in Kashmir, mobbed by crowds wherever he went. According to the comedian, political rallies would empty out if he was passing by; 'curfew-like conditions' prevailed when the show was aired every Saturday night. It is said, Farooq Abdullah, newly crowned leader of the National Conference, was not pleased. Even less so when he heard the new nickname people were using for him—Ahad Raaz.

In Urdu and Persian, *hazaar dastaan* means a thousand stories. The phrase carries echoes from elsewhere. A thousand stories told over a thousand and one Arabian nights by Scheherazade as she tries to stave off death. Stories carried by winds and wars to all parts of Asia. In Kashmir, *hazaar dastaan* has become the name of a bird, the blue whistling thrush, which sings in a thousand notes.

Ahad Raaz could also sing in many different notes, changing tune as he moved across his kingdom, explains Josh, who wrote the series. It is one tune in Chari Pathri, Foolish Hollow, which is definitely not Kashmir; one tune in Garam Pathri, Warm Hollow, which is definitely not Jammu; and one tune in Rajdhani, the imperial capital, which is definitely not Delhi.

It was remarkable that they had convinced Doordarshan, the normally stodgy public broadcaster, to run the show in the first

THE BUFFOON KING

place. Their cover lay in comedy, in the allegorical worlds and upside-down words of *bhand paether*. Nobody was mocked directly. Viewers joined the dots for themselves.

According to Bashir Budgami, who produced and directed the serial, Ahad Raaz resembled the *badshah* in *Darze Paether*, the rapacious bon vivant who demanded women and chickens as tribute. Here was a buffoon king. His *wazirs* bled him dry. When he got carried away, they administered the '*shahi dokkur*', the great hammer. One blow to the head and Ahad Raaz would be out cold. He would wake up crying, '*triesh, triesh,*' water, water, but courtiers knew he was really asking for something stronger. For the *badshah* was a slave to his excesses. Usually found draped around his two mistresses, Zoon and Mehrjaan, he was not above a spot of *badtameezi*, bad behaviour, with any other woman who came his way. '*Sharab, kebab, sex-vex*'—booze, food, sex—Josh sums it up.

Any resemblance to Farooq Abdullah was surely purely imaginary.

By the time *Hazaar Dastaan* went on air, 'Wazir-e-Disco' had already had his first stint as chief minister. Sheikh Abdullah had died in 1982. His son, in the best feudal traditions of South Asian political parties, was considered his natural successor. Despite being afflicted with occasional flashes of autonomy, Farooq Abdullah seemed to fit the image of the prodigal son with his golf-course-building, motorcycle-riding ways, not to mention his adventures with actresses. Tongues were clicked.

It did not help that many felt the junior Abdullah ran a rickety administration. Nothing seemed to move except for money as it disappeared from the state exchequer into ministerial pockets. Rumours of his incompetence came from all sides. The Congress, directed by then Prime Minister Indira Gandhi in Delhi, took a lively interest in painting Farooq Abdullah as antinational after he won state assembly elections in 1983. Instead of propping up a state government in Kashmir, the Congress had wanted to win the elections itself. Many in Kashmir were also quite done with National Conference governments, and not just because of Wazir-e-Disco.

There was a charge in the air in the eighties. You could feel it, says one journalist. A concatenation of ions that crackled into protest every now and then. Men bursting into the cricket grounds at Srinagar to dig up the pitch when India played the West Indies. Crowds booing the Indian team. Student rallies cutting across downtown Srinagar. Power cuts and a rise in electricity prices setting off demonstrations that turned fatal in 1988 and also turned power transformers into objects that somehow conspired with the state. Everyday irritations that would sharpen into something more—a cold, incandescent rage against the Indian state itself. By the eighties, the National Conference was India.

With the Indira–Sheikh accord of 1975, a contrite Sheikh Abdullah had signed away Kashmir's demand for self-determination. He didn't insist on the autonomy guaranteed under Article 370 in its original form either. Maybe he had tired of being locked up every time he had differences with Delhi or maybe he had changed his mind. Either way, after decades of holding out and holding on to the hope of a plebiscite, the Sheikh was in accord with Delhi. Anger against the accord was perhaps not immediately obvious. When he died in 1982, the Lion of Kashmir still had enough of a fan following to line the streets. Forty years later, his tomb is barricaded to protect it from angry vandals who call him traitor.

Nowadays, the Sheikh is blamed for everything, laments Taing, his amanuensis. For decades, Taing insists, the Sheikh was genuinely loved for giving land to tillers and building hospitals and schools. But even Taing is forced to admit that the Sheikh's refusal to fight on was keenly felt after the 1981 historical film *Lion of the Desert* released to packed audiences in

THE BUFFOON KING

Kashmir. That was in 1985, the same year that *Hazaar Dastaan* hit the small screen.

'In this our twentieth century, almost every nation in the world has at some time been in conflict, the oppressors and the oppressed, the victors and the vanquished,' the film began.[1] The titular Lion of the Desert was an aged, worried-looking depiction of the Bedouin leader Omar Mukhtar, played by Antony Quinn. Mukhtar had started life as an imam and a teacher before taking up arms to fight the occupation of Libya by fascist Italy. Crowds watching this heroic portrait in the Valley made some unflattering contrasts with the late Lion of Kashmir, who had also started out as a schoolteacher.

At the end of the film, Omar Mukhtar is hanged. His words echo in the skies as crowds march across the sands: 'We will never surrender. We win or we die. And don't think it stops there. You will have the next generation to fight; and after the next, the next. As for me, I will live longer than my hangman.'[2] Audiences in Kashmir might have recalled that the Sheikh went to jail but preferred compromise to death. They might have remembered Jammu and Kashmir Liberation Front militant Maqbool Bhat, hanged suddenly in Delhi's Tihar Jail the year before. Then they might have thought of the Sheikh's heir, who did not show any sign of a fight as Delhi played havoc with his government.

A former police officer, who worked with the crime branch in those days, had gone to buy his daily *paan* one afternoon when audiences burst out of the Regal Cinema near Lal Chowk. They had just watched Omar Mukhtar go to his death. They were ready for anything, the officer recalls. Slogans broke out, damning the government, demanding *azadi*.

No surprise, then, that the film was quickly removed from movie theatres. It had created problems for the National Conference, reflects Taing.

But that didn't stop a poster war breaking out in parts of Srinagar. 'Sheikh *saab*'s people removed the [movie] posters,' recalls a National Conference worker who lived in downtown Srinagar. 'So other people got angry and removed National Conference boards.' He had left the Valley for a while that year. When he returned, he took a *tonga*, a horse-drawn carriage, back into downtown Srinagar. The *tonga* driver warned him Kashmir had been swept by a *sabz inquilab*, a green revolution. There were green flags everywhere, a sign of allegiance to Pakistan and to Islam.

But these were not the only constituencies that had tired of pro-India politicians. Anger against the government in those years could be catabolised into many elements. Some had seen their hopes for *azadi* dashed, others for autonomy. Some were finished with Kashmiri politicians who had let Delhi play puppet master for decades. You voted for one government and a different one came to power in Jammu and Kashmir, recalls the journalist. Then there were more quotidian grievances. In the countryside, the Sheikh's land reforms might still have commanded loyalty. But a specific urban discontent was spreading among educated middle classes, explains historian Hakim Sameer Hamdani. There were no jobs. Medical seats went to the children of the politically connected. Nothing happened without a bribe.

Dissent was quickly put down so the anger had nowhere to go. It did not register in the Indian press, too busy hunting down the foreign hand that was apparently responsible for the country's troubles. The local press, according to a shawl maker in downtown Srinagar, was worried about irking the government. So movies and other forms of entertainment became political events.

Lion of the Desert had rattled the government. But public broadcasters were quietly letting dissent leak into their programmes. According to one Doordarshan officer, this was unusual as such channels were wrung dry of subversion before they could reach the public. But according to a former Doordarshan director, this was not out of the ordinary. Across the country, regional branches of Doordarshan were broadcasting political satire. It was allowed. Maybe the semblance of dissent helped them maintain credibility as a public broadcaster and not a government mouthpiece, speculates the journalist.

Starting from the mid-sixties, breakfast in Kashmir meant tuning into Radio Kashmir to listen to *Zoon Daeb*. It spoke of public grievances through the story of an ordinary Kashmiri family. It is said, government officials were instructed to keep up with the show even if it made them squirm. The show ran for two decades, winding up around the time *Hazaar Dastaan* went on air. Turning rage into laughter, Ahad Raaz had found his moment in a decade where all the old arrangements were being questioned.

'Every week, we expected this politician or that to be roasted,' says the shawl maker, a fan.

Listening to the radio or watching TV was often a community affair in the eighties. Men huddled over radios in street corners, discussing the latest government scandal or the Miandad six, still fresh in cricket news.[3] Maybe one family in the neighbourhood had a television set, so on Saturday night they were expected to keep an open house. By eight o'clock, everyone had poured in, the air thick with conspiracy. *Hazaar Dastaan* was going to start. If you had followed the political events of that week, you could probably predict the storyline.

'Whatever happened, we showed it on screen,' say the makers of the show. And what a lot happened in that decade.

* * *

Ahad Raaz left Foolish Hollow for Warm Hollow every winter. One year, he returned to find his kingdom stolen away by his *wazirs*.

The buffoon king had five ministers. Wazir Kalam, the Big Minister; Wazir Hutmut, Minister Nothing; Wazir Talukpyet,

Minister Upside Down; Nyer Kak, a Kashmiri Pandit, who was deaf; and Ali Chacha, who was mute. Also hovering around the edges of his court was Nibir Karate, a strong man in more ways than one, with a habit of swinging his club as if preparing to strike.

Big Minister was close to Ind Raaz, the emperor stationed in Rajdhani, who held paramountcy over Ahad Raaz's kingdom. In a shocking turn of events, Big Minister had conspired with the imperial powers to place Nibir Karate on the throne. Minister Nothing, who was also involved in the intrigue, might have had ambitions of his own, but he was only in charge for two days. Faced with such perfidy, Ahad Raaz lost the power of speech. He wandered mutely in his former kingdom, reduced to penury, supported only by the loving ministrations of Zoon and Mehrjaan.

What a coincidence that just months before the show was aired Farooq Abdullah had faced a similar mutiny. The Congress in Delhi had grown impatient after years of taking out unruly National Conference leaders and replacing them with more docile National Conference leaders. But a determined bid to win the state assembly elections of 1983 came to nothing, much to Indira Gandhi's alleged annoyance.

It was then found that many legislators in Farooq Abdullah's government, starting with his brother-in-law Gul Shah, had bitter complaints against him. Thirteen legislators suffered a sudden loss of confidence in the chief minister. The matter was given a most sympathetic hearing by Jagmohan, then governor of Jammu and Kashmir, who lost no time in dismissing Farooq Abdullah.

Gul Shah became chief minister with the support of the Congress, forming a government that made up with force what it lacked in legitimacy. For instance, the new chief minister developed such a fondness for curfews that he came to be known as Gul Curfew. Khalida Shah, who was his wife and

THE BUFFOON KING

Farooq Abdullah's sister, headed the breakaway faction of the National Conference.

Some customs had clearly not changed since the times depicted on *Hazaar Dastaan*. As in the Dogra era, elected state governments still migrated from the cold Kashmir Valley to the warmer plains of Jammu every winter, a long and complicated bureaucratic exercise quite unironically termed the Durbar Move. Some characters might not have changed either. Did Gul Curfew share the thuggish ways of Nibir Karate? Did Big Minister sound like Ghulam Mohiuddin Shah, another National Conference heavy? This was left to viewers and the politicians themselves to decide. It is said, Khalida Shah was nicknamed Zoon after Ahad Raaz's lovely mistress. But here the analogies get mixed up, for Khalida Shah was busy drawing more National Conference leaders into the rebel fold, while Zoon was tenderly mopping her vanquished lover's brow.

Anyway, these petty rivalries hardly mattered when both Ahad Raaz and Farooq Abdullah lived on the whims of the *markaz*, whether it was Rajdhani or Delhi.

* * *

Ahad Raaz's relationship with Ind Raaz worked like this. The buffoon king owed the emperor his allegiance and depended on his munificence to run a debt-ridden kingdom. The emperor used the five *wazirs* to keep a close watch on Ahad Raaz, lest he dream of secession. There seemed to be little danger of that. When Ahad Raaz visited Rajdhani, he was at his wheedling best. Give me a few more coins, Your Majesty, the buffoon king argued—it won't make you poor and it won't make me rich.

When the emperor asked for accounts, Ahad Raaz did not have much to say. He really did not know where the money went, why his subjects insisted on starving and why his *wazirs* were always renovating their palaces or buying new horses. Once, one of the ministers offered to explain state expenditure to Ind Raaz. He gave such an account that Ind Raaz fainted, his head spinning with numbers. Ahad Raaz's sudden downfall proved he wore the crown at the emperor's pleasure.

Viewers gathered around the television on a Saturday night would have recognised this state of affairs. Less than two years after he was sworn in as chief minister, Gul Shah was swapped for Governor Jagmohan, the *markaz*'s man in Kashmir, who was now who was now in charge of running the state. Jagmohan took over in a glow of self-abnegation—'I have the opportunity to show the nobler, the purer, the more radiant face of power'—but was swapped six months later for Farooq Abdullah once again.[4]

Wazir-e-Disco had made a swift recovery. After writing a tract entitled *My Dismissal*, in which he blamed Jagmohan, the Congress and defectors within the National Conference for his dismissal, he had entered negotiations with the *markaz*. Indira Gandhi was shot dead by her Sikh bodyguards in October 1984. Her son and successor, Rajiv Gandhi, was more willing to make up. Once more, an accord was sealed, the second in little more than a decade between a Gandhi and an Abdullah. Once more, a tenuous return to power was watched by an increasingly sceptical public.

That Delhi would pull strings in Kashmir had become common sense in the Valley. But the *markaz*'s power was not restricted to deciding who formed government in Jammu and Kashmir. After decades of intrigue, it was seen as a mysterious, malevolent influence that spread over every part of life.

Any misfortune could be put down to '*markaz ki chaal*', the centre's trickery. 'If we failed our exams, it was *markaz ki chaal*; if the power went off while we were eating, it was *markaz ki chaal*,' says the shawl maker from downtown Srinagar.

The sense of being controlled by a dark, distant power would intensify with the *haalaat*. In 1990, word spread that the main

THE BUFFOON KING

water tank in Srinagar had been poisoned and that food packets distributed by the army could turn men impotent. In 2016, it was polio drops, rumoured to be lethal and administered to thousands of children before panic spread. But these were the more sensational outings of the *markaz*. To date, *markaz ki chaal* has also been held responsible for a number of covert operations.

The sudden proliferation of tipper trucks in Srinagar.

The sudden proliferation of high footpaths that have wrecked Kashmiri knees.

The sudden proliferation of dogs that ensures no one walks on the streets after dark.

The sudden proliferation of alien alligator fish in Dal lake.

The sudden proliferation of Russian poplars that shed balls of fluff coating the countryside in white and causing allergies in spring.

Apart from the security camps, the detention centres and the concertina wiring that spreads across the Valley like an invasive weed, these daily harms are seen as war by other means, emissaries of a state that does not wish you well. Then there is the other *markaz* across the Line of Control, which sends its soldiers to fight in Kashmir. Many in the Valley believe it fights their war. Others cannot shake off the sense that Kashmir's fortunes are not for Kashmir to decide, that it is constantly pulled this way and that by the magnetic force of two rival *markazes*.

But that came later. Back in 1986, *Hazaar Dastaan* may have survived precisely because of *markaz ki chaal*.

Feathers had been ruffled in Kashmir. No scam or conspiracy escaped the show's notice. No authority was spared, religious or secular. For instance, Ahad Raaz's court hosted a Shahi Pir, a Grand Cleric, who did little more than flutter pleasantly around the throne. Could the producers of the show be blamed if the Mirwaiz's followers saw him in the Shahi Pir?

The Mirwaiz in question was the chief cleric of Srinagar's Jamia Masjid, a hereditary position that had accrued political power over the centuries. Since the thirties, the pro-Pakistan Mirwaiz of the Jamia Masjid had battled with Sheikh Abdullah and his National Conference. Those who followed the Mirwaiz were called Bakra, or sheep, and those who followed the Sheikh were, predictably, called Sher, or lions. The furious Sher-Bakra rivalry had defined the politics of Kashmir for decades, leading to pitched battles in downtown Srinagar. But Maulvi Mohammad Farooq, the Mirwaiz of the time, was an agile politician. In the seventies, having built his reputation agitating for a plebiscite, he suddenly decided to support opposition parties fighting the Congress in Delhi.[5] Then in the eighties, before the *tehreek* started, he seemed keen to make peace with the Abdullahs. These frequent changes of heart were not always popular.

According to Budgami, Maulvi Farooq's followers had threatened action against the show. 'If you see yourself in the clerics of *Hazaar Dastaan*, please repent and mend your ways,' Budgami had shot back. They fell quiet. Years later, the conciliatory Mirwaiz would enter the pantheon of the *tehreek*, an honour earned in blood after gunmen widely believed to be from the Hizbul Mujahideen entered his home on the banks of the Nigeen lake and shot him dead. But that was later, when the furies of the *haalaat* meant there was no telling who was what, when both killers and those they killed commanded obeisance. This was before, when everyday politics brokered truces so implausible they ended up as Saturday night entertainment.

A minister told Budgami they were scared to make any move because they would end up on TV the next Saturday. The inevitable legal notice arrived sometime in 1986, after forty episodes had been broadcast. Ahad Raaz was often called Ahad Kaniul. This was an insult to the *kaniul* community, basket weavers who lived on the banks of the Wular lake, the notice apparently said. The word '*kaniul*' had started out as a name for the community but had expanded over time, acquiring pejorative undertones. It

THE BUFFOON KING

had become another name for a buffoon. But the lawyer who delivered the notice, said Budgami, was less concerned with the dignity of the *kaniul* community than with the dignity of the National Conference. He had been deployed by a National Conference leader in downtown Srinagar. *Hazaar Dastaan* went off air that weekend. According to Budgami, the poor lawyer's wife and children went on strike against him because he had tried to stop the show. The notice was withdrawn. *Hazaar Dastaan* was back on air after a fortnight.

Was the National Conference trying to ban the serial? Yes, no, maybe. There is no reason why all answers cannot be true at the same time.

Taing acknowledges the notice might have come from zealous members of the National Conference. But he claims the party was not bothered by *Hazaar Dastaan*. It was all a bit of fun; his wife loved watching the show.

Budgami insists the interregnum was needed because the show was changing from black and white to colour. But he also thinks the management at Doordarshan had misread the legal notice as an official stay order. According to him, the Doordarshan director at the time had grown jumpy. He summoned Josh and Budgami and asked them to tone down the satire. They replied they would not; satire was the heart of the show.

This much is certain: someone in Srinagar was growing uneasy with the programme. Uneasy enough to send tapes of *Hazaar Dastaan* to be vetted at the Doordarshan headquarters in Delhi. The *markazi* office was delighted with the show. They wanted to broadcast it on national TV but Josh and Budgami refused. The humour of *Hazaar Dastaan* was distinctly Kashmiri, they said; it depended on tricks of language, on references that would not work with a national audience. In Kashmir, the show was allowed to go on.

It cannot be confirmed if the *markazi* office was secretly pleased with a satirical show that mocked Kashmiri politicians who nursed ambitions of regional autonomy. It cannot be confirmed, either, if they had noticed that the actor who played Ind Raaz was the spitting image of Rajiv Gandhi. The show had not been kind to Ind Raaz, an apoplectic despot who destroyed governments for breakfast. But then, Josh pointed out, the jokes were in Kashmiri. The *markaz* wouldn't understand.

* * *

In 1987, Jammu and Kashmir was headed towards assembly elections. 'We also had elections,' said Josh, who still has a habit of slipping into first person when speaking of Ahad Raaz.

If the buffoon king wanted to win back his kingdom, he would have to run for elections. Nibir Karate was also a candidate. So was Big Minister, who had abandoned the role of kingmaker to take a stab at the job himself. Campaigning was fierce. Ahad Raaz chose to sing and dance at his rallies.

At this point, Josh and Budgami decided to democratise the script. They ran an audience poll asking who should win the election that would be televised. Josh says they got three sacks full of votes. Ahad Raaz had won a landslide victory. Two years of being knocked out by the great hammer had given him a loyal fandom.

If only electorates worked the same way. After the Rajiv–Farooq accord, the Congress and the National Conference were in alliance as they went into polls. Opposition to the ruling alliance came from a new quarter. The *sabz inquilab*, the green revolution, had turned into a loose political grouping called the Muslim United Front, which consisted of the Jama'at-e-Islami and other parties of a religious bent.

A businessman in downtown Srinagar remembers seeing an MUF rally at the Eidgah, a vast field where community prayers are held on special occasions. It was heaving with people, mostly young men, who listened hungrily as the leaders told them to do their duty—lead a religious life and resist the political status quo.

THE BUFFOON KING

But when the election results were declared, the MUF had barely won any seats while the National Conference and Congress alliance had swept the elections. Voters were not buying it. What explained Amira Kadal, they demanded, where Mohammad Yusuf Shah, a schoolteacher with a flair for oratory, was slated to win the seat for the MUF? Suddenly, the votes turned in favour of Ghulam Mohiuddin Shah, the alleged Big Minister of *Hazaar Dastaan*. And what explained Handwara, where Abdul Ghani Lone, another opposition candidate, complained ballot boxes had been magicked away and counting agents arrested?[6] It was the same story in booth after booth. The elections, it was widely believed, had been stolen.

Looking back, journalists in Kashmir feel that even at the height of its popularity the MUF did not stand a chance of forming the government. But it was expected to win enough seats to press for its demands and influence the legislative agenda. Now it was clear the *sabz inquilab* could never start from the legislative assembly.

Along with a sense of injury, an idea was taking root in Kashmir: electoral politics had been given a chance but it did not work. Many of the leaders and polling agents of the MUF left the electoral fold, never to return. Mohammad Yusuf Shah melted across the LoC to become Syed Salahuddin and eventually lead the Hizb. His polling agent, Yasin Malik, crossed over to join the Jammu and Kashmir Liberation Front. In North Kashmir's Sopore, the Jama'at's Syed Ali Shah Geelani did win his seat. But he would resign two years later and help found the Hurriyat to agitate for *azadi*. He was joined by Lone and the young new Mirwaiz, forced into politics after his father's assassination.

The MUF and its insurrections are not written into *Hazaar Dastaan*. 'We did not touch all that,' said Josh.

Maybe they feared jokes about the MUF would not go down so well with viewers in Kashmir. Or maybe they had planned for a simpler show, where kings were mocked, hit on the head and then restored to power. Guns, bodies, agencies, new armies springing up every day—these were too messy for the script.

* * *

Hazaar Dastaan ran for twelve more episodes after the short break in 1986. In the closing episode, Ahad Raaz takes off his royal robes and introduces himself to the audience. He is only Nazir Josh, an actor and no *badshah*, he explains as he takes a bow.

'Ahad Raaz had won in the show and Farooq had also come back to power,' said Josh. As he saw it, this was a good time to wrap up. He was already on to his next role as Jumma German, a cowardly policeman who had gone to fight in the German War, otherwise known as the Second World War, but then decamped because the war proved too much for him.

Budgami feels *Hazaar Dastaan* might have gone on forever had there not been 'pressure', although there wasn't 'open pressure'. He was transferred out of Kashmir twice, first to Delhi and then to Jalandhar. He suspects these were not routine transfers—'I was victimised'.

When the show ended in early 1987, there was public outrage. Crowds mobbed Josh when he went on picnics. Television sellers petitioned him with urgent pleas. Before *Hazaar Dastaan*, they would sell one TV set a week. Afterwards, they were selling three or four. The show needed to return; their business depended on it.

It was not to be. Over the next decade, there would be little filming in Kashmir and the Doordarshan offices would become a set piece for the *haalaat*. A Doordarshan officer sitting gloomily at his desk more than thirty years later remembers it well. There, five feet away, is where a grenade exploded while he was working. There, by the toilets, is the spot where a rocket launcher landed, killing an employee. And there, in that bend of the corridor, is where he saw a harmonium lying abandoned one day and assumed it had been left behind by folk musicians. Upon closer inspection, it turned out to be wired with bombs, which were defused but not before they left a protesting crater in the wall.

There was Lassa Kaul, director of Doordarshan Srinagar and a Kashmiri Pandit, shot dead in February 1990. There would be more killings in the decade to come—anchors, producers, stringers and singers who worked for Doordarshan. It did not matter who was what. The Valley was at war with the Indian state, and as most people saw it, Doordarshan was the state.

What survived? Not *Hazaar Dastaan*, not the original episodes, forty in black and white, twelve in colour, stored in the VTR format, each reel the size of a small and ancient tyre. They had not been converted into newer formats and even if the *haalaat* had not arrived there would be no machines left to play the reels. Officials privately complain that the public broadcaster's archives had always been shambolic. Tapes were squirrelled away by employees or sold to scrap dealers; manuscripts were used to light fires on winter nights. Of the little that survived, much was carried away by the floods of 2014.

Ahad Raaz briefly shimmered into view a few years after the show ended. Josh reprised his character to sell television sets, perform in live shows and film short sketches later uploaded to YouTube. But it was not the same as the original fifty-two episodes that had once created curfew-like conditions in the Valley. With the public archives in Srinagar gone, Ahad Raaz has turned into stories, a thousand stories, passed on from mouth to mouth.

It would seem that *Hazaar Dastaan* had lost to its adversary. Farooq Abdullah went on to win many more elections after 1987. So did his son, Omar Abdullah. Yet, decades after it was taken off air, *Hazaar Dastaan* has left powerful traces. It lives in fragments of plot still remembered by Josh and Budgami. It is found in words and gestures. Men in their fifties still copy the swing of Nibir Karate's club. They chuckle over the boing-boing sound made by the great hammer as it landed on the buffoon king's head. They still use the name Ahad Raaz for a very thin man or a very silly man. And in the worst days of the *haalaat*, they might remember a line often repeated by the buffoon king, a benediction turned into a curse. '*Khoda karnei reatchh, gode karin na tza.*' May God protect you, he will not protect you.

PART II

POSSESSION

5

RAANTAS

Ghosts emerge from a blurring of time.[1] In places that have known conflict, ghosts are shadows of the past that exist as absences, as silences, as tics of language, as the hope of long-delayed justice, as heart wounds passed down from mother to child.[2] Kashmir has many such ghosts. Then there are reports of ghosts as ghosts, possession and visitations from the dead, the undead, the disappeared.[3] Kashmir has such ghosts too. Sometimes, ghosts are a metaphor for what cannot be said. Haunting reveals that which is meant to be concealed; it is a way in which abusive systems of power press on the substance of everyday life, especially when their abusive nature is denied.[4]

The story of the *haalaat* is often, quite literally, a ghost story.

Not that Kashmir was new to ghost stories when the *haalaat* arrived. Demons and monsters of a wide variety had haunted its streets, fields, woods for centuries. There were many stories about them. Stories of warning.

For instance, it is said that the village of Akingam is not named after the flight of Gannak at all but a different disappearance worked by a different woman. A *raantas*, a demonic woman who preys on men. Her feet are turned backwards; her hair and nails grow long. The secret to the *raantas*'s powers lies in her hair. She can move boulders up mountains, bound as fast as speeding cars, carry off grown men. Cut off her hair and she loses her superhuman strength.

Akingam is said to be a very old village, as old as Kashmir itself. But some say this happened just forty or fifty years ago. A band of men from the village went into the forest to collect wood. The *raantas* took one of them. She kept him in her cave and had babies with him. Seven or eight years passed. One day, another man from the village went into the woods and heard screams from the cave. He tried to extricate the captive and the *raantas* took him. When another man from the village was sent to the rescue, the *raantas* took him too. And then another, and then another.

One by one they all went, until there were no men left. And that is how Akingam got its name. *Akh* (one)—*niu* (taken)—*gam* (village), the village where they were taken one by one. The story doesn't say about the women left behind.

In other stories, the *raantas* is destroyed. Take the folktale about the *raantas* and the *khor*, a stock character in Kashmiri villages, someone who has lost all his hair to a disease and possibly some of his wit too. The *raantas* kidnaps this particular *khor* with the intention of pounding him to a fine chutney.[5] Twice he escapes from the sack in which she had bound him. Twice she catches him again.

She takes him home, only to be betrayed by her daughter, who falls in love with the *khor*'s smooth, bald head. When the *raantas* is sleeping, the girl ties her mother's hair, the source of her powers, to a pillar so that she won't wake up. But the daughter of a *raantas* can also be destroyed by her hair. As she is preparing to marry the *khor*, he grabs her hair so that she cannot move. Then he brings a pestle down on her head, again and again, until she is dead. Having laid waste to the *raantas*'s household, the *khor* escapes.

The *khor*'s exploits are pure story. Nobody knows where they happened or when. But across Kashmir, everyone knows someone who was taken by the *raantas*. It happened to their neighbour, their relative, or a boy from the next village. One journalist said his friend's father had been taken by a *raantas* for some years, although he was too polite to ask the friend for details. Another journalist in Srinagar said that, on a winter night quite recently, there was a ghostly woman banging on his door, saying she was cold, asking to be let in.

Beware of strange women who turn up at night complaining of the cold. PB, who grew up in the mountains of Ganderbal district, said her uncle narrowly escaped a *raantas*. He was working in the power department at the time and posted at a lonely outpost in Gutlibagh. It was winter and it had been snowing. Around midnight, he saw a woman at the window saying she was cold and that she wanted to be let in. He thought she must be a Gujjar woman who lived nearby. All they had for homes were wooden shacks that barely held together. What is your name, he asked, and she told him. It was the name of someone he knew, so he asked her to come in.

When she entered, he noticed that her feet were turned backwards and that she seemed to shrink away from the glowing heater. It is said, the *raantas* can change shape, taking on the faces of people you know, speaking in familiar voices. But she cannot hide her fear of heat or fire. And she cannot turn her feet the right way round.

The *raantas* got straight to the point. She wanted to marry him. And why not, said the power department official politely as he inched towards the phone in the next room where he quietly called the police. He kept up a steady chatter until he could hear police vehicles outside. When the *raantas* heard the cars, she scratched him in fury and ran away. He blacked out and did not wake up for two or three days.

He left his job and went back to his village, but the *raantas* did not leave him alone. She would turn up at the village, asking again and again, why did you betray me? PB remembers her uncle being brought back to the village, the screams of the *raantas*.

Sometimes, the *raantas* arrived when the shadows lengthened in the paddy fields. PB has heard about a man they called '*raantas niu*', the one taken by the *raantas*. He had been building a hayrick late one evening and was perched on top of the pile while his wife handed him bundle after bundle of hay. The mountain of hay grew and grew. He lost track of how long he had been on the hayrick. When he looked down, he saw he was a long way from the ground and the woman below was not his wife. She told him to jump on her shoulders. He jumped. She carried him away and kept him in her cave for twelve years.

They had children, half human, half monster. Every day, she went out to forage for food, often human flesh and bones. For years, he watched her go out, how she held up her comb to the rock that sealed the cave entrance, how it rolled back. One day, he too held up the comb and made his escape. When he returned to the village, everybody scattered from him in fright. His nails and hair had grown long. Nobody remembered what he looked like, not even his wife. Only after he had bathed and shaved did they recognise the man they once knew.

He went back to his old life, but for a year the *raantas* returned to the village, shouting for him to come back, for what would she tell their children?

A woman who grew up in the mountains near Qazigund, the last major town in the southern end of the Valley, tells a similar story. There was a couple in her village who went out to their cowshed one night. While the woman went into the shed, the man lingered outside in the vegetable patch. A mistake, for that is when the *raantas* took him.

Once more the cave, his hair and nails growing long until he resembled his captor. Once more the escape as the *raantas* went out to get food. How long had he been in the cave? Long enough that his wife could not recognise him at first. The night he went home, the *raantas* banged on their door, shrieking that he should be returned.

A young woman in Anantnag town says her tutor's friend nearly got taken by the *raantas*. He had been visiting Anantnag town from Kokernag, up in the hills. As evening fell, he set off on his bike, refusing invitations to stay in town for the night. Somewhere on the road from Anantnag town to Kokernag, he saw a beautiful woman asking for help. He was startled. What woman would be out alone at this hour?

Then he happened to look down and saw her feet were turned backwards. He sped up but there she was again, turned into a row of boulders stretched across the road, certain death for speeding bikes. But the tutor's friend was a skilled cyclist. He whipped the bike around and escaped.

Only KM's grandfather could fight off a *raantas*. He lived in the mountains of Bandipora district, a giant of a man, about seven feet tall, given to eating entire cauldrons of rice at a time. One night, the moon was so bright he thought it was day and went to the forest to cut wood. Once he was done, he tied two logs to a rope and slung it over his shoulder. After a while, the logs seemed strangely heavy.

He turned around to see a *raantas* sitting on them. He told her to get off but she would not. So there was nothing for it but to fight her with his bare hands. They battled for hours, until dawn broke and the *raantas* fled. When people from the village arrived, they found great swathes of forest torn apart. KM's grandfather had to spend two months in a hospital after that.

The *raantas* caught men who went out at night, men who went where they were not supposed to go. Very often, women told these stories to their children and grandchildren at bedtime to stop them from going out after dark. But beyond the warm square of the blanket, the men of the house were also listening. The warning in the story—do not stray. Stories drew a charmed circle around the home, keeping everyone indoors and everything as it should be.

For the night is crowded with terrors in Kashmir. There is the *raantas*, also called the *daen*, with her feet turned backwards and her dangerous sexual appetites. There is the *van moenu*, or forest man, cousin to the yeti, who lives in the woods. The wolf-like *bram bram chok*, a spectre with a lamp on its head. The cat-like *yachch*, who calls two and a half times, *wuf-wai, wuf-wai, wuf.* It wears a fez. If you can steal the fez, untold wealth will be yours. But if you try and you fail, a dire fate awaits you. Some say the *yachch* is only a cat sneezing. Still, if you hear it call at night, stay indoors.

These monsters have their time and place. The *raantas* or the *daen* appears in winter. So does the *bram bram chok*. The *yachch* in early spring. None of them can enter your home without *ijaazat*, permission.

When the *haalaat* arrived, there were new terrors abroad in the night. They did not keep time with the seasons. Not all of them asked for permission.

In this blood-haunted time, boys disappeared, then reappeared with guns. They strode openly through the Valley in the early years of the *haalaat*, declaring parallel governments and knocking on doors at night to demand food and shelter. Crowds flooding the streets believed, in the early days, that *azadi* was around the corner; it would come tomorrow.

But this dream of freedom came with boots. Farooq Abdullah's feeble government was disappeared in January 1990, along with the legislative assembly of Jammu and Kashmir and the pretence of elections. For six years, there were only governors, sour bureaucrats and former security men appointed by Delhi. And there were forces. Thousands of military and paramilitary troops bussed into Kashmir in slow, green convoys. There were the Rashtriya Rifles, the counterinsurgency wing of the Indian Army hastily put together in 1990. They painted '*Dhridta aur Veerta*', resolve and bravery, on the gates of new camps and hurtled down village roads flashing a skull and crossbones logo, quite failing to reassure the population they were apparently sent to protect. They were men who covered their confusion at suddenly being transported into an unquiet valley with gratuitous violence.

Forces took possession of fields and woods, street corners and school buildings. Camps and interrogation centres emitted men from other places who did not speak Kashmiri, who sometimes knocked and sometimes didn't as they entered homes at night. The camps also sucked people in; they were taken behind iron gates and never seen again.

Those who remember the early years of the *haalaat* describe them as a frenzy of hope and death, a period of madness when all regular politics disappeared. Nothing was in its place. It was, to use a well-worn phrase, a 'time out of joint', where the normal paces of history had stopped, where the present did not quite belong to itself.[6] How could it? Five hundred years of *zulm* were being fought in the present, where the shape of future terrors were finding their outline.

A black veiled shape appears on the horizon around the time the camps spread across Kashmir. As it draws nearer, it reveals glints of metal, a flash of talons. It is given different names in different towns. *Daen*, *raantas*, or just plain *bhoot*, ghost. Old names for a new terror which dissolves the boundaries between inside and outside. It does not stay in the streets. It presses on windows, it enters homes, bodies and minds.

For a few months in 1993, there is a period of intense panic. The *haalaat* take the shape of a *daen*, invading towns and villages across the Valley. The mass panic dies out in a few months but tales of ghostly visitations crop up through the decades that follow. Stories haunt stories. Nearly a quarter of a century after the steel *daen* walked the Valley, the braid choppers arrive.

6

THE STEEL *DAEN*

At the mention of the *daen*, the twelve-year-old boy reappears briefly in the forty-year-old man's face. Yes, he knows of the *daen*. He has seen it. The memory is filed away as a scene from a movie.

It is night, sometime in 1993. For weeks, ZM and his family have been sleeping in one room on the ground floor. Everyone sleeps early. They live in Dalgate, a neighbourhood in Srinagar where the Dal lake trails off into a channel that meets the Jhelum. It takes its name from the sluice gates that guard the Dal. Their house is in the lower reaches of the Takht-e-Sulaiman, the hill that rises from the banks of the Dal lake and looms over southern Srinagar. They sleep with knives and hammers under their pillows. ZM is very pleased with the small pocket knife he has squirrelled away under his own pillow.

That night they hear something in the street outside. It is a robotic noise, something like a mechanical roar. Everyone rushes upstairs, one of his uncles leading the way armed with a meat cleaver. A window is opened, and ZM sees something leaping away. It reappears about thirty metres away, a black shape clinging to their neighbour's first-floor window. It did not climb but jumped straight up. Then it drops to the ground in one smooth movement. It is like Batman or some other comic-strip superhero.

If he saw it now, he would not believe his eyes; he would laugh.

In those days, no one laughed. Uncanny events were reported. A young man in the neighbourhood had gone out one evening telling his family he would not return that night. But late at night they heard his voice outside the door, his and a woman's. Something did not seem right so his father decided against opening the door. When the young man got home the next day, they asked about the nocturnal visit. But I did not return at all before morning, he said.

The mountain had always been prone to haunting. Everyone knew the story of the stranger who had turned up at a local supply shop one night to ask for oil. Eyeing him warily, the shopkeeper said he would not let him in but could hand over the oil at the gate outside. The stranger took the oil and lit a small lamp that was perched on his head. When the lamp was lit, the shopkeeper later said, he lost his senses. He must have followed the stranger for he woke up screaming high up on the mountainside several hours later. That would have been a *bram bram chok*, everyone concluded.

But that was in the seventies or eighties, before the *haalaat*. This new haunting was different. It started around ten or eleven every night with knocks on the door and stones hurled at windows, forcing families into a single room where they ate and slept or just waited out the dark. If they needed to use the toilet, which was usually in an outhouse in the courtyard, they had to go in groups. It is said, the haunting forced a permanent architectural change in Kashmir. Toilets have moved from outhouses into the main house ever since.

The creature stalking the neighbourhood was called a *daen*. It was very tall; some said it was three storeys tall. It often wore

THE STEEL *DAEN*

'spring boots', weapons-grade footwear that enabled it to jump to the height of several storeys and walk up walls. Many called it a steel *daen* as they could swear they had seen a metal carapace beneath the black sheath. Others said it had long, steel claws, curved like those of a bear.

Two features of the haunting were noted in Dalgate. First, even the street dogs stopped barking at night. In the morning, their necks were ringed with scorch marks, leading everyone to speculate that the *daen* drank their blood. Second, many reported that when an alarm was raised, the *daen* disappeared into the mountain above. A military camp lay in that direction.

'We used to call it a *daen*,' says ZM. 'But this much is certain—it was not a *bhoot daen*.' It was not a ghostly ghost.

* * *

'In a new anti-"Freedom Movement" campaign, the authorities have adopted a fresh strategy in which the Kashmiris have been deprived of their nocturnal sleep and rest for about three months now,' says an article in *Greater Kashmir* dated 19 August 1993.[1]

This would put the date of the *daen*'s first appearance sometime in May 1993. It started in Bemina, then a suburb of Srinagar, close to the Jhelum river. A 'strange dressed creature' was entering homes to molest women and slash men's faces and bodies, the article continues. When neighbours tried to give chase, they got beaten up.

Curious affinities had been noticed in several localities. When anyone tried to wrestle down a *bhoot* or a *daen*, it seemed to disappear into a bunker or scoot off on a security vehicle. In Rainawari, an escaping ghost backed into a mosque and brandished a small gun at an angry crowd before it was rescued by forces. In downtown Srinagar's Wazapora, a badly beaten ghost was able to send a signal through a watch-like transmitter before passing out. Within minutes, Wazapora and the neighbouring

Maharajganj were under a security cordon, men, women and children dragged out and beaten while the ghost was smuggled away. In Dalgate, the ghost had killed. It had pushed a man off a three-storey building before vanishing into a security bunker.

The director general of police had 'coolly and blatantly' passed it off as the work of 'miscreants', the article continues, its sentences taut with rage by now. The ghosts roamed at night. Even beggars and dogs who wandered at night were shot down by forces; how come nobody had managed to shoot a ghost yet? Quite clearly, this was aimed at creating a 'fear psychosis' among people. Some claimed the ghost was a ploy by government agencies to split public opinion and cut down support for the movement. Others claimed ghosts were unleashed at night to provoke militants into reacting. Once they revealed themselves in pursuit of the ghost, security forces would rush to the spot and lay a cordon. The article works up to a grand and blistering finale. 'Do they think that in this age of modern technology, Kashmiris would believe in superstitious nonsense like "Bhoot"?'

Several articles blaze with the same rage, that Kashmiri stories should be turned against Kashmiris themselves, that they should be taken to be slaves to superstition. They were no longer the illiterate public of centuries past. An editorial published in *Greater Kashmir*, entitled 'The Kashmir Horror Show', is scathing.[2] It seemed the *Zee Horror Show*, a popular television serial of the time, was no longer 'restricted to the idiot box'. Its vampires, which had 'developed a fancy for the fairer sex', now appeared in crowded localities at night, even areas turned into 'fortresses' by armed forces. The government had released a statement saying these apparitions were aimed at fomenting disaffection; the editorial writers are plainly sceptical. Unless the government could actually prove who the ghosts were, it could be assumed that these creatures who appeared in curfewed nights were manifestations of another 'ill-conceived security gimmick'. Kashmir may

THE STEEL *DAEN*

be a 'land of Fairies and Ginnies', but it was certainly not a land of fools.

As sightings spread, ghosts appeared frequently in news reports and editorials. The local press had grown loquacious since the political upheavals of the eighties, holding up politicians and governments to a close and lively scrutiny. While the *haalaat* had placed much of the press under siege, it also had a galvanising effect, giving rise to a sudden efflorescence of dailies and magazines in English and Urdu. Take, for instance, *Greater Kashmir*, which started life as a periodical in 1987, the year of the infamous elections, and became a daily in 1993, the year of the *daen* and the year that *azadi* parties came together to form the Hurriyat. The newspaper quoted official sources where available but reserved most of its space for the popular version of events. In those early years, many of its editorials and op-eds echoed public sentiments, which supported the *tehreek*.

Then there were the public broadcasters, Doordarshan Srinagar and Radio Kashmir. The shooting of Doordarshan Srinagar director Lassa Kaul had made it unpleasantly clear that the Valley was no longer safe for them. Both moved their news operations out of Kashmir. Doordarshan Srinagar stationed itself in Jammu for about three years. Radio Kashmir migrated to Delhi. The running joke was that every broadcast started with a lie. 'This is Radio Kashmir,' the newsreader would announce, even though it was really Delhi. Programmes on both channels were vetted so that no anti-national content slipped through. But one editor seems to remember a song, played frequently on Radio Kashmir in 1989, which was a veiled call to arms.

Either way, by the time Radio Kashmir moved back to Srinagar, it had been freshly injected with national feeling and scrubbed free of irregularities. The first news broadcast from Srinagar after the interregnum was aired in June 1993. Before that, 'irritants', such as how the channel would refer to key figures, had to be sorted out.³ Even though the news would be read in Urdu and Kashmiri, neutral English words were to be used when referring to militants, the prime minister of India, the president and the governor. There was very little original reporting since it was still dangerous for channels associated with the state to send out stringers. Local journalists from other news outlets grew increasingly peeved because such channels seemed to cherry-pick lines from their reports to suit a statist narrative.

Thirty years later, the archives of the public broadcasters are in disarray. Officers and former officers who worked there in the nineties have no memory of covering the *daen* panic. But journalists working for the local press remember. Old copies of *Greater Kashmir* and other local dailies may be found at the archives of the Press Information Bureau, an agency of the Indian government that hands out official news to the media. The Srinagar branch of the bureau is quartered at the Press Colony. Its archives are in a room with tall cupboards that is kept locked at all times, as if storing classified documents or contraband. News pages from the nineties are bound in massive cardboard files. Open the files and a cloud of dust and headlines rises up.

The columns of *Greater Kashmir* suggest a war was fought on the genealogy of the *daen*. Two theories seemed to exist, one carried by public channels such as Radio Kashmir, the other by *Greater Kashmir* and various privately owned local dailies. This is the side of the argument I found preserved in the reports and editorials of *Greater Kashmir*, still jousting with officials long gone from the Valley and *sarkari*—governmental—programmes long forgotten, a war waged on shadows.

* * *

Thirty years later, the *tonga* driver in Ganderbal district in central Kashmir still has scars on his wrists and on the back of his neck. They take him back to the day he met the ghost.

THE STEEL *DAEN*

Once again, it is night in the summer of 1993. The *tonga* driver does not go out after dark. He has three young children to feed and wants to keep his life. Every day, he prays that night won't come. It comes like *qayamat*, doomsday.

Houses in this part of Ganderbal do not have walled compounds yet so any intruder—man, woman, spectre—can glide up to the house undetected. Metal nails will then knock on windows and metal nails will scratch those who stray outside. Around ten or eleven every night, people pull out steel plates and vessels and start beating on them, a collective exorcism to drive away the ghost.

That night, the clanging has started again and there are rumours that the ghost is on the prowl. The *tonga* driver decides to go check on his brother, who lives next door. He sets out with his father and takes a shovel with him. The moment he steps out, taloned fingers grab his neck. He swings his shovel and it strikes metal. The ghost is wearing a helmet.

He wriggles free but six or seven more ghosts swoop in. They wear uniforms but their faces are covered with cloth and they have claws of steel. They pin him down and beat him, shooting at the ground near him all the while. Then there is a torch in his face and a voice he recognises. It is the inspector of the local Border Security Force camp. He is flashing his torch and saying, 'This is a *civil* [civilian], not a *milton* [militant], let him go.' So they let him go, leaving him to drag his battered body back to the house.

The next morning, soldiers from the BSF camp are at their door. They yank his daughter out of his arms and pull him out of the house, beating him as they bear him away to the camp. You tried to kill one of us, they say as they administer electric shocks to his body until his ears bleed.

He thinks he will die in that camp but a day later the local police take him into custody. He is charged with attempted murder, but really the police are quite grateful. He has solved the mystery of the ghost. He has, in fact, become something of a hero. At the Srinagar hospital where he is taken to recover from his wounds, the patient in the next bed is so impressed he offers his home-cooked lunch of mutton curry as tribute.

But the case will drag on for years. None of the witnesses will ever show up to testify. Finally, the court will close the case. Decades later, he will receive a letter from the ghost. When he sees the name on the letter, the *tonga* driver will realise he knew the ghost, a soldier at the local BSF camp. The ghost will want to meet in person to apologise for the trouble he caused. But the *tonga* driver will not go—what if it's a trap?

* * *

The haunting picked up in August 1993, about three months after the *daen* first appeared. On 1 August 1993, a young couple and their child were killed by BSF men who stormed their house in Daribal in downtown Srinagar. The child's weeping grandmother told *Greater Kashmir* he had gone out to get milk but suddenly ran back into the house and bolted the door. Minutes later, forces burst in.[4]

Ajmer Singh, a BSF man, was arrested for the murders. But the government was still prickly about it. It was suggested that Singh was really a Pakistani agent working as part of a larger conspiracy to light fires in Kashmir. One government spokesperson complained that such killings could be avoided if only people cooperated more and militants did not take refuge in ordinary homes. The arrest cut no ice with the public; neither did the government's complaints. 'Ajmer Singh's arrest a "Face saving device"'; 'An attempt to legitimise killings,' ran the *Greater Kashmir* headlines on 7 August 1993.

Anger that rippled through the neighbourhoods of downtown Srinagar could not be contained by curfews. When crowds defied the curfew and spilled out into the streets, BSF men opened fire

THE STEEL *DAEN*

again and protesters were killed.[5] The crowds doubled. Community kitchens were set up and tents were pitched on the street.[6] Other areas of Srinagar and other towns in the Valley were now lighting up with protests.

It was around this time that the *daen* started paying frequent visits to downtown Srinagar, scattering crowds and forcing everyone indoors at night. The sequence of events did not go unnoticed.

Protests had become routine after the Daribal killings, noted a report by a local human rights group published in *Greater Kashmir*.[7] Demonstrations continued into the night, after evening prayers, when crowds would gather to shout 'pro-freedom and anti-India slogans', the report said. Curfews and shootings by security forces had done little to dampen protests. 'All of a sudden, whole of Kashmir was gripped with the fear that "ghosts" have been roaming during nights.' The *daen* had succeeded where guns and curfews had failed.

* * *

Nights in Dalgate, 1993, have found a new rhythm. This is how it goes. As darkness falls, doors are bolted; everyone is locked in. Everyone except the groups of boys appointed to the neighbourhood patrol. They keep watch at street corners.

Inside, there are others keeping watch, armed with fifteen-litre tin canisters that once held oil but are now filled with stones. When they rattle their canisters, it is a code. Watch out, the *daen* has arrived. The message is picked up by the nearest mosque, for there are mosques on every other street, which then makes the announcement from its loudspeakers. Watch out, the *daen* has arrived.

Everyone spills out into the street, beating on their tin canisters to drive away the *daen*. Militants hiding in nearby homes are also part of the crowd. Should search operations start, this is

DAPAAN

their best bet. Soon enough, forces form a cordon around the area and start searching houses. They are only trying to restore order, forces say. But this much is clear. When the *daen* appears, soldiers soon follow. They don't often enter the neighbourhood during the day.

Days in Dalgate have their own rhythm. In fields and public parks, militant groups hold parades. Protest marches from different parts of the city converge at the United Nations office at the bottom of the Takht-e-Suleiman.

The solid colonial building is the relic of a time when the ceasefire line dividing Kashmir was considered temporary and a plebiscite quite imminent. Since then, the Indian government has told the UN observers to please leave and the office in Srinagar has pulled up its drawbridges. Very few people are seen going in or out. Its gates are always closed. But the 'UN *chalo*' marches resurrect old promises as they draw up to the implacable gates.

Crowds chant in rhythm. '*Hum kya chahte? Azadi.*' What do we want? Freedom. '*Pakistan se rishta kya? La ilaha illallah.*' What is our relationship with Pakistan? There is no God but God. In other words, a relationship of shared faith. '*Yahan kya chalega? Nizam-e-Mustafa.*' What will run here? The rule of the Prophet Muhammad. In other words, no more Indian laws.

At night, some of the mosques play the song '*Jeeve, Jeeve Pakistan*', Long Live Pakistan, to boost morale. Because if daytime belongs to the *tehreek*, the night belongs to the *daen*.

They still call it a haunting, but they know it is something else. Word has spread that Maruti Gypsies have been seen disgorging strangers into the streets of Dalgate. Boatmen who live in and around the Dal chase the *daen* through the tall grasses of Chinar Bagh one night. They drive a harpoon into the escaping figure and draw blood. Then the creature seems to make off in a Gypsy.

They also know now that there is no *daen* drinking the blood of stray dogs. The marks around their necks are made by a cor-

THE STEEL *DAEN*

rosive substance, possibly gunpowder. There could only be one explanation. It is meant to terrify the dogs into silence when strangers enter the neighbourhood at night.

What will run here? A mechanical roar seems to arrange itself into words—the rule of fear.

* * *

But in Zurimanz village on the banks of the Wular lake in North Kashmir, HG cannot believe his luck. He is only eleven years old but he has been chosen for the night patrol.

In this quiet village, mostly home to boatmen and fishermen, the arrangement had to be vetted by the army camp just outside. They said go if you must, but you have to carry lanterns and keep to the village limits. If there is a crackdown, local patrols must disband and go home.

The patrols have been formed after the *mohalla* committee called a meeting. Weeks earlier, a non-Kashmiri ghost was caught trying to enter a home in the neighbouring Watlab village. He spoke Punjabi or Hindi, the residents of Watlab are not sure which, but it was the language of the military. Showing admirable restraint, they did not beat him up once they caught him but handed him over to the local police, who sent him back to the camp he came from, no doubt.

Greater Kashmir reports, however, that forces are also looking for a ghost as part of their anti-militancy operations, an 'artificial bhoot' who has disappeared somewhere around the Wular lake.[8] It is not clear if this is the same ghost from Watlab.

Either way, ever since the non-Kashmiri ghost was discovered, the nightly disturbances have spread to surrounding villages. HG's aunt has seen a hand with metal nails at the window. It disappeared when she raised an alarm. There are rumours that people have been scratched, although no one has seen the wounds.

The people of Zurimanz are no strangers to disturbances. The village is also called 'Bangladesh', a name borrowed from war. In

DAPAAN

1971, as East Pakistan burned, the village of Zurimanz caught fire. As Bangladesh rose from the ashes of the war, Zurimanz was also rebuilt. The name of one calamity became attached to another, and Zurimanz became Bangladesh.

So when the nightly disturbances show no signs of going away, the *mohalla* committee calls a war meeting to discuss what is to be done. It is decided that ten boys will patrol the village every night. A roster is drawn up, and HG has to press his case. He feels extremely important as he steps out with older boys at night, armed with lanterns and a sense of camaraderie. They do rounds of the village and sometimes stop for a cup of tea. Years later, when much more blood has spilled and much more has been lost, he will remember the haunting as a pleasant adventure.

* * *

'"Bhoot" keeps people on toes in valley,' said the lead article on the *Greater Kashmir* front page on 26 August 1993.[9] The last twenty-four hours had been particularly unquiet.

In one town, a ghost had entered the residential quarters of the Jammu and Kashmir Police, forcing them to open fire. Central forces stationed nearby seemed to have taken strong exception to the firing. In North Kashmir's Baramulla district, it had dragged out one Shakeel Ahmed, but when local residents sounded the alarm, it decamped after throwing Ahmed into a well. In Shopian town in South Kashmir, it had briefly kidnapped a boy. More sightings were reported in other parts of the Valley.

There was another curious detail. Militants of the Hizbul Mujahideen and Al Barq claimed to have 'arrested some mysterious creatures which still are lying in their custody'. The article did not say who or what these mysterious creatures were.

The spectres kept changing shape. On 30 August, a report cited government sources who said the ghosts were militants and security sources who claimed it was Pakistan's Inter-Services

THE STEEL *DAEN*

Intelligence haunting by proxy.[10] The same report also cited militants who said the ghosts, 'nailed and shrouded spectral beings', were sent by Indian security forces.

In Mehjoor Nagar, a neighbourhood in uptown Srinagar, people were up at night chasing away 'wild creatures', who they reckoned were burglars in disguise, making the most of the panic to rob a house or two.[11] Some thought the creatures looked like 'well-built' men dressed in a burqa without the opening for the eyes.[12] One of them had entered an attic and run its hands over the face of a sleeping woman, who woke up, screamed and fainted. But in Bagat Hyderpora, where the city of Srinagar thinned out, the ghost was a woman.[13] She was found slumped over in a veranda one evening, sporting bandaged limbs and a nasal plug. She claimed she was from Charar-e-Sharief, a town known for its mediaeval Sufi shrine. When given chase, she disappeared into a security bunker.

Sometimes, there was no ghost at all. A girl in downtown Srinagar panicked after her braid got caught in a latch.[14] Two brothers in Budgam took each other to be the ghost in the dark. People were seeing ghosts everywhere. Journalists remember a flood of tip-offs every day, frantic phone calls and photographs showing scratch marks apparently made by spectral talons.

There was a proliferation of hands.

An editor for an Urdu daily in Srinagar got a call from a woman late one night. Could he please send a reporter immediately? She was being tickled silly by the *daen*. In Sonwar, close to the Srinagar army cantonment, a man was sitting on his balcony one evening when he felt a hand on his shoulder. It was a woman's hand with painted nails. He thought it was his sister, Lily. 'What, Lily?' he said as he turned around. And then he saw it was not Lily but a *daen*.

Such were the manifestations that there was no telling what form they would take. Beneath psyops, fear psychosis and area domination, beneath conspiracy, disaffection and anti-national activity, beneath the grand schemes of this side or that, lay smaller things. Family feuds and battles over property, pranks and private demons. It was so many things at once, there was no telling what a ghostly visitation could do. It could leave you tickled or it could leave you dead.

* * *

August is hot in 1993. Families have been driven outside because of the heat, braving the *daen* to get a decent night's sleep. One morning, men waking up for dawn prayers in a North Kashmir locality are met with a horrifying sight.

Their neighbour lies in a pool of blood. Chunks of flesh have been gouged out of his sides and he has scratch marks all over. It is as if a pair of talons have been to work or the claws of a big cat. They call a doctor, but it is no use. He has an hour of life left in him.

His wife and four children had been sleeping next to him in the garden. The family never heard or saw the killer. They only woke up when the neighbours raised an alarm.

The house is built on a desolate patch of land with paddy fields sloping away on one side and orchards on another. It has no compound wall, so the bloodied body is visible to the whole neighbourhood.

By now, the *daen* has made several appearances in North Kashmir so they have set up a local patrol. The neighbourhood patrol did not see anything that night either. But two nights earlier, they saw a black shape in spring boots leaping away from the house.

The family files a police complaint against 'unknown persons' but the investigation never goes anywhere. A local newspaper reports that a man has been killed by 'shadows'.

* * *

'Next time think more plausible,' runs the headline of a *Greater Kashmir* editorial published on 4 September 1993. The night before, Radio Kashmir had broadcast a 'special news-reel' after the regular evening news. It had been advertised in advance so many people would have tuned in.

The special news reel had started by saying the ghost had been busted, which piqued audience curiosity even more. But then they proceeded to play a 'pre-recorded statement from some youth in captivity'. This unfortunate had apparently confessed that he was employed by the Hizbul Mujahideen to play ghost and spread fear; some fifty other 'locals' had also been engaged.

'Rude and crude propaganda' was the verdict in *Greater Kashmir*. It was misinformation designed to malign the Hizbul Mujahideen, the editorial explained, and there were obvious gaps in the story. Fifty, even a hundred times fifty hired ghosts could not account for the scale of the haunting. Why did these apparitions only materialise in security strongholds? And how exactly were they able to escape detection by a hawk-eyed public? The biggest error, however, was to suggest that an organisation like the Hizbul Mujahideen, which commanded so much popular support, which handed out as many press releases as any government explaining its methods and policies, could ever, would ever need to, stoop to 'Operation Bhoot'.

It was a term that had become familiar by then, 'Operation Bhoot', along with 'Operation Sarkari Jin'—Government Djinn.[15] Several articles traced the genealogy of the ghost back to West Asia. It was said to have walked first in Israel, where the Mossad had used ghosts to drive out Muslims living near the Al-Aqsa mosque in Jerusalem. Then it travelled to Punjab, where Indian security forces used it to curb Khalistani militancy. In Kashmir, it was allegedly used to stop the movement of militants and the flow of arms while keeping people paralysed with fear.[16]

Most articles were dead serious, some less so. 'Operation Sarkari Jin: A Grand Flop Show' borrowed the name of a show by the Punjabi comedian Jaspal Bhatti.[17] It imagined an official document outlining the government's spectre policy. This was designed to subsume the rebellious Kashmiri public into the 'turbulent, aimlessly gushing national mainstream' while also stopping the 'flux of misguided elements across the line of factual control'. It would create a gulf between 'misguided youth' and 'frightened pigeons', that is, the gullible public. Ghosts had to be pressed into service because crackdowns had failed.

In the imagined policy document, Operation Sarkari Jin was necessary because 'what cannot be done overtly must be done covertly', 'pigeons can be frightened easily', 'dark hours of the day are conducive to execution of dark deeds', and 'what Akbar the great could not achieve by direct fight with Kashmiris in the past, could be attained by him through treachery, treason and proxy'. Ghosts would be nominated from every zone of the Valley. Tortured youth and those amenable to bribes would also be enlisted in the scheme. The official document concluded that policy outcomes, sadly, had not lived up to expectations. Operation Sarkari Jin had, in fact, flopped.

Jokes apart, a journalist who covered the haunting still recalls official statements on the need for 'night domination', when militants were on the move. In 1993, there were thousands of militants in the Valley and forces could not dominate the night through checkpoints alone. So the *daen* was sent to do battle.

The former crime branch officer seems to concur. Militants moving through localities at night needed a place to stay and people were quite willing to let them in. Instead of forces getting into direct confrontation with residents, why not invent a character who would do the job? Such a character had to be interesting and people-friendly, the officer explained. Apparitions were not new to Kashmiri politics. In the sixties, for instance, there was a creature called the *trounz* setting fire to haystacks in villages. According to the former officer, it was a plot by opposition parties to agitate rural Kashmiris and spread rebellion against Bakshi's government.

In 1993, after the initial panic, the *daen* seemed to be losing its powers. On 10 September 1993, *Greater Kashmir* published an opinion piece entitled 'Fatal Visits', slyly inviting readers to compare the haunting with a recent trip to Kashmir by Rajesh Pilot, then India's internal affairs minister.[18] According to the article, both 'Operation Ghost' and the official trip had ended without much tactical advantage to forces. Kashmiris were still ready to fight and die.

* * *

ZM often confuses the *daen*'s visits with the big crackdown in Dalgate in October 1992. That is the day when they take his cousin, recently returned from Goa. Trouble has been brewing for a while. A few days before the crackdown, soldiers questioned his cousin—did he have *samaan*, weapons? He said no, he didn't.

ZM is too small to be forced out into the playground for the crackdown but when he hears about it later, he can picture it as if he were there. Men from the neighbourhood have been ordered to the playground and told to sit in rows. They settle in for the whole day. What they never mention about crackdowns, apart from the cold, the hunger, the fear, is the boredom of being outside all day with nothing to do. His cousin wants to change rows so that he can be with his friend. It will help pass the time.

He is wearing red pyjamas, so when he gets up to change places, the soldiers notice him. Do they haul him up for his audacious choice of clothes or his seditious desire to make the best of things, to chat with a friend instead of swatting flies in the field, listening to the tattoo of his heart against his ribs? They say he would have been hauled up anyway because the *mukhbir*, the informer, the cat, has it in for him. The *mukhbir* had wanted to marry a girl from his family but his family did not like the match. This is payback.

The soldiers take ZM's cousin and three others, load them into a military car and drive away. In the evening, ZM hears the sound of gunfire and is conscious of a sensation he cannot name. The next morning, they will be shown four bodies. Militants, the soldiers will say, pointing to the guns they have planted on the four dead men.

The four men are not killed on the field. They are taken to a desolate spot near the power receiving station, the place where the forests start and spread upwards to the Shankaracharya temple, and shot dead.

* * *

As of 29 August 1993, at least four people, including two women, have been killed during ghostly visitations.[19] But who knows what the real death count is. Murderous ghosts stalking the Valley are not such big news as one might think.

Few journalists have spent time investigating the incidents. They can barely keep up with the news. In the morning there is a grenade blast, seven people killed. By evening that is stale news. More are killed and scores injured in a violent crackdown. Almost every morning, the front page of *Greater Kashmir* leads with a death count. It is often in double digits. People have died in gunfights, in raids, in custody, in trucks, in ditches, in fields, in rooms, and what difference does it make whether they died by ghostly hands or mortal?

There is very little ordinary politics in the news pages of 1993, hardly any bickering between parties, speculation on elections, talk of peace talks. Instead, there is pure event. Sopore, where the year has started with a massacre, is turning from a 'liberated zone' into a town of barbed wire.[20] The frontier regions of Uri and Keran have been emptied out by migration across the Line of Control.²¹ Mass rapes are reported in the villages of Budgam district.²² Daily life has stalled in Bandipora.²³ The hunt for 'guest militants', foreign fighters, has begun.

It is the season of 'catch and kill', young men picked up by agencies and dying in custody in such numbers that it can only be official policy, not mere accident. Operation Ghost is suspected to be an extension of Operation Catch and Kill. Young men disappearing into thin air, apparitions floating up windows—it is all the same thing.

It is all the same thing, even if you are a young girl who lives in uptown Srinagar, believing yourself exempt from the haunting. You go about your school day quite unmoved by the bombs going off in the next street. But like everyone else in Kashmir, you pray that night will not fall. There is a gunfight between militants and soldiers near your house, and your father says everyone might have to leave the area if this continues.

And it is all the same thing if you are a boy in South Kashmir's Kulgam district woken up one night by the sound of adults rushing outside to drive the ghost away. It is no different from that other night when everyone rushed outside because militants had come to kill two Kashmiri Pandits who had taken shelter in the village headman's house. All the women from the surrounding houses had gathered outside, had tried to protect the Pandits, but the militants fired in the air, forcing them to scatter. Then they shot the Pandits.

It is all the same thing when militants kill the relative of an Ikhwan, a renegade, and leave his body on the road. It lies there for a while, nobody daring to touch it. An old man who lives nearby, a poor old man who sells odds and ends from a donkey cart, ventures out to cover the body so that it won't be eaten by dogs. But as he is leaving the body the Ikhwan arrive and, taking him to be the killer, shoot him dead.

It is all the same thing, it is all the same thing, the ground still shaking from the impact of the last grenade, the walls still

DAPAAN

rattling with the burst of gunfire, the shape of things so blurred they come unstuck from themselves, and in this confusion of shapes, a new, dark shape. The *raantas*, she walks.

7

THE BRAID CHOPPERS

HB and her son have just finished their morning tea. It is around eleven in the morning and she goes out, bin in hand, meaning to throw out the trash. Two men she does not know are hanging about on the street. Outsiders, she thinks, probably looking for a place to rent in Srinagar.

She and her family rent rooms in a neighbourhood of walled gardens and high metal gates. Spare rooms here are often rented out to students and professionals from other towns, staying in Srinagar to study at coaching institutes or work in government jobs. People are always flowing in and out of this part of town.

HB starts walking and the men walk behind her. She quickens her step but it is too late; one of them has pulled her to the side of the road. She sees his hand reach into his pocket and reappear with what looks like a spray. After that, she doesn't know.

When she opens her eyes next, the ground is beneath her cheek and a neighbour is bending over her. Next to her lies the thick coil of her hair, recently chopped off her head.

* * *

DAPAAN

It does not start in Kashmir. In June 2017, women in Rajasthan report their hair has been cut off by late-night marauders. It is widely believed to be the work of a *churail*, a witch, cousin to the *daen*.[1]

From Rajasthan, the braid choppers travel north to Uttar Pradesh, Delhi and Haryana, where they shape-shift into witches, god-men, cat-like creatures.[2] Not satisfied with this loot of braids, they travel further north into Jammu, where residents quickly ban strangers from entering villages. So they travel up the Banihal tunnel and enter the Kashmir Valley by September 2017.

Now here is a rich harvest. In about a month, they collect over two hundred and fifty braids. At least a hundred and five first information reports, FIRs, official complaints that must be investigated, have been lodged against them with the police. But what can they do? As one police officer complains, you cannot catch ghosts.[3]

They work their way up from the hills of the southern districts into the dense neighbourhoods of Srinagar. Then they spread across the countryside before hitting the towns of the north.

If Kashmir offers rich yields, much better than anywhere else, it also appears more ready for them. In street after street, they find bands of young men armed with sticks and torches, ready to give chase or beat them back. It is almost as if they have been recognised.

They do not know yet that ghosts can be haunted by other ghosts. Stories can wake up sleeping stories. They do not know yet that the women they attack in Kashmir, long declared a 'disturbed area' by the government, are well acquainted with ghosts.

* * *

Late one evening in 2017, JM hears a shriek from the fields behind his house in Ganderbal district and rushes out with a paper knife he has kept for just such an occasion. Several other

THE BRAID CHOPPERS

men patrolling the neighbourhood have also reached the field. They find a woman who says a man in a burqa crept up on her and tried to cut off her braid. JM and the men comb the area, flashing torches into muttering bushes and patches of tall grass. The woman shrieks again, this time from the edge of the field. They dash to the spot, flicking their torches here and there. Nothing.

JM is a teenager and not, strictly speaking, allowed outside with the neighbourhood patrol. But he has been itching to go and kept the paper knife ready. He is not quite sure how he will use it should he come face to face with a braid chopper but thinks it best to be armed.

Since last year, when forces killed Burhan Wani and the protests started, he has felt himself to be at war. He has seen his friend wounded by tear gas shells fired by the police and then arrested for allegedly setting fire to a school building. His friend spent four months in jail and was only released when there was another fire in Ganderbal, apparently by the same culprit, and his lawyer argued it couldn't possibly be him. Every killing and wound, every rumour of police or paramilitary action against protesters fuelled more protests.

The year turned amid a flood of arrests. The crowds started thinning, everyone tired and heartbroken but still seething. That is when the rumour of braid chopping started, spreading through the streets like acrid fumes of tear gas.

Now it's back to the streets. These are not ghostly ghosts; these are political ghosts. These are psyops designed by central agencies to keep people from the streets. These are cruel and deliberate humiliations planned by the government. At the very least, these are *nebrim*, outsiders, with sinister designs on Kashmir.

The People's Democratic Party, which heads the state government, calls it an attack on the Kashmiri ethos.[4] The National Conference, now in the opposition, holds rallies protesting against the government's failure to nab the braid choppers.[5]

DAPAAN

The Hizbul Mujahideen releases an audio message saying it is a ploy by agencies to make sure no one opens their doors to militants at night.[6] It is no use for the police chief to protest that all his anti-militancy operations have been stalled because of the panic.[7]

Hurriyat leader Syed Ali Shah Geelani, gaunt veteran of the *tehreek*, has seen it all before. Remember Operation Ghost, he says, remember Catch and Kill.[8]

* * *

In stories told about braid choppers, the *raantas* walks again.

The woman with the golden earrings recognises the signs. Noises in the outhouse—some houses in downtown Srinagar have escaped the architectural changes of the nineties and still have toilets in the courtyard—then footsteps echoing down the street. After that, she and her downstairs neighbours stay up at night for weeks.

She knows how this goes. She has lived in this tall house for decades and has ghosts of her own to mourn. She has lost her husband and son here. These knocks on the window and noises in the street, these are not ghosts. It's the military, what else?

Her five-year-old grandson has seen the braid choppers. After his father died, he moved to Habbakadal, another old neighbourhood in Srinagar, to live with his mother and her family. When the braid choppers come to Habbakadal, he is there.

It must be around one at night. He is woken up by the sound of someone landing on the lavatory roof in the courtyard. When he looks out, he sees three masked figures in black. He starts shouting, which wakes up the adults in the house, who start shouting as well. The three figures melt away. He thinks he sees two women and a man. The man carries a pair of scissors and one of the women a sort of spray. They all wear spring boots.

But the visions of the night fade in daylight. The next day in school, he does not tell his friends about what he has seen. He

THE BRAID CHOPPERS

will tell no one at all until, five years later, a visiting journalist asks his grandmother about braid choppers.

Women who say their hair has been cut off are eager to talk at first. But they suddenly find themselves accused by their own stories. While HB says the braid choppers are flesh-and-blood men, others cannot tell who or what attacked them. They are men in burqas, black shapes, shadows. As weeks pass, the public outrage is mixed with something else. It is suspected that stories of braid chopping no longer speak of dark forces outside but of a derangement within. As if three decades of disturbance have finally moved into the bodies of women, symptom bearers of the *haalaat*.

Older stories about the *raantas* and the *daen* have often been used to indict women. Those who claim to have seen a *daen* confirm that she stores her powers in her hair. When she speaks, her hair switches from side to side as if she's preparing to spring. And then you can do anything she says, anything, as your eyes follow her hair back and forth, back and forth. Women who leave their hair open, women who speak too loudly or do not obey, are often called *daen*, disapprovingly.

In the Kashmir Valley, *raantas* and *daen* are names for the same creature. But in the Pir Panjal mountains, they are not the same, says the former crime branch officer, who was posted in Doda district in the seventies. Here, a *raantas* is a supernatural being, her feet turned backwards. A *daen* could be any woman—your mother, your sister, your wife. She can read the Quran backwards to wield power over men and have them do her bidding.

Folktales have always warned against the excesses of ungovernable women; everyone grew up knowing the *raantas* was defeated when her hair was cut off. After the *haalaat* arrived, she acquired the features of military vehicles—a body and nails of steel, a mechanical roar. Her monstrous desires, which had pressed against the walls of Kashmiri homes for ages, did not wait for permission to enter. But she still came from outside. In the narratives of women attacked by braid choppers, the distinctions between outside and inside grow blurred. Who is the *raantas*, and who is her prey in these stories?

* * *

HB only properly regains consciousness in hospital. She is later told that staff from a nearby school gave chase to the attackers but they disappeared. For months, she is beside herself. She goes into depression and has to see a doctor.

Six years after the braid chopping panic, a psychiatrist in Srinagar says the narratives of the women who got attacked are irrational. One woman said her braid chopper came out of the wall. Another woman said he climbed in through a tiny window. Such things are physically impossible, sighs the psychiatrist; the only explanation is that the women cut off their hair themselves.

He uses an old-fashioned word, 'hysteria'. Until the nineteenth century, it was believed that only women were prone to hysteria, the madness generated by a wandering womb, sometimes linked to demonic possession, causing 'ungovernable emotional excess'.[9] It was only in the twentieth century that both men and women were found to suffer, a diagnosis brought on by the world wars, where soldiers in emotional distress displayed hysterical symptoms.[10] Still, the word did not lose its associations with possessed and ungovernable women.

After 1980, hysteria was no longer formally studied as a psychological disorder.[11] Symptoms linked to it were attributed to dissociative disorder. This is how the psychiatrist describes the hysteria of women who say their hair has been chopped off, as a form of dissociation. For a brief period, the women are beside themselves, severed from their conscious minds. Patients in such a state are suggestible, he says. When they see reports and social media posts about braid chopping, they imagine it is happening to them.

THE BRAID CHOPPERS

Hard to say what disturbances prompted this dissociation from the self. Earlier, the psychiatrist recounts, they treated patients with post-traumatic stress disorder, struggling to deal with the after-effects of bombs, raids or sudden and bloody loss. As the years wore on, the cases changed. The *haalaat* made itself felt in quieter ways, a thrum of insecurity that entered the bones: no jobs, schools closed for months, everyday life suspended as everyone held their breath and waited for peace. Rumours went viral, the symptom of a society that has become suggestible because it is not well.

Hard to say what psychic pain is so unbearable that the only way out is to escape yourself and take on another identity. To be so dispossessed that you can be possessed. There are many forms of dissociation, the psychiatrist explains, including possession syndrome. The belief that another being has taken hold of your mind and body.

Stories of possession have always floated around in villages. JM's father, who has an interest in the occult, knows something about possession. He spoke to a *raantas* after summoning her into a man's body. You may only call a *raantas* after midnight. That night, JM's father took the man's hand and blew on him. Then he told the man to close his eyes and imagine himself outdoors, next to a school building nearby. The man closed his eyes and was transported to the school in his head. The *raantas* saw him there and entered him. JM's father knew she was in the man's body when his feet turned backward.

When JM's father was growing up, he had also been told not to go out after dark as he would be taken by the *raantas*. He did not believe these stories until he grew up, and then he found that such creatures did not merely wait outside. According to JM's father, the *raantas* is no different from the *djinns* of Islamic mythology. *Raantas, van moenu, djinns*—they are all wind. They move like the wind, passing through trees, forests, mountains, human bodies. This is the dread. You could turn into the thing that you fear, your feet turning backward, your voice speaking in their voice.

* * *

Kashmir officially became a 'disturbed area' in 1990. That is, a place of such unnatural disturbances that it needed unnatural laws, like the Armed Forces (Jammu and Kashmir) Special Powers Act. Soldiers could search houses without a warrant and open fire to put down such disturbances. Unless the *markaz* allowed it, and the *markaz* rarely did, they could not be taken to regular courts over these operations. It was understood that certain things happened in the line of duty in disturbed areas.

The Valley continued to report disturbances even after the law was imposed. Bomb blasts and gunfights, yes, but also other agitations. It is said, soldiers conducting a search operation in the villages of Kunan and Poshpora raped many women who lived there.[12] (It did not happen, the army said. Probably not, the government eventually said.) It is said, a bride was raped on her way to her new husband's house while forces turned their guns on the wedding party.[13] (Unfortunate, caught in the crossfire, the government said at first. The BSF later court-martialled two men and demoted two others.) It is said, two women, Asiya and Neelofar, were raped and killed before their bodies were set adrift in a stream in Shopian district.[14] (They drowned, concluded the Central Bureau of Investigation; doctors saying otherwise were working for Pakistan.) Other disturbances were not even reported. Suppressed or denied, such disturbances haunted official records. They rippled through towns and villages as rumours, manifestations of an unquiet valley.

The government's strategy to curb militancy was to make Kashmiri women the first target of security operations, claimed a *Greater Kashmir* column from 1993.[15] They were allegedly molested during crackdowns, when men were forced outside and women remained indoors; they were also attacked in ghostly incursions by the *daen*.

In Anantnag district, the ghosts never left, even after the panic of 1993 died down. In 2004, there was a ghost trying to enter homes in Anantnag town. One man, a father of four daughters, said they spent a night of terror when the ghost almost broke into their house. So every household with young women locked its doors and kept vigil after six in the evening. They tried complaining to the police. The police replied with some salty comments—your wives and your daughters have lovers who try to enter at night.[16] One evening, residents of a locality on the outskirts of Anantnag town decided they had had enough. As the disturbances started up, they poured outside and ambushed the ghost, delivering a few well-placed blows. He seemed to be a *sardar*, a Sikh man who wore a turban and spoke no Kashmiri. The ghost reportedly confessed to being a Rashtriya Rifles soldier.[17]

Invasions continued, some less ghostly than others. One night in 2005, a soldier barged into a house in Dooru, a village close to Anantnag town, stabbing and killing a girl.[18] Her family claimed he had seen her a few days earlier and was struck by her beauty; he came calling that night to rape her. Having stabbed the girl, the soldier bolted into the night to escape. But the night had other plans for him. As he rippled through the fields, men from a nearby Central Reserve Police Force camp took him for a militant and shot him dead.

Ghosts were back again in 2013, this time in Anantnag district's Nowgam village. Stones were thrown at windows in the night, causing a fifty-five-year-old woman to die of a heart attack.[19]

It was not just Anantnag. In the villages of North Kashmir, teenage boys set up a night watch for the ghost till the end of the nineties. By then, it was generally accepted that these were not ghostly ghosts. They came from camps. As mass protests raged in 2008, a little girl in downtown Srinagar was told not to go out of the house after dark. Her father said that soldiers these days took no prisoners; they just ate people straightaway.

Forces, which included camps, soldiers as well as personnel required for infrastructural support, had been confused with spectres even before the *haalaat*. In 1981, Alison McDonald, a Scottish teenager, disappeared in the mountains of Sonamarg in Ganderbal district. She had been staying with her friend at a run-down hotel in the mountains. One day, she went out trekking on her own and was never seen again. Police officers from Srinagar were called in to investigate several days after the disappearance. By then, crucial evidence available in the first twenty-four hours after any crime had disappeared. Still, the investigation seemed to lead to the employee of a nearby Beacon camp. Beacon is a project of the Border Roads Organisation, which is owned by the Indian defence ministry and tasked with building infrastructure in Jammu and Kashmir. The case was hushed up and the employee was transferred soon afterwards. Instead, it was rumoured that the *van moenu* took her. It is said, the forest monster, who is very large but has very short arms, will take lone women and disappear with them underground.

The girl's body was never found, and stories continued to sprout from her disappearance. PB, who grew up around Sonamarg, had heard the owner of the hotel where the teenager was staying might have kidnapped her for money. In 2007, the girl's father detected the ghost of a Skye accent in certain words used by Hizbul Mujahideen leader Syed Salahuddin. He suggested the militant commander might have picked it up from his kidnapped daughter.[20]

But the *van moenu* rumour lingered in the Sonamarg forests. Forces and mountain monsters remained entangled in other stories told here. In 1995, people in Sonamarg claimed to have seen an injured *van moenu*, brought in for treatment by soldiers.

THE BRAID CHOPPERS

The local police, however, found no evidence to support the reported sighting.[21]

* * *

When the braid choppers arrive in 2017, BB and her sister, who live in Anantnag town, know what to do. They lock themselves up in the house after dark and listen for sounds in the courtyard. Such disturbances are not new. Everyone knows who is behind this, even if the first information reports, or FIRs, against the braid choppers charge 'unknown persons' with 'outraging the modesty' of their victims.

Both sisters cover their hair when they leave the house. Most women do. They see it as part of their Kashmiri Muslim identity. Some wear a *pootz*, a scarf that is tucked behind the ears and knotted at the back. It keeps hair out of your face when bending over paddy fields or a cooking pot; it also keeps the dust out of your hair. Others wear a hijab, a headscarf fashioned according to Islamic prescriptions, framing your face while covering your hair and neck. BB sometimes just throws a dupatta over her head when going out or meeting men outside the immediate family.

If braid choppers can take your hair, what else can they take, many women demand. To have your scarf ripped off, to be suddenly rendered braidless feels like being stripped, not just of your modesty but also of your religious and cultural identity.

But the panic dies out as suddenly as it started. By the end of October 2017, just as Delhi sends an interlocutor, a soft-spoken former intelligence officer tasked with embracing all Kashmiris, the braid choppers leave the Valley.[22] Not many ask who they were anymore or pursue the charges of outraging modesty. The police point out all the women were alone when they were attacked and there were no witnesses. Psychologists cautiously start speaking of mass hysteria.

Hysteria may have been dropped from medical books, but it has returned as a metaphor for political and cultural life in the twenty-first century, used to describe conspiracy theories, social media panics, the frenzy over populist dictators.[23] As if entire societies are afflicted by the ungovernable emotions that women have carried for centuries.

Six years after the braid choppers disappeared, questions linger under an uneasy silence. Was it psyops or ungovernable emotional excess? Were they agencies or militants? As with the *raantas* of the nineties, they seemed to be many things at once. An elderly man in Anantnag district was pelted to death with bricks, mistaken for a braid chopper when he went out early in the morning to relieve himself.[24] A young man visiting his girlfriend at night was beaten by local boys.[25]

The former crime branch officer believes that, in some localities, braid choppers may have been useful to forces trying to keep the peace after a turbulent year. It may not have reached the *markaz* or even high up in the Jammu and Kashmir government; maybe it was just a ploy used by local commandants. But the psychiatrist in Srinagar says no, the braid choppers of 2017 were very different from the steel *daen* of 1993. This was no psyops or counterinsurgency operation.

Journalists covering the attacks cannot decide. There must have been external forces acting on the women—how else would one of the victims find herself in a room locked from the outside? But they also remember the haunted eyes of the women they interviewed. Many of them looked, well, disturbed.

* * *

Six years later, the women attacked by braid choppers turn away journalists and cameras. They were called hysterical for sharing their stories, disbelieved and shamed. Now everyone has forgotten and their shame is theirs alone. They will not speak. They don't remember. The braid chopping happened a very long time ago.

The silence has become a haunting that presses on the daylight and lives in walls. It lives in the walls of a house in downtown Srinagar. Rooms have been added to it since 2017. It has become a tall, narrow townhouse with several floors, five cats coiling around the staircase and a sense of something blazing behind curtains.

DK appears at the door, her strong, lovely face loosely framed by a dupatta. She is wary at first. Then she makes a decision—come in.

Yes, it happened to her youngest daughter. They call her Jaanu, beloved. Yes, Jaanu is home but she will not talk. Anyway, come upstairs into this room.

It happened one afternoon in her mother's house, DK begins. Jaanu and she were visiting. Everyone was lingering in the first-floor kitchen after lunch when Jaanu said she would leave for tuition. Her tenth-grade board examinations were just months away and this was crunch time. She left. Ten minutes later, her grandmother went into the landing and declared, 'Jaanu's dead.'

The girl was lying on the floor, her severed braid next to her. They tried to wake her up but she would not stir. Finally, her brother gathered her in his arms and took her to the hospital. She stirred more than an hour later and they thought it best to take her home. But at home, they noticed a dark fluid dribbling out of her mouth. It looked like poison so they took her back to the hospital.

This is what Jaanu told them later. On her way out that afternoon, she had passed the bathroom on the first floor. Someone must have been lying in wait there because she felt something hit the back of her head before she fell to the ground.

DK, however, remembers there were no scars on the back of her daughter's head. Some boys ran after the attackers, although later on it is not clear whom they were chasing, ghosts or men, one man or two. As news of the attack spread in the neighbourhood, protests started up.

Late evening a week later, it happened to Jaanu's aunt as she sat in the veranda of her house, which is in the same downtown neighbourhood. She thought she saw a figure in black before it brought an iron rod down on her head. When she woke up, her braid was gone.

At night, local boys patrolled the streets, but it wasn't enough. For months, DK and her whole family slept in the ground-floor kitchen, guarding Jaanu with their bodies. She was the youngest; she had to be protected. After the attack, Jaanu had plunged into a twilight world. She would not go to her tuition classes; she hardly went out at all. The principal of the school where she studied came home to speak to her, which helped a little. When it was time to write her boards, DK took her to the examination hall and brought her back home safe.

In the six years since then, Jaanu has finished school and gone to college. They have started thinking of getting her married. The attack is hardly spoken of anymore unless it crops up on social media.

As the mother speaks, someone walks up the stairs and slams the door shut from the outside.

DK has told the story quietly so far, but now her voice rises, acquiring notes of anger. They are unconscionable, these pictures online, taken in the chaos after the attack and published in local papers. Every time someone posts them on social media, DK goes to war for her daughter. Would they post these pictures if Jaanu were their sister, she demands. Did they have no sense of a woman's honour? Some things cannot be mentioned again, especially when Jaanu is going to get married soon.

When her story is done, DK gets up and walks to the door. She finds it locked from the outside. There is no anger left in her voice, not even surprise, as she leans out the window and calls to someone downstairs. Let us out, beloved, she says.

8

GHOSTS IN THE GROUND

It is said, ghosts walked in the mountains of Anantnag district. They walked in Panchanthal and they walked in Brariangan, a few kilometres apart, cloaked in green, part village, part forest. Orchards and mustard fields merge into pine groves and deserted mounds, but more on that later.

Everyone knew they weren't ghosts like that but they called them ghosts anyway. Well, in Panchanthal, they called the intruders '*bhoot*', ghost. In Brariangan, they sometimes called them '*tasarruf*', the Kashmiri and Urdu word for possession. As if it was such an intimate haunting that it had entered the bodies of those who lived in the village.

These were creatures you sometimes saw and sometimes didn't. Sometimes they wore uniforms and sometimes they didn't. Sometimes they were masked; sometimes they were vague shapes in the dark, for they always moved at night.

Their presence was mainly felt through the traces they left. Stones thrown at windows. Stories of them trying to break into homes. SP, who lived in a particularly desolate part of Panchanthal, said they had left home for eleven days at the height of the visitations. When they got back, all the windows were broken and their things strewn around the house.

No one can remember when exactly this happened. It was long after the *raantas* scare of 1993. Perhaps in 1999 or early 2000. Residents of both Panchanthal and Brariangan are certain that the ghosts never came back after the spring of 2000, after the killings. But more on that later.

The stories of Panchanthal and Brariangan are shadowed by the story of Chittisinghpora, another village in the Anantnag mountains. Three places bound by blood, killings that no one ever answered for. They are ghostly in more ways than one. For ghosts may be tricks of language that draw attention to the unresolved nature of crimes. Ghosts are phantom histories that have been suppressed or will not be admitted on record. Ghosts are sometimes not people at all but places rendered thin by the past.

* * *

It is said, the killers were men in uniform. They were army men. No, they were militants from the Lashkar-e-Taiba. No, they were Ikhwan, renegade militants turned counterinsurgency militia. They had been playing cricket with local boys in the months leading up to the killings, observing the rhythms of life in the village: when people went out, when the streets were deserted, when you might find men at the gurudwara and the women safely inside. After the killings, they never came to play cricket again.

This much is certain. On the evening of 20 March 2000, as United States President Bill Clinton prepared to land in Delhi, a group of men entered Chittisinghpora with the intention to kill.

The village is bookended by two gurudwaras. It is said, Sikh families settled here in the time of Maharaja Ranjit Singh, who added Kashmir to his empire in 1819. Sikh rule in Kashmir, both brief and disastrous, ended in 1846. But Chittisinghpora

GHOSTS IN THE GROUND

remained, pine and walnut groves closing in on its homesteads, a small village of ardent Sikhs. They lived on good terms with their Muslim neighbours but were largely aloof from the *tehreek* that raged around them. Which is why they had also been spared the crackdowns and raids that spread across the rest of the Valley. Searches here were a civil affair.

That evening, when the men in uniform announced they were on a search operation as they had got word of militants hiding in the village, no one was very alarmed. It was Holi, a Hindu festival to mark the arrival of spring where revellers douse each other with coloured liquid or powder. Someone remembers the men had faces stained with colour.

There was a holiday calm about the day. The gurudwaras had emptied after evening prayers. A few men were returning from the fields. Dinner was waiting for them at home. Someone remembers they had chicken curry that night. At some point, the lights went out.

Men were rounded up in two groups, one at either gurudwara. A few of them were still making their way back home. Others were picked up from their homes. Then they were lined up against a wall and shot at close quarters. Giani Rajinder Singh, a priest, was still in one of the gurudwaras when the gunmen arrived. In his memory the shots have grown so loud he reckons they would have been heard in villages six to seven kilometres away.

Afterwards, women and children from the village made for a large house behind the Gurudwara Singh Sabha Samundri, drawing together for safety. Giani Rajinder Singh and two other men stumbled through the dark to Kehribal, several kilometres away, to call the police. Chittisinghpora did not have phone lines at the time. It was midnight before the police reached the village. Of the thirty-six men rounded up that night, only one survived.

And Chittisinghpora entered the map of Sikh martyrdom. They were martyrs because they were targeted even though they were innocent, says a nineteen-year-old from the village, pointing to the pictures of the thirty-five dead. It is the summer of 2023, and he is standing in a memorial hall at the Gurudwara Singh Sabha, built over the spot where their last rites took place.

He thinks about them all the time, these men who died before he was born. He knows their names and what they did for a living, who was related to whom. He reads feverishly about the incident and is keen to fill in any visitor who will listen. In Punjab, a predominantly Sikh state where he studies law, everyone knows of his little village. They know of it because of the killings. Chittisinghpora has become a name that summons the dead. They walk with us, says the nineteen-year-old. Everywhere we go, they walk with us.

* * *

Four days after the Chittisinghpora shooting, there were visitors in Brariangan, further up the mountains. It was not a crackdown, just regular night movement, say residents of the village, echoing the language they used to describe the earlier haunting. Invisible creatures moving at night. Night movement.

Abdul Rashid Khan remembers it was around two in the morning. He was at home then, as were his brother, Mohammad Rafiq Khan, and his father, Jumma Khan. The night movers, men in army uniform, broke the door and entered their home. They wanted guides to show them the way to Shangus, a village lower down in the mountains. The brothers, then barely out of adolescence, offered to go. But the men seemed to think they were too young to be reliable guides. They picked their father, Jumma Khan, a farmer in his mid-forties with a long beard and an air of solidity. They said they would be back in half an hour, but they never returned.

In the morning, Rashid went down to the police station at Achabal and filed a complaint that his father was missing. That

GHOSTS IN THE GROUND

same night, soldiers had taken another man from Brariangan, also called Jumma Khan.

On 25 March 2000, the day after they took his father, Rashid heard about a shooting in the Pathribal forests just above Panchanthal. On the news, the government was claiming the men killed in the shooting were militants. Rashid found it strange. Bullets were still flying but the dead men had already been declared militants.

In Panchanthal that morning, SP had woken up to a crackdown. Several villages were under a cordon; militants had been trapped and the army warned everyone to stay indoors. SP cannot remember such a big operation before that spring day in 2000. For hours they huddled in cold rooms listening to the sound of *dhamakas*, blasts, in the forests above. There were no settlements up there, only a few scattered shacks used by nomadic Gujjar herders. Later, Gujjars who lived nearby were asked to bury the dead.

When the guns stopped, they heard five men had died in the forests above Panchanthal. The army and the special operations group, SOG, claimed they were foreign militants from the Lashkar-e-Taiba, the killers of Chittisinghpora.[1] Forces had surrounded the hut where they were hiding, said the police, and the militants died when it caught fire during the gunfight.[2] Their bodies were charred or battered beyond recognition.

In Brariangan, they listened to the updates with growing unease. The men taken on 24 March had still not returned. Rumours about the Pathribal gunfight were snaking into surrounding villages. Someone had recognised the bodies when they were being buried. They did not seem to be foreign militants.

Protests had already started when word spread that four more men from Brariangan had been held on the night of 1 April.[3] It was said, two others managed to escape from custody. The army, they claimed, was planning to finish off the four men still held captive, just like they had killed the five men in the Pathribal forests. Protests gathered steam. The four men were reportedly released. But in Brariangan, all suspicions about the Pathribal gunfight were confirmed.

On the morning of 3 April, there were public announcements, recalls an old man in Brariangan. The village was to march. If the authorities could not hear protests in the hills, the protesters would go down to the district headquarters in Anantnag town. They were to march all the way to the district commissioner's office in the heart of the town. It was to be a long walk, but they were used to long walks.

The old man remembers the sky was blue that day. Shops and businesses were closed in protest. Almost everyone in the village joined the march. Return us our Pathribal bodies, the crowd chanted. They had walked several kilometres downhill and reached a traffic crossing in Brakpora, on the outskirts of Anantnag town. There was a camp here, housing Central Reserve Police Force and SOG troops. That was where the firing started. The old man fell down and remained pinned to the ground as people ran over him. He remembers the mustard was golden in the fields then.

Rashid and Rafiq were part of the crowd. As the shooting started, Rashid saw his brother fall next to him, hit by a bullet. Rashid lay down on the ground hoping the bullets would miss him. The crowd started breaking up. Some tried to get to hospitals with the injured, but CRPF men along the road started beating them up—women, children, everyone. Others ran through by-lanes and narrow streams leading off from the main road.

Eight people died in the Brakpora shooting, seven of them from Brariangan. There was no telling whom the bullets chose, whom they spared. The old man got up and made his way to Anantnag town through one of the by-lanes. Rashid survived. Rafiq did not.

GHOSTS IN THE GROUND

In ten days, Rashid had lost his father and his brother. More deaths followed. Rafiq's young wife was soon married off again. She left behind her daughter as she moved to her new home. The child died not long afterwards, barely a year old.

Those left behind were doomed to a half life. Rashid and Rafiq's mother has been ill ever since. Rashid is now about the same age as his father was when he disappeared, a man with a thick, black beard and a vitality that casts a force field around him. Over the last two decades, he has appeared in newspaper reports and television clips, asking for justice. But he describes himself in ghostly terms: I do not consider myself alive.

* * *

Justice or reparation grows spectral in societies that have lived through conflict, writes the legal scholar Jaco Barnard-Naude in his essay on truth and reconciliation in South Africa and Rwanda.[4] Justice is the spectre that haunts the law. It exists as an impossibility because it seeks to bring redress to the irreparable, that which is without remedy, that which cannot be changed. In post-apartheid South Africa, reparation is thought to be necessary to transitional justice. But no reparative measures can bring back the dead or heal the wounds of the living. So to strive for justice is to ceaselessly strive for the impossible. To Barnard-Naude, this ceaseless quest becomes an act of hope.

To the families of the dead in Kashmir, hope is a stretch. Forty-eight people died in two weeks in the spring of 2000 and no one was really found guilty. If justice is an ever-receding spectre, they fight simply against putting the ghost to rest.

In the days after the Brakpora killings, police officials suggested that it was militants who opened fire within the crowd; if forces had fired at all, it was in self-defence.[5] Then the Pandian commission, appointed by the state government, named four CRPF men and three SOG men as the accused. The Union home ministry refused permission to prosecute the CRPF, a central paramilitary force.[6] In Kashmir, a few junior members of the state police were suspended but no one was arrested.

In the years that followed the killings, the fate of the Chittisinghpora case grew entwined with the Pathribal case. If the men who died in Pathribal could be proved to be civilians and not the killers of Chittisinghpora, the latter case would gain new life. But nothing now remains of the Pathribal case except a plea filed by the families of the victims in the Supreme Court, asking for the case to be reopened. It has disappeared into the labyrinth of appeals, objections and public interest litigations that eternally wait their turn in Delhi. Rashid has stopped tracking its fate. And anyway, he fears going to Delhi, where Muslims are attacked and made homeless by bulldozers. In 2014, an army court closed the case and acquitted the accused. But the plea in the Supreme Court still haunts the system.

Back in April 2000, protests had compelled the administration to exhume the Pathribal bodies. Rashid and others had rushed to identify what remained of their relatives. There was not much to go by. The curve of a back that looked familiar. A ring with a stone in it. Rashid's family thought they recognised his father, Jumma Khan, by his missing tooth, but forensic reports claimed the body's teeth had been freshly broken. They broke four of his teeth, Rashid says, to hide the tooth that had always been missing.

Physical evidence, the stories told by blood, skin and bone, was rendered shadowy through the course of the investigation. The bodies were so burnt or mutilated they could not be reliably identified. So Rashid and other families gave blood samples that could be matched with DNA samples taken from the bodies. They were sent to forensic labs outside Kashmir. In 2002, it was revealed that the Anantnag administration had tampered with the samples.[7] This had happened twice. Lab experts visited Kashmir to collect samples for a third time. It had become clear

GHOSTS IN THE GROUND

the local police and administration were not keen on finding the killers. The case was transferred to the Central Bureau of Investigation, with its headquarters in Delhi.

Cold-blooded murder, the CBI concluded in 2006. The third round of DNA tests had revealed that the bodies belonged to the men taken from Anantnag and not to foreign militants.[8] For a while, they lived again in official records: five innocent men from Anantnag district, kidnapped by the army for the purposes of 'Operation Swift', a security blitzkrieg which was to show that the Chittisinghpora killers had been found and punished. Five men whose bodies were burned or dismembered so that they could not be identified when the 'After Action Report' on Operation Swift was written up to say Chittisinghpora had been solved, terrorists sent by Pakistani intelligence and hiding in the Panchalthan forests neutralised. The story of the staged encounter made it to the national press so a public outside Kashmir now heard their names. Jumma Amirullah Khan and Jumma Fakirullah Khan from Brariangan; Zahoor Ahmad Dalal, picked up from near his home in Mominabad; Bashir Ahmad Bhat and Mohammad Yousuf Malik, taken from the outskirts of Anantnag town.

As the case went through the courts, flesh-and-blood men turned spectral again. The army argued its soldiers could not be tried in civilian courts as they were protected by the Armed Forces (Special Powers) Act. In 2012, the Supreme Court ruled the army could choose whether they should be tried in civilian or military courts. The army chose military courts. Twelve years after the killings, Rashid and other relatives were asked to give evidence all over again, this time to the army. At first, they chose not to go. The army had started hearings at a camp in Nagrota in Jammu district, about two hundred kilometres away from Brariangan. It would take a day to get there and never mind the cost. When the case was shifted to Awantipora in the Kashmir Valley, they went, swallowing their fear as they entered the gates of an army camp. But in January 2014, the army acquitted all the accused, claiming the 'evidence recorded' was not enough to convict them. It refused to let the families see the summary of evidence that led to this conclusion. Now, once more, Jumma Amirullah Khan, Jumma Fakirullah Khan, Zahoor Ahmad Dalal, Bashir Ahmad Bhat and Mohammad Yousuf Malik were men without bodies. The charred limbs and torsos found on the mountainside in Pathribal were bodies without names.

So nothing now remains except the plea in the Supreme Court, listed repeatedly for hearing but never heard. It stands for a phantom story, the story told by victims, allowed to live for a while in the official processes of justice as the case wound through police investigations, inquiry commissions and court hearings, but then killed off through these very processes.

* * *

Two stories flickered against each other in Chittisinghpora. There was the government version—militant groups backed by Pakistan deliberately targeted minorities in Kashmir and aimed to destabilise India–US talks as Clinton visited.[9] Within days of the attack, police and paramilitary forces were patrolling the village, apparently to reassure its terrified inhabitants. Luminaries descended on Chittisinghpora. The government offered some measure of compensation to the families of the dead. A few shell-shocked residents interviewed by television channels initially agreed the intruders were Lashkar-e-Taiba militants.

But the fiction of the Pathribal militants was quietly retired by security agencies. They first arrested one suspect, then another, but never managed to build a case against them. Periodically, there are reports of Lashkar operatives arrested in other terror cases confessing to the Chittisinghpora attacks, which appears to confirm the government's thesis. No prosecution follows.

As the years passed, the other story gained strength in Chittisinghpora. Agencies did it. Why else would the investiga-

GHOSTS IN THE GROUND

tions go nowhere? In 2017, when an outlet called *Sikh News Express* interviewed KS Gill, a retired lieutenant general of the Indian Army, many felt vindicated. Gill claimed the attack was propaganda. It was staged by the Indian state to show Clinton that Pakistan targeted minorities. He said the attack was carried out by the Ikhwan, aided by friends in the lower echelons of the army.[10]

The nineteen-year-old at the gurudwara in Chittisinghpora points to another text, or the absences in the text, as evidence. In 2006, former US secretary of state Madeleine Albright published a book featuring an introduction by Clinton. As he fondly perused his memories of the Albright years, the former president mentioned the 'Hindu militants' who killed in Chittisinghpora. After howls of protest in India, the publishers hastily agreed to remove the phrase. What did the Clinton administration know, the teenager demands. Why was it so important to bury the reference?

Now, many residents of Chittisinghpora dwell on details that back the second story. The attackers chanted Hindu slogans; they called each other Hindu names; they wore army uniforms and were still covered in Holi colours.

With the crime unresolved, Chittisinghpora remained disturbed. A former police officer remembers being sent down to the village on the second anniversary of the killings. He found people in a state of panic. An army officer had visited the village, asking for cars. It happened a lot in Kashmir, the army requisitioning private vehicles for military work, people handing over the keys because what choice did they have. But in Chittisinghpora, it felt like a flashback. They thought the same men had come back, the assassins in uniform, says the former police officer. They believed it was a conspiracy against Sikhs and they would have to leave Kashmir, just like the Pandits.

* * *

DAPAAN

In May 2023, the mountain villages of Anantnag district are veiled in rain. It drips from walnut branches, through the droop of willows, down the sad bark of deodars, falling on the darkening earth there, there, there.

Maybe it is possible for landscapes to be haunted by traumatic events.[11] The stories people tell about them, meanings poured into a stretch of road, a stream, a grove, ensure that memory seeps into the land itself. Time grows blurred in these places.

In public records, the three tragedies from the spring of 2000 are named after the places where they occurred: Chittisinghpora, Pathribal, Brakpora. But the patch of the Pathribal forests where the killings of 25 March 2000 took place is largely uninhabited. It is the village of Panchanthal that bears memories of the staged encounter. The traffic crossing in Brakpora has long forgotten the people who died there on 3 April 2000. It is Brariangan, which lost nine of its inhabitants, that commemorates the killings of 25 March and 3 April 2000. So in the private records of grief, a different triad of names emerges: Chittisinghpora, Panchanthal, Brariangan.

After the spring of 2000, the *bhoot* never returned to Panchanthal and Brariangan. Inhabitants of the villages cannot say whether the ghosts were militants or soldiers. No one ever caught a ghost. But they will say this—if you chased the spectres, they melted into security cover within a few hundred metres, and why was that?

The Anantnag mountains were unquiet in the first decade of the *haalaat*. In the upper reaches, the last Kashmiri villages trail away into vast forests and lonely valleys, no man's land between the Jammu and Kashmir divisions. Early in the *haalaat*, foreign militants who had crossed the Line of Control were often led here by guides.[12] Every other family had a son who had joined up. Militants strode through villages quite happy to show off their new guns. Forces were thin on the ground.

GHOSTS IN THE GROUND

There was one police station for every fifty villages, says the former police officer. Attempts to spread out further were often thwarted. For instance, around the late nineties, a police post was set up in a private house in Larnoo, a village in the Shangus area. If people went there with complaints or requests, militants would turn up and say they would take care of it. Eventually, more police posts were set up. The militants allowed it, says the former police officer, because the local constabulary was Kashmiri.

Even the army would not make frequent incursions into the Anantnag mountains. A camp was added to the ammunition depot at Khundru. This is where the 7 Rashtriya Rifles unit that carried out the Pathribal operation was stationed. Its jurisdiction arced across a wide radius of villages, including Chittisinghpora, Panchalthan, Pathribal, Mominabad, Sheerpora and Brariangan, all places touched by the events of the spring of 2000.[13] But smaller camps were largely absent in the early nineties. If the army conducted operations, they were elaborately planned, with masses of men and weapons.

From the mid-nineties, the Ikhwan started making inroads into the mountains from bases in and around Anantnag town. They were renegade militants who had changed sides to work with the army and other counterinsurgency forces, which denied working with them. But it was an open secret. Residents of Anantnag district remember Ikhwan camps nestled close to army camps, army personnel walking with their arms around Ikhwan fighters as if to say, they are with us. The Ikhwan would sit in the forest department office next to the police lines in Anantnag town, says one resident, and no one in the authorities objected. They ran a money racket around the district court complex, and no one complained.

Officially spectral, bound by no code of law, civil or martial, the Ikhwan were left—in a phrase frequently used by security officials and ministers—to 'break the back of militancy'. They built networks of informers, helped with crackdowns, targeted militants and laid waste to villages to break the back of militancy.[14] Eventually, the Ikhwan became a target for militant groups and were forced to retreat into their camps, which meant they lost touch with their network of informers. By the late nineties, they were becoming a bit of a liability. Many were absorbed into counterinsurgency units of the local police or killed.

The army and official forces often worked in the shadows through the nineties, acting through proxies. By the middle of the decade, the militancy had grown and splintered. Various armed groups were trapped in interlocking rivalries and truces.[15] These fractures could be used to weaken them further. In Brariangan, Panchanthal and Chittisinghpora, at least, the shadows seemed to disappear after the killings of 2000. Forces moved into forests and villages. An era of more direct confrontation between forces and militants had started.

In Panchanthal, a camp was set up where the Pandit *mohalla*, or neighbourhood, used to be. The Kashmiri Pandits who lived there fled in 1989 and 1990 as they came under fire from militants. Maybe the haunting started then. The Pandit *mohallas* of both Panchalthan and Brariangan are now stretches of open land where the ground dips and rises in soft undulations, sometimes crusted with brick plinths. They might have been ancient burial mounds and not the remains of houses that were inhabited around thirty years ago.

SP says they were friends with the Pandit families who lived in Panchanthal. They would visit each other. If they ran out of rice or sugar, they would run over to their Pandit neighbours' home to borrow some and vice versa. It is said, the Pandits were the biggest landowners in Panchanthal. Their absence left large swathes of deserted land in the village. Soon after they fled, their homes were burned down. By whom, the residents of Panchalthan will not or cannot say.

GHOSTS IN THE GROUND

But as the Pandit *mohalla* was emptied out, the few Muslim households there were isolated, leaving them more vulnerable to the *bhoot* visitations of the late nineties. After the spring of 2000, when the army set up camp on the deserted mounds of the Pandit *mohalla*, it rubbed up against the walls of these households. Over time, the large-scale violence of the early *haalaat* petered out. Residents say the camp wound up in 2015. Now the mounds are open to the sky again, ravens wheeling in the pines above, each year's sun and rain clothing them in a new layer of grass. Only those who live in the village remember what was once there, the laughter and feasting, the guns and then other guns.

* * *

Chittisinghpora and Brariangan have built 'ghost-places', where haunting is performed in public.[16] They are memorials to the dead where the past takes place again and again. Ghost-places will not put the dead to rest. They insist you remember; they tell you how to remember.[17] They remind you the past is unresolved.

Outside either gurudwara in Chittisinghpora, there is a bullet-riddled wall facing the street. This is where the men were lined up on the evening of 20 March 2000; this is where the bullets that went through their bodies buried themselves. Above each wall, looming over the street, are pictures and names of the dead.

At the Gurudwara Singh Sabha, there is a new memorial hall. It marks the spot where the dead were cremated. Here, too, the pictures of the thirty-five men hang on the walls. Above them is another portrait, summoning the ghost of an older rebellion. This is Jarnail Singh Bhindranwale, who led the Khalistani militancy in Punjab and was killed in Operation Blue Star, the nine-day siege of the Golden Temple in Amritsar by the Indian Army under the orders of Indira Gandhi in 1984. His picture belongs there because he too was a martyr, explains the nineteen-year-old. The men who died in Chittisinghpura are to be imagined in this continuum of fallen braves.

DAPAAN

But outside, there is a freshly painted caption:

On 20th March, 2000, late in the evening at 07.50 pm, some unknown gunmen with barbarity martyred 35 innocent Sikhs of the village Chithi Singh Pora. This was the day, when the then President of the United States Mr. Bill Clinton was on an official visit to India. Unfortunately, on this day, 35 Sikhs from miniscule minority of Kashmiri Sikhs, were martyred by the tyrants with severe brutality.

Unknown gunmen and tyrants who have no name have turned into spectres in an unresolved story of the past. The caption reminds visitors that this was an attack on a minority, much like the calamities faced by Kashmiri Pandits. It creates a space for demonstrations every year on 20 March. Relatives of the men who died and members of local organisations gather outside the gurudwaras to address the government. Over the years, most of the pleas have settled around the subject of compensation. Sikhs in Kashmir are a persecuted minority like the Pandits, say local community leaders, but they have not received the same kind of material redress. Then they return to that original question: tell us, who killed our men? We demand an impartial investigation, an international investigation.

In Brariangan, protests have been snuffed out. Every year on 25 March, the village would gather outside the graveyard for the nine people from Brariangan who died in the spring of 2000. It's not much—unmarked graves girded by a rough stone wall on the village main road. Easy to miss but for the board outside, brightly painted with the names of thirteen people, the five killed in Pathribal and the eight killed in Brakpora. These are the dead that the village claims for its own specific grief. Every year on the anniversary of the Pathribal killings, they held a special *namaaz*, prayer. Then they gathered around the board holding placards: 'Reopen Our Case', 'Remove AFSPA', 'We Want Justice'. For years, these protests appeared to take place with the tacit consent of the administration. But a few years ago, the local police warned

GHOSTS IN THE GROUND

them not to hold a public event. Rashid was not surprised. Ever since Kashmir lost autonomy in 2019, he explains, such protests have been discouraged.

As public protests die out, only the official version of Pathribal remains. Five foreign militants who shot the men of Chittisinghpora were killed in the forest that day. Strangely, this is a version that now keeps Jumma Khan and Jumma Khan alive. Suppose it is true, says one resident of Brariangan—suppose the men killed that day were foreign militants and not people from our village. Where did the men from our village go, then? In twenty-three years, they have not returned.

PART III

LOSS

9

SINGING BODIES

At weddings, women sing of death. Weddings are for remembering.

'Dilbar o, dil kar samandar
Adanyer manz maidanas
Chaapyo, chaapyo, Kokernagas, chaapyo,
Taityos Burhan bhai commander,
Tenui lod manz maidanas.'

Oh beloved, make your heart an ocean
Before you leave for the battlefield.
There was a cordon, there was a cordon in Kokernag,
Our brother, Commander Burhan, was caught in it,
He fought on that battlefield.[1]

The women are singing of Burhan Wani, the Hizbul Mujahideen commander who was killed during a gunfight with forces in Kokernag, in the mountains of Anantnag district, on 8 July 2016. But when TK sings, she is really singing of her own brother.

He too joined the Hizbul Mujahideen. He was barely twenty when he died during a gunfight with forces in Bandipora district in North Kashmir in 2000. His origin story is similar to Burhan's. According to TK, he too had taken up arms because he could take no more *zulm*.

Bandipora in the late nineties was the fiefdom of the Ikhwan commander, Kuka Parray, who fed on fear. Living in a valley where they were widely considered traitors and fair prey for militants, Parray and his men survived by extreme violence. Kill or be killed. Be known by the havoc you wreak so that people will not dream of crossing you. Kuka Parray had won elections, held at gunpoint, in 1996. This gave him a new sheen of legitimacy.

The first time TK's brother left home to join the Hizb, he was still a teenager. It happened after the incident with the Ikhwan. He was with his cousin when a group of Ikhwan drew up in front of them in a car. They got out, beat up his cousin and left. When the Ikhwan beat you, you took it; you did not fight back. Her brother could not come to terms with this humiliation, TK says, so he took up arms.

Eight times, they brought him back home. Eight times, he left again. When he was killed, three years after he first joined the Hizbul Mujahideen, in a gunfight about ten kilometres from his home, he was a Pakistan-trained militant. But TK says he had no first information reports, FIRs, to his name. As with Burhan Wani, no one knew of any violent crime committed by him.

TK got married a couple of years after her brother died. When the women at her wedding sang to the beloved, asking him to make his heart as big as an ocean, they took her brother's name. When they described the gunfight where he died, they named a village in Bandipora district.

The militant's name and the place of his death may be changed every time you sing the song. Commander Ishfaq, Commander Maqbool, Commander Zakir. They died in battle in Tral, Sopore, Kokernag, Srinagar. No town or village has been exempt from the *haalaat*. Every woman singing, TK says, will be thinking of her own brother; there is not a dry eye in the room. A private grief enters the public through these songs.

* * *

Wedding songs often became tombs for the dead after the *haalaat* arrived in Kashmir. They carried the memory of lost bodies.

Traditionally, women have sung *wanvun*, slow, solemn songs that start up a few days before the main ceremony, heavy with the enchantments of the moment. Every *wanvun* is sung to the same tune, composed of three notes, and set to a six-beat rhythm, divided into cadences of three. There are no accompaniments, just the sound of women's voices. They sit in two groups. One group starts the song, the other responds.

The chorus starts with an invocation: '*Bismillah kaerit haemai wanvune / Sahibo azwalo sonuyai*'. In the name of God, we begin our song / O Prophet, come to ours today. And the household enters a wedding fugue.

Wanvun tell the story of a wedding in song. There is a song for every part of the ceremony, explains poet Naseem Shafaie. A song to bless the wood used for the cooking fire, a song for the grinding of the spice, a song for the sifting of the rice, a song for the onions, the ginger, the garlic, a song for the barber, the tailor, the cook. When the food is cooked, when hands are painted with mehndi, when the groom is shaved, when the bride is dressed, when the gifts and the guests arrive. A song greets the groom when he reaches the bride's home. A song announces the *nikkah*, the religious ceremony to marry the couple. There is a pause when the wedding vows are solemnised. Then again a song for the bride as she leaves her home.

Nobody remembers who came up with the songs anymore. They have been passed on from mouth to mouth by generations of women. Earlier generations knew them by heart. As memory fades, some women have them written down in notebooks. New *wanvun* may be composed on the go, says Shafaie. Older ones may also be tweaked for detail—the names of the couple getting married or the village where they will live. Jokes may be introduced, about the groom's large nose, say, or the bride's fondness for sweets. Sometimes the world intrudes—floods, fires, deaths, taxes, curfews, *hartals*, militant commanders.

In 2012, Ather Zia, an anthropologist, attended a wedding in Bandipora district. She found women singing songs for the disappeared and odes to militants along with the traditional *wanvun*.[2] Grief and joy have converged in social occasions, Zia writes, and *wanvun* do the vital work of memory-keeping in a time of censorship. As lived experiences are suppressed in official histories, everyday social spaces become crucibles of memory. *Wanvun* carry women's memories, in particular, as they sing of lost husbands, brothers, fathers and public heroes.

There were *wanvun*, sung in 2016, that contained the news of Burhan Wani's death. ZB, a researcher in Srinagar, remembers going for his cousin's wedding soon after the killing in Kokernag. Wedding banquets were being cancelled amid *hartals*, curfews and an endless internet shutdown. Local newspapers filled their classified sections with the same notice, repeated over and over again, only the address changing: invitation cancelled, regretfully, because of the prevailing circumstances; wedding rituals to be carried out with utmost simplicity.

ZB and his mother had set out for his cousin's house through downtown Srinagar. They were preparing the rice for the wedding feast that day, washing it and sifting it and singing. The streets and bridges of the old city, usually a tangle of traffic and gossip, were empty. 'It was just the two of us and the military,' ZB recalls. At the sadly depleted wedding party, women sang of desolation.

'You are a lonely groom,
Leaving at a time when the streets are empty.'[3]

SINGING BODIES

But the song that spoke of loneliness bound listeners together in a community of suffering, making sense of the upheavals that had choked off the ordinary currents of life. It connected you to what was happening all around, ZB explains.

Poetry, writes Suvir Kaul, forms a conduit between individual and shared suffering. Every time a poem of personal sorrow is read, recited or sung, others bear witness and connect it to their own experiences. In such a way, a political community is formed, forged by shared experiences of violence and loss, recognising itself as a community under siege, impelled to resist what it identifies as the source of its suffering.[4]

There was something about weddings, the warmth of bodies drawn together in a room, everyone wreathed by the fragrance rising from cooking pots while the voices of neighbours and aunts lapped around them. There was something about weddings that dissolved individual grief into a larger community.

Wanvun were often threaded with personal memories. Other songs of remembrance, composed especially for the dead, were also sung. So were the sad love songs of Habba Khatoon. As if words of longing could recover lost bodies.

* * *

TK keeps her grief in a trunk. It contains the following items. One *pheran*, bullet-holed. One batsman's glove, faded but otherwise intact. One maroon pocket notebook, a hole in the centre where a bullet passed through. One picture of a dear friend, a militant, long dead. One letter in neat handwriting: take care of our parents now that I have crossed the Line of Control. Several sets of clothes bought for Eid in 1997, '98, '99, never worn. One skull cap. One string of prayer beads. One school identity card bearing the picture of a boy with the shadow of his first moustache on his lip. One nail cutter. Personal effects. Effects of a body when the body is gone.

DAPAAN

Also in the trunk, one A4-sized exercise book filled with the thoughts of a militant in hiding. There are poems by Mohammad Iqbal and verses from the Quran. There seem to be original verses, composed in English: 'Life is believing / Believing in the best / Life is blooming / Blooming in the worst. // Friends come and go / To carry on the show, / It is your own self / That you must know.' Then there are pages and pages of meticulous notes, questions and essay-style answers, on *All My Sons*, Arthur Miller's mid-century play about a family haunted by war and the dirty business of war. TK says it was part of her course in college. Her brother must have been making notes for her while he was hiding out in the forests.

Each year, for twenty-three years, she has taken out the things in the trunk, put them out in the sun and put them back again. Her children never knew her brother but they have a name for him, Shahid Mama, Martyr Uncle. His cricket bat, fiercely guarded by his nieces and nephews, is propped up against a wall.

TK has a notebook of her own where she writes poems. She composed a song for her brother in 2019. It imagines the bridegroom he never became. But mostly, it is a poem about her own grief.

> I live in thoughts of you day and night,
> Sometimes I cry, sometimes I sing.
>
> Whom do I tell of my grief?
> And who will listen to me?
> I can never tell you, brother.
>
> I would colour your hands with mehndi,
> I would dress you up in a turban.
> But your body returned in blood-stained clothes,
> Darkness fell on the light of my life.
>
> I have kept your books,
> I have kept your clothes scented in attar,

SINGING BODIES

> You promised me you would return,
> I have kept my gaze on the door.[5]

She does not say if this song about a lonely grief has ever been sung at a wedding or at a funeral. While wedding songs darkened with the *haalaat*, funerals of militants were marked by a frenzy that seemed almost festive. When young men died in gunfights, they were sent off into the other world as bridegrooms, their hands darkened with mehndi, their bodies showered in rose petals and wedding confetti. Both weddings and funerals dwelt on the beauty of lost bodies.

RB, who grew up in Dooru, part of Anantnag district, would steal away for protest marches in the early nineties. At a march led by women, she remembers seeing her neighbour, a girl still in her teens, chanting slogans in a frenzy. Later, it was conveyed to her, in chaste euphemisms, that the girl had been dating a militant. Not married or engaged, just dating. Until he was killed in a gunfight with forces.

At weddings after that, RB noticed how the girl spoke of her lost love, her hair streaming down her back, her face wet with tears, dissolved in grief. She did not sing of his deeds in battle. She sang of the person she had lost: his eyes, his skin, his hair. Other women gathered around her would also watch, silent in the presence of such emotion. As they watched, a strange elation would take hold of the group.

Surely such grief reclaimed him as a body that must be mourned? When forces shot down militants, press statements would say, 'terrorists were neutralised'. Not killed, just neutralised, because killing required acknowledging life in the first place. In the Indian national public, militants figured only as a 'threat to life'.[6] Pictures of their bodies, neatly arranged with weapons and ammunition, appeared in newspapers. Neutralised, like a negative charge. These were not 'grievable bodies', with lives and pasts and a common human vulnerability.[7] In the national public, it was outlawed to mourn such bodies. In Kashmir, songs of remembering retrieved the grievability of militant bodies. As they resisted the national consensus, they also became a form of defiance.

While the girl sang of her lover's body, she was also conjuring up the physicality of a fighter. Odes to the strength and beauty of Kashmiri militants were quite common in those days. They were also exaggerated, RB observes dispassionately. It was the same with the *mehmaani mujahideen*, the guest militants who had come from Pakistan, Afghanistan and beyond to fight in Kashmir's war. RB remembers hearing stories of gigantic mountain men who could eat fifty chickens in one go. But when they surfaced in the villages to ask for food or deliver gun salutes at funerals, it turned out these fighters were quite ordinary men, badly in need of a wash and a change of clothes.

Burhan Wani's physicality was more verifiable. The tall, young militant had become a familiar face on social media. Unlike earlier generations of militants, Burhan and his group had dispensed with masks and scarves, revealing their faces to the public. They had also shed their loose *pherans* to wear fitted t-shirts and military fatigues. When people speak of Burhan Wani today, they speak, among other things, of his beauty.

* * *

As news of Burhan Wani's death spread that July evening, NF started running towards his house. She lived in Tral and had pored over his pictures for years. Now she needed to see his face before it was gone forever. The brief gunfight in Kokernag had ended around six in the evening. By the time his body reached his home in Sharifabad, on the edges of Tral town, it was past two in the morning. NF says she was the first woman to see his face after he died. It would go on to become a famous body, photographed thousands of times. People took pictures of his body, NF says, because they loved him.

SINGING BODIES

In the weeks and months that followed, a new song was sung at weddings. It is said, the women of Tral composed it after Burhan's death. They mourn Burhan *bhai*, brother Burhan, but theirs is also a political grief, marshalled to rally the forces of the *tehreek*.

'Who will now hurry you back to Tral?
Who will run where Burhan's footsteps once fell?'[8]

The very land seems to be mourning the militant. To the women of Tral, the death means a loss of the political language wielded so effectively by Burhan. It is a blow to the ambition that 'Kashmir will become Pakistan', which is the Hizbul Mujahideen's stated goal. Even his boots were worth more than all the cement used to pave the railways, the women sing, gesturing to the Indian government's attempts to answer Kashmiri political demands with promises of economic growth. They name other militants in Burhan Wani's group who will carry on the fight. Finally, the singers wish 'a dog's death' on the *mukhbir*, the informer, who tipped off forces about Burhan's final hiding place.

Over the next couple of years, wedding songs mourning Burhan Wani spread outside Tral as well. These were mostly *gyawun*, songs performed by both men and women, accompanied by music. But they were often written in the voice of the grieving mother. 'Oh son, oh my son, in which graveyard should I look for you,' lamented a well-known wedding singer in North Kashmir's Kupwara district. 'May your mother's life be sacrificed on this bullet-riddled chest.' In another song, the mother asks if the '*shahid*', or martyr, is still hurting from his wounds. Is he not hungry, is he not thirsty, she wonders. While the vivid bodies of the dead are invoked, the bodies of the living crumble away in these songs. The mother's body has turned to ashes with pain. The father worries about who will carry his coffin when he is dead.

The first wedding songs for Burhan Wani were sung at his funeral, *wanvun* turned heavy with grief. Pictures from the day show Muzaffar Wani sitting quietly over his son's body as a crowd surges towards them. Like thousands of others, he takes pictures of his son's face on his phone, as if recognising his grief is not quite his own, his son not just his own. This is a public death and a public grief.

If militant funerals were big, Burhan Wani's funeral was the biggest of them all. Nearly a decade after he was killed, the people of Tral remember it with quiet pride. They had been called upon to host all of Kashmir and they had stepped up to the task.

Spectacular numbers circulate about the attendance at the funeral: fifty thousand, one million, five million. 'Eighty percent of the Kashmiri youth turned up.' 'People from Banihal to Kupwara came here on foot.' Banihal, which links Jammu to the south of Kashmir, is about eighty kilometres away. Kupwara is at the northern end of the Valley, over a hundred kilometres from Tral.

Certainly, as the militant commander was laid to rest, thousands rushed to see him. Tipper trucks made for Tral, disgorging people instead of stones. A curfew had descended on the Valley, so many walked. Where the roads were sealed, they took secret routes through forests and mountains. Tral opened its doors to them, cooking meals, laying down mattresses. 'People were sleeping on the streets,' says PK, who had kept an open kitchen for about ten days.

After being taken home, Burhan Wani's body was borne along by the crowd to the Tral Eidgah, the community prayer grounds, not far from the bus stand where, it is said, he was beaten by forces so many years ago. Here, the body lay in state. Sabzar Bhat and Zakir Musa, part of Burhan's cohort in the Hizbul Mujahideen, materialised at the funeral for a gun salute. Then they wove through the crowd of mourners, distributing juice. It is said, the funeral prayers were read over forty times, not just in Kashmir but also in Pakistan and Saudi Arabia. It was not just Muslims who mourned him, people in Tral like to say—the local

SINGING BODIES

Sikh community had also set up a *langar*, a community kitchen distributing food for the funeral.

With militants breaking cover and crowds breaking curfew, the funeral was a vast open secret in the heart of Tral. Elsewhere, forces were cracking down on protesters. In Tral, police and CRPF camps were attacked by crowds, but forces chose to lie low. This was a maelstrom of feeling they could not enter.

The crowd swirling around the body at the Tral Eidgah wavered between grief and joy. For six years, they had been holding their breath for this day. 'Every time there was an encounter, we thought this was the last day of his life,' says CW, a twenty-five-year-old who grew up in Tral. Now the day they had feared had come, but Burhan Wani could not be grieved in the ordinary way, for reasons that belonged to this world and that.

Burhan's death was no ordinary death because he died fighting, CW explains. 'What is most important is his cause, not his death,' he says. 'People come, they go, they die. The cause remains.' CW himself had a close friend who took up arms a few years after Burhan Wani died. He was swiftly killed. 'It left a hole in my heart,' he says. But he still took pride in the militant, who had gone willingly to his death. Both Burhan and his friend were martyrs in his eyes. So while family and friends privately grieved the person they had lost, the public body of Burhan Wani was offered up to paradise at his funeral.

A new sense of purpose seemed to fill the mourners at the funeral. Political slogans whipped through the air. The Tral Eidgah vibrated with songs played on mosque speakers. '*Choan Burhan, moan Burhan / Os shah sawar, tsoan Burhan.*' Your Burhan, my Burhan, / He led the vanguard, our Burhan. '*Drav Burhan akh masiha / Nyer toh ath vaas kaerit.*' Burhan was a messiah / Now we must go shake his hand. In other words, we must also join the *tehreek*.

It was a tide of feeling that would bear many more towards their own death. For years, the ecstatic grief of militant funerals had driven boys to leave home and take up arms. It is said, some left straight from the funeral, not stopping for second thoughts. They knew they were going to an early death. According to officials, in the decade after the 2008 protests, there were rarely more than three hundred militants at any given point of time, and the number was usually much lower.[9] At least a third were foreign fighters from across the frontier. A hundred or so local boys armed with rifles stood no chance against one of the largest armies in the world. They did, however, hope to win a psychological war, a battle for morale in the Valley. 'It was our bravery,' says CW. 'It was also madness,' he adds.

Militant funerals in this decade became a place to enact rage, grief and defiance. Forces stayed away from Tral the day Burhan Wani was laid to rest, but they often arrived at other militant funerals, emptying pellet guns and tear gas shells into crowds chanting *azadi* slogans. Sometimes mourners responded with a hail of stones. Ordinary civilians, electrified by the death before them, were now pitted against forces. Without public funerals, CW feels, 'that sentiment has no outlet'.

Because such funerals no longer take place. The totemic power of militant bodies had worried state authorities for years. These bodies had to disappear. When the Covid-19 pandemic broke out, they stopped handing over the bodies of militants killed in counterinsurgency operations to their families. Pandemic rules, the authorities said; public funerals could spread contagion like wildfire. Instead, the bodies were buried in graveyards far away from the villages where the militants had once lived. Only a few relatives were allowed to visit the graves and say a hushed prayer. But then the pandemic waned and bodies were still secreted away after gunfights. The authorities seemed to be thinking of other contagions that could spread at funerals.

* * *

SINGING BODIES

TK did not go to Burhan Wani's funeral but she sang songs for him at weddings. She also has a poem for him in her notebook, written in the coded language common to Persian, Urdu and Kashmiri poetic traditions. As with the poem about her brother, it is written in the voice of the waiting woman. As in the Kashmiri public sphere, the body of the militant has disappeared. It has become an absence that runs in the blood and sap of the living world.

> The flowers have bloomed again,
> And the cuckoo and swallow have returned again,
> All the gardens are filled with colour again.
> Who will tell my Burhan
> Your mother is waiting for you?[10]

The garden is a country where it is summer and eternal winter at the same time, for though the birds have returned, Burhan will not see them again. Gardens recur in Urdu and Kashmiri verse, often dramatising a state of mind as well as a political order. But TK may be drawing more specifically on the poetry of Ghulam Ahmad Mahjoor. In his poems, written during rebellions against Dogra rule, Kashmir is a garden is full of possibilities. The flowers there are waiting to come to fullness, the birds waiting to be uncaged through political change. Mahjoor imagines the gardener as an agent of revolution. His poem 'Arise, O Gardener', which became an anthem for the *tehreek* in the nineties, is a call to action for a new political order.

> Come, gardener! Create the glory of spring!
> Make Guls [flowers] bloom and bulbuls sing—create such haunts![11]

In the poem, Mahjoor is hopeful that political action will bring a Naya Kashmir, Sheikh Abdullah's alternative to the Dogra state. It is another matter that by the time he died in 1952, Mahjoor is said to have lost hope in the National Conference and its promise of Naya Kashmir, turning into the bitter, satirical poet of the salt shortage.

TK writes in an ageing *tehreek*, where political mobilisations killed generations of young men but change did not come. More than two decades after her brother died, she will not let go of her loss. Maybe it was grief for her brother that lit her passion for the Burhan Wani group. She tracked them as they rose to fame in Kashmir, trying to find her brother's story in their stories. She linked her life to theirs. Zakir Musa, once rumoured to be Burhan's successor, was killed in May 2019, the same day TK's nephew was born. She named her nephew after him.

As the militants of the Burhan Wani group died one by one, as seasons of protest swelled and waned, TK's notebook filled up with poems. In these poems, Kashmir is marked forever by loss. But this insistence on loss is a fight against forgetting. As she spends her days in quiet rooms, TK has chosen the only form of political action that is open to her, a melancholia that keeps alive a relationship with the past.

10

MELANCHOLIA

Freud writes that melancholia is mourning gone wrong, turned inwards, born of the mind's inability to detach itself from the object of its loss because it doesn't know what exactly it has lost.[1] But later, he suggests melancholia is not so different from mourning, that maybe it is loss becoming part of the architecture of the mind.[2] Loss accrued in the mind's interstices, a thing made of memory and longing. That which you long for can never die. Longing creates new objects to long for. When mourning ends, the past is done. Melancholia holds more regenerative properties for the past, creating it again and again as it grapples endlessly with loss.[3]

What was lost to the Kashmiri public when Burhan Wani died? A whole body of songs and stories tries to speak of it. But the object of loss remains unreachable so the stories multiply—it was this, it was this, no, it was this.

It is said, Burhan Wani once asked an officer in the Territorial Army to meet him by the Jhelum river at Anantnag town. When the officer got to the river, he found no one there. But glistening on the riverbank was a bar of freshly used Lifebuoy soap. The choice of antiseptic soap, favoured by soldiers and government health campaigns, was like a grenade.

It is said, another time, Burhan Wani went to meet then Chief Minister Mufti Mohammad Sayeed in Bijbehara. Mufti was visiting his hometown in Anantnag district for a rally. Burhan walked up to him in disguise and hugged him. Later, he sent word to the ageing chief minister—it was me that you hugged at the rally today. It is also said that this story was enthusiastically spread by Sayeed's People's Democratic Party, which wanted a share of the militant's popularity.

After he went underground in 2010, Burhan Wani turned into stories. Over time, they would spread to all parts of Kashmir, but the four districts of South Kashmir—Pulwama, Anantnag, Shopian, Kulgam—were the thickest with stories. These were also the districts where a new phase of militancy thrived the most. Tral, where Burhan Wani grew up, is an administrative division of Pulwama district, consisting of a small town that trails off into mountains, orchards and forests. Tral was at the heart of the stories. Suddenly it seemed as if stories of Burhan flowed down mountain streams, appeared in rocks, rose with the flight of ravens from pines. The wind in the apple orchards carried it to the fruit *mandi* and then into the markets of Tral. Burhan had melted into the landscape.

He certainly seemed to have a knack for hiding in plain sight. Women in Tral talk about the time he was bathing in a river and soldiers were walking past. They did not recognise the teenage bather, hardly more than a child, as the famous Burhan Wani. While soldiers and the police were watching the Valley for signs of Burhan, he made it clear that he was watching them. It is said, he once called up a policeman and asked him what he was doing in Tral, adding that he liked the colour of his jacket.

Traders from Tral started getting concessions all over Kashmir because they were from Burhan Wani's home turf. Small boys in

MELANCHOLIA

South Kashmir started playing a game of catch called 'Burhan, Burhan'. The group of players was divided into policemen and militants. Pieces of wood did duty as guns.

In many stories, Burhan is like the king in the folktale who goes out in disguise to mingle with his subjects. Or like a Sufi mystic given to shimmering in and out of his disciples' lives. These are myths of affability and public service. It is said that he gave money to poor families, whether they were Muslim, Hindu or Sikh, to marry off their daughters. That he was anxious not to give trouble, unlike earlier generations of militants who barged into homes demanding dinner and shelter. That he was spotted eating food people had thrown away. Many reported hosting a well-mannered boy who carried no weapons but helped around the house and in the orchards. He worked for a Kashmiri Pandit household in Shopian district. He even appeared in North Kashmir, toiling away in the orchards of the family who gave him shelter. Both stories end the same way. When he was leaving, they asked what his name was and he replied, with all the modesty of a superstar, 'I am Burhan.'

Others never found out. It was only when he died, and his picture was everywhere, that they discovered Burhan Wani had come to stay.

He was a son to mothers, a mentor to young boys, a brother to young girls. When it was suggested the handsome, teenaged militant had a girlfriend, people bristled. This was *markaz ki chaal*—put out a salacious story to sully his good name.

Burhan Wani was loved because he was good, they say in Tral. Did he not forgive *mukhbirs* who may have given away militants? While the government painted him as an Islamic fundamentalist, did he not assure Sikhs and Pandits that they were welcome in Kashmir? Did he not tell Kashmiri policemen that they should join the *tehreek*, that he did not want to attack them as he did not want to spill Kashmiri blood? Most important is the myth of his innocence. Burhan Wani, they say, took up arms but never killed anyone.

But in one early story, Burhan and a few others are said to have stolen into an army camp in Tral, stabbed some soldiers and escaped. A photographer who had gone to cover a gunfight in central Kashmir's Budgam district spoke to a Sikh soldier who was part of the military cordon surrounding the house where militants were trapped. Burhan, the soldier said in tones of awe, had blazed out of the house, raining down a storm of bullets.

Then again, there are rumours that he was really working for Indian agencies. How else could he have survived six years underground when other militants died within months?

Everything is true, nothing is true. Burhan Wani was militant, terrorist, freedom fighter. He was fighting a secular battle against state oppression, he was fighting a religious battle for an Islamic state, he was fighting a political battle to merge with Pakistan. This much is certain: during his half a decade as a militant, he was deeply, wildly popular. His fame shot through the Valley like an electric charge, with common talk spreading onto social media, which was suddenly everywhere. Nearly a decade after he died, the myth of Burhan Wani grows infinitely more complex within a community still trying to make sense of his loss.

* * *

Militants in Kashmir have always been trailed by myth. In the streets of downtown Srinagar, boys sang of the death of Ashfaq Majeed Wani, one of the first to join the Jammu and Kashmir Liberation Front when the *tehreek* started. He was killed in a brief shootout near Firdous Cinema, a movie hall that had been turned into a camp in the city. It is said, he was about to hurl a grenade at the camp when he was shot. So downtown boys sang, '*Manz athas bam phatiyo / Ashfaq Wani lagiyo*'. The bomb burst in his hand / Ashfaq Wani, I would have died for you.

MELANCHOLIA

In the countryside, the landscape and its spirits silently formed ranks around militants. GP remembers his uncle, the militant commander in North Kashmir, had a lucky escape once. As soldiers advanced, his uncle sprinted up a willow tree and hid behind a bundle of wood that had been trussed up and stored among the branches to wait for winter. In his panic, he had forgotten his slippers under the tree. A *djinn* saw the slippers and removed them, so the soldiers passed by without suspecting a thing. They know this happened because the *djinn* later appeared in the dreams of GP's cousin, who was given to dreaming of *djinns*, and told her how he had saved the militant commander's life.

By the time Burhan Wani became a militant, the internet had arrived, turning Kashmir into a 'networked public'.[4] Connectivity and the spread of social media were transformative for the *tehreek*, reconfiguring the way it worked. Already, the internet had revealed its powers during the mass protests of 2008 and 2010. Anyone armed with a phone camera could document the protests, and anyone with access to the internet could see them. The pictures and videos went viral. 'Rage boys' in skinny jeans and quiffs, handkerchiefs covering their faces, throwing stones in a cloud of tear gas and pellets. These images were meant to speak of both rebellion and state oppression.

This flurry of images and the online conversations that followed lived around the edges of traditional media. But as the years passed, they would enter the local press. A viral video would be covered in news reports. Journalists would post breaking news on social media first. Until a crackdown post-August 2019, the local press remained adversarial to the government and largely sympathetic to popular sentiments, but it had been feeling the heat for a decade before that. Despite being channels of dissent, most outlets depended on government advertisements, one of the many political ironies of Kashmir. Central government funding for certain leading dailies was halted after the protests of 2008 and 2010. Local cable channels were told to stop news broadcasts in 2010. But information, and rumours, spread anyway. The government responded with internet shutdowns that ran into weeks or even months. A mutinous public used virtual private networks to go online and log in to proscribed websites, until even having a VPN connection was declared seditious.

For about a decade, social media carried the language of rebellion. It catalysed ebullient, chaotic protests that did not depend on the old information channels or even, to a certain extent, on the traditional political leadership of the *tehreek*. It also supplied new objects for the *tehreek*, a photographic record of *zulm* that flowed into households across Kashmir, images of rage that birthed new rage. Kashmiri rappers would sing of them. Men sitting around a *pe'end*, or shop front, would discuss them. It soon became clear that if photos and videos circulated online released energies for civil protest, they could also bolster armed rebellion.

While he lived, Burhan Wani helped spread the myth of himself through the internet. Some videos address the question of the *tehreek*; others reveal Burhan and his cohort ranging the forests and mountains of South Kashmir. 'They understood how to use social media,' says CW. 'It was not just the gun. It was to show we are free here in our land—we exist and we will exist.'

But this Facebook folklore was supported by a cloud of stories that never made it to the internet, that often lived in places where the internet never reached. Not all stories spread with the wind. Rumours started before breakfast, when men went to buy fresh flatbread from the bakeries. They went home and told their wives, who then spoke to other women in the neighbourhood. Journalists in South Kashmir believe at least some of the stories were spread by overground workers and supporters of the Hizbul Mujahideen, others by agencies. Kashmir was an information

MELANCHOLIA

war, after all, in which stories told by the *tehreek* competed with those spread by the state.

What came first, the videos or the stories? Would the videos have resonated among ordinary Kashmiris if the songs and stories did not already exist? Or did the videos set off an eddy of songs and stories? In a networked public, the changes worked by digital technologies do not stay online. They enter the veins of the offline world, reconstituting it in their wake.[5] They are in turn shaped by the societies and power structures they inhabit.[6]

Even the offline stories about Burhan Wani seemed to gain a virality that stories about earlier militants did not. And long after Burhan Wani's death, the pictures and videos remain points of reference. They stand in for the original object of loss, still radiating stories, still raising questions that refuse to die. Who was Burhan Wani? What did he stand for? What did his death mean for the *tehreek*? The online traces left behind by the twenty-one-year-old militant now form a map of melancholia.

* * *

Nobody is quite sure of the first video released by Burhan Wani. A journalist in South Kashmir thinks it was a video of Burhan directly addressing the camera with a message, shortly after *The Guardian* published a profile of him in 2013. In Tral, they think it was a cricket video—a quiet clip of Burhan playing a match in someone's courtyard while another militant stands guard, carrying a gun. There was, of course, more than one cricket video. A second video shows Burhan and others in military fatigues playing cricket in an orchard, believed to be somewhere in Shopian district. Burhan is batting.

The videos pushed back against the idea that 'terrorists' were alien creatures, all ideology and no humanity, explains QA, a skinny young man in his twenties who grew up in Tral. They also spoke for the multitudes who supported armed groups.

'Burhan showed that we are good people, we love good things, we love cricket and singing songs,' QA says.

When not fighting for *azadi*, Burhan was apparently thinking about cricket, the reigning obsession of every decent man in South Asia. In Kashmir, as in all parts of India and Pakistan, cricket fandom is often seen as a conduit for cultural or political affinities. When India plays Pakistan, most Kashmiris will be glued to their phones and television sets, many silently praying for Pakistan to win. Silently, because loud support can get you arrested. There are also more intimate connections in South Kashmir. Bats made from Kashmiri willow are used by famous cricketers. Burhan Wani grew up not far from Sangam, the region where the Jhelum meets the Veshav river, where most of the bats are made.

The militant in the videos plays a confident game. But in Tral, people remember a child scared to play with older boys and scolded for rookie mistakes. Some say he was a fast bowler rather than a batsman. Many of these matches would have been played in Dadsara, a village in the mountains of Tral. This was Burhan's *nanihal*, home to his mother's family. This is where he went to school and spent much of his childhood. It is said, this is where the scared child became a militant and changed his game while he was at it.

The student in Dadsara was very clever, a class topper, even though he took up arms before he could sit the board examinations in tenth grade. These are the first of the qualifications that mark the lives of middle-class South Asians. They give you definition. For instance, you might be 'tenth class pass' or 'tenth class fail'. If you score high marks or, better still, top the exam, you are certified for life as a good person. Many like to point out, not without a touch of middle-class pride, that the boys who joined up in the new phase of militancy were highly qualified, from very good families. They recite the credentials of militants long gone, as if they are still prospective grooms. Ishaq 'Newton' Parray was a tenth grade topper. Zakir Musa studied engineering in Chandigarh. Manan Wani was a PhD scholar from Aligarh Muslim University. Burhan Wani may not have graduated but his father was the headmaster of a government school. This was an educated militancy, it is said—they knew what they were doing.

Burhan had always liked uniforms; he was not too particular about which one. Some say he had wanted to sit the entrance exam for the National Defence Academy, where he could train to join the Indian military. But then again, they remember that when he was in ninth grade, he had run away with five friends to cross the Line of Control but was caught and turned back. It was his innocence, they say, for the LoC was not what it had been in the early nineties, when thousands crossed over. Since then, it had turned into a metalled beast snaking through the mountains; barbed wire spiking its back; the light catching the sparkle of CCTV cameras; thousands of Indian and Pakistani soldiers lined up 'eyeball to eyeball', as news reports liked to put it, red-veined eyes both angry and tired from watching each other. There was no chance a group of fourteen-year-olds would be able to make it. Maybe Burhan thought wearing a uniform, any uniform, meant being able to control the circumstances that bound most Kashmiri lives. 'The Kashmir conflict was always on his mind,' says QA. 'Why this injustice, why are we being terrorised—it used to be stuck in his head.'

It is also said, Burhan Wani's fight was about *zulm*, but it was not just about *zulm*. Decades of rebellion do not live on one thought alone. Apart from dissensions stirring within Kashmir, hot winds rising from the plains of the subcontinent had always scattered ideas in the Valley. Maybe Burhan's journey into militancy was foretold by his family's history, shaped by social and religious movements that had swept across South Asia. Tral is a bastion of the Jama'at-e-Islami. Its founder, Sayyid Abul Ala

Maududi, a journalist and Islamic scholar born in Aurangabad, had marched in the anti-colonial movements of the early twentieth century. His early writings suggest Maududi was not opposed to armed struggle if it was in the interest of truth or justice, as he saw it.[7] He also preached a form of political Islam that involved winning state power to spread Islamic tenets until all secular legislatures became irrelevant, replaced by *nizam-e-Mustafa*, the order of the Prophet.[8] It is said, Burhan's father's side, in particular, had strong links to the group.

The Jama'at had started life in British India in the forties, but the group splintered with the borders drawn after 1947. More esoteric aims were shelved for a while; each faction grew preoccupied with its own regional concerns. Jama'at-e-Islami Jammu and Kashmir is sporadically banned by the Indian government. It is distinct from Jama'at-e-Islami Hind, the main Indian branch. The Kashmir branch has deep roots in the Valley, absorbing all its tensions and dilemmas. Its sympathies have tended towards Pakistan, where Maududi relocated after Partition despite his reservations. But for nearly two decades until 1987, local leaders of the Jama'at contested elections held under the aegis of the Indian state.[9] The Jama'at had a steady electoral base in North Kashmir, especially in Sopore. The star candidate from Sopore, Syed Ali Shah Geelani, later became the most formidable leader of the Hurriyat.

The Jama'at in Kashmir has long been entwined with the mythology of the *tehreek*. As one journalist puts it, till the eighties, you were either for the National Conference or for the Jama'at. Kashmir was already teeming with groups and parties, each with its own ideas about *azadi*, but these were the two dominant schools of thought. When the National Conference abandoned plans for self-determination through a plebiscite, he says, many of its supporters found themselves making common cause with the Jama'at.

MELANCHOLIA

It is said, Jama'at leaders were invited to Pakistan in the early eighties and were asked to form an armed group but they refused. It is also said that, as militancy gained ground, there were misgivings within the Kashmiri Jama'at leadership about patronising an armed group. Having rejected electoral politics after 1987, some had wanted to keep to their original projects—running schools and charities. But other leaders argued that most socio-religious groups in Kashmir had acquired an armed wing; the Jama'at risked fading into irrelevance if it did not follow suit. They finally lent support to the Hizbul Mujahideen, even though such ties were not openly acknowledged, and in 1998 a battered Jama'at officially distanced itself from militancy.

Maybe the Hizb found the Jama'at instead of the other way round. Several Jama'at leaders lived in Sopore and surrounding areas. Residents recall how, in the eighties, these parts were also home to a number of fighters who had joined the Afghan mujahideen as they battled Soviet Russia. The fighters had returned to Kashmir with weapons, lone wolves with no group to call home. Many of them now banded together in the Hizbul Mujahideen, which declared itself the 'sword arm of Jama'at'.[10] More men would join up from all parts of the Valley, turning the Hizb into the largest Kashmiri militant group. Several belonged to families that supported the Jama'at. Between the two sides of Burhan Wani's family, about five or six men became Hizbul Mujahideen militants.

Residents of Tral also recall a more intimate family history, one of childhood games and attachments, a young boy trailing behind his older cousins. Nothing extraordinary about this, except it leads to that fateful choice. Burhan was close to his cousins in Dadsara, especially the four sons of his uncle Bashir Mir. Nayeem, the eldest son, joined the Hizb in 2009 after dutifully completing his BTech degree. He was killed in 2010. Adil joined up soon after his death. He was killed in 2014. A third brother, Kashif Mir, would follow them into the Hizb in 2021. He too was killed.

When Burhan disappeared from his home one October evening in 2010, it was Adil who is believed to have led him away. In Tral, some say it was Adil who revived a fading militancy and took it online; Adil who was divisional commander of the Hizb in South Kashmir.

An audio clip shared in 2013, while Adil was alive, is still remembered in Tral. It went viral. Militants were trapped in a gunfight with forces and last calls were being made. One of the militants asked Burhan to pray for forgiveness on his behalf. He was killed not long afterwards. But Burhan Wani was now known to a larger public.

Adil himself was killed in a gunfight in 2014. Sometime later, Burhan became divisional commander of the Hizbul Mujahideen, not just in the south but in all of Kashmir. That was when the videos started in earnest. Burhan's videos spoke not just of death and martyrdom but of inhabiting a Kashmiri landscape with no barbed wire and no checkpoints. Snowball fights in the mountains, long afternoons in the orchards, treks along a green stream, cold hands glowing in the light of a fire. All of that was lost with the death of Burhan, the headmaster's boy who said his prayers, topped his class and played cricket. But that was not all that was lost.

*　*　*

There is a photograph that most people in Kashmir will recognise. It went viral in 2015 and was strung up in parks and graveyards. Eleven men, very young, dressed in fatigues, are posing with guns in an orchard. They form a dense knot of bodies, leaning on one another, arms flung around each other's shoulders or knees. Everyone is tilted towards Burhan Wani, who is at the centre of the group.

MELANCHOLIA

Most of them, like Burhan, have an origin story of *zulm*. They were detained after protests, summoned to police stations as children, beaten up, tortured, until they could take it no more. That is why they took up arms, or mostly why. Eleven men, all now dead except for one.

He is top right in the picture, standing slightly aloof from the others. A man with deep-set eyes and a short, thick beard, as if his face does not have enough space for all the features in it. Tariq Pandit, who survived because he was arrested and jailed. In Karimabad village, where he grew up, it is said that he was a *mukhbir* and surrendered in order to live. It is said, his mother died of a broken heart because of the charges against him.[11] On the extreme left is Naseer Pandit, also from Karimabad, no relation. If Tariq Pandit's features look densely packed, Naseer Pandit is lanky and loose-limbed. He was once a policeman. His father says he ran away with his service rifle after being mocked by his colleagues for trying to bust a drug racket. He was killed within a year.

Looming in the foreground is Sabzar Ahmad Bhat. It is said he was once a drug addict and a thief. But then he met Burhan, who steered him away from addictions into piety. There is another picture of just the two of them, Burhan with his arm around Sabzar, who towers over him. A nickname from his former life lingered even after he joined the Hizb. Sabzar Don, who made up with zeal what he lacked in complexity.

Pictures and videos of men in combat uniform, embracing each other, signalled a cohesion in militant ranks not seen before or since. It is said, Burhan Wani kept the Hizb together. He also drew other armed groups closer, a sharp contrast to the early years of militancy, when armed groups had often clashed with one another. Different ideological wellsprings lay at the source of various armed groups in Kashmir. The JKLF, which claimed to fight for a secular independent Kashmir, gave up arms in 1994. But the Hizb still thrived, linked to the Jama'at and its political

Islam. As the *haalaat* aged, other groups from Pakistan gained ground, the Lashkar-e-Taiba and the Jaish-e-Mohammad, with their suicide bombers and their nostalgia for religious wars fought in the nineteenth century.

The ideological fine print may have mattered only to the leadership stationed in distant cities, explains a journalist in Srinagar. Teenagers joining up in Kashmir were not always particular. Most often, they joined this group or that for functional or incidental reasons. It depended on which group was dominant in their village, which militant leader recruited them. In the Burhan Wani years, these distinctions grew even more blurred to the public as he seemed to draw the support of Lashkar and Jaish cadres, QA says. After him, the militancy fractured once again, many in Tral point out.

It is telling that Zakir Musa is absent from the poster of eleven militants. He was born Zakir Rashid Bhat in Tral's Noorpora village, the son of an affluent government engineer. His father, it is said, was close to the Jama'at. But Zakir's teenage obsessions were cars, bikes, new hairstyles. Something changed after he went to the engineering college in Chandigarh, something elemental. In 2013, he dropped out and joined the Hizb. Zakir Rashid Bhat became Zakir Musa. Once again, it is said, Burhan played reformer, turning the spoilt sports car enthusiast into a devout fighter. Like with Sabzar, there are pictures of Burhan with a paternal arm around Zakir's shoulders. But Zakir Musa was a creature of more complicated desires. His unsmiling face in group photos suggests grievance. Others may revel in the Kashmiri landscape, but Zakir remains unmoved. Songs and games, folk tales about friendship and betrayal are not enough to sustain him.

In Tral, some remember disquiet in the Hizb before Burhan Wani took over. Adil Mir had started resenting Pakistan's control over the Hizb. Some say his objections belonged to both this

MELANCHOLIA

world and that. Adil wanted a Kashmir free of Indian and Pakistani control because he had tired of nation states altogether. He seemed to have drifted towards more puritanical forms of Islam which dictated that you could not pledge your allegiance to anything other than divine power. The Jama'at-e-Islami's experiments with political Islam, its acceptance of Pakistan as an interim political arrangement, did not cut it. It is also said, Adil's problems were really organisational. He was growing restive with the local Jama'at leadership, which was said to take orders from Pakistan.[12] He seemed ripe for mutiny against Syed Salahuddin, who had been managing the Hizbul Mujahideen from the other side of the LoC for years. 'He felt Pakistan was running a dictatorship here,' says QA.

So strong was the discontent in militant ranks that when Adil was killed in 2014, it was rumoured in Tral that the Jama'at-e-Islami had got him shot on the orders of Pakistan. But then Burhan became divisional commander. 'He investigated the matter and found Pakistan was not involved,' says QA. It is not clear how Burhan established this, but tensions were put to rest for a while.

They rose to the surface again after his death. Sabzar Bhat and Zakir Musa were now well-known faces of the Hizb, both rumoured to be Burhan's successors. By early 2017, Zakir Musa was starting to acquire a celebrity to rival Burhan's. During India–Pakistan cricket matches, crowds in South Kashmir chanted 'Musa, Musa' every time Pakistan hit a boundary. Then, in May 2017, an audio clip was shared frantically across WhatsApp groups.

The cold, soft voice on the recording was believed to be Zakir Musa's. He was clarifying a few things. Kashmir was a religious, not a political, war. The *azadi* they should fight for was '*azadi barai Islam*', freedom for the sake of Islam. Their fight was for '*shariat, shahadat* and *khilafat*', Islamic laws, martyrdom and a caliphate. They could not give in to the temptation of nationalism.

If the leaders of the Hurriyat kept insisting otherwise, he would have to behead them and string up their heads in Lal Chowk. The threat apparently applied to all political leaders, including the venerated pro-Pakistan Geelani.

The clip was heard in appalled silence. In that grief-stricken year after the death of Burhan and the mass uprising, many in South Kashmir had found solace in the idea of *shariat, shahadat, khilafat*. Electoral democracy had not brought peace or justice, they reasoned; maybe an Islamic government would. But beheadings? Threats against Geelani?

The Hizb and the militant leadership in Pakistan quickly distanced itself from Zakir. In Tral, some remember Zakir's father trying to explain that his son had no real quarrel with the Hurriyat; he was only tired of some local Hurriyat leaders who were corrupt. Even Zakir seems to have realised he had gone too far. He put out a second clip explaining that he meant Geelani no harm but had a bone to pick with anyone claiming to fight for a secular state. Nobody was going to die for that.

In July 2017, Zakir announced he had started a new group. It was called the Ansar Ghazwat-ul Hind and claimed ties with Al-Qaeda. The group took its name from a hadith, or saying, attributed to the Prophet Muhammad. According to some interpretations, it prophesies a battle that will lead to the Muslim conquest of India and the consolidation of an Islamic caliphate. Despite the hype, not many joined the new group. Even during Zakir's lifetime, it was a lean group of ten to twelve militants. By the time Zakir was killed in a gunfight in Dadsara in 2019, it was struggling to survive.

Four years after his death, many in Tral are bitter about Zakir Musa's legacy. QA suspects he was deployed by Indian agencies to divide the Hizb. At best, he says, Zakir was just a rich, spoilt boy who did not really have a base beyond pockets of Tral and downtown Srinagar.

MELANCHOLIA

But what of Burhan Wani, beloved cousin of Adil, burier of hatchets, expansive divisional commander who had embraced both Sabzar and Zakir? Which battle had he fought in Kashmir? He was constantly refracted through a shifting cloud of rhetoric. Which Burhan you saw depended on who you were.

* * *

'The police [are] demoralising us, have repeatedly misbehaved and tortured our families. They too have families, but we won't harm them [their families] as we belong to the same Allah and our *Sharia* doesn't allow us to do that.'[13]

It is Burhan Wani in August 2015, flanked by two militants standing guard, a gun resting on a Quran before him. He is asking Kashmiri boys to join the Hizbul Mujahideen. He is asking them to join because Kashmiris must be protected from the Indian state.

Burhan was of the land, says a researcher in Srinagar, and he used the vocabulary of a specifically Kashmiri political struggle. What he emphasised most, what he understood best, was *zulm*. Many claim that even as he exhorted boys to take up arms against state oppression, Burhan spoke of a militancy that followed the rules of war. Some call him the Bhagat Singh of Kashmir. Others see him as a Kashmiri folk hero in the model of Ashfaq Majeed Wani. But Ashfaq Wani had been part of the JKLF, whose aim of an independent nation state was well defined. What political future Burhan imagined is harder to divine.

He is said to have mended bridges with Geelani and the militant leadership in Pakistan, reaching out to Salahuddin and even Hafiz Saeed of the Lashkar-e-Taiba. As the researcher points out, Burhan Wani was the first Kashmiri militant officially acknowledged by the Pakistani government. After his death, then Pakistani President Nawaz Sharif praised the 'young leader' at the United Nations General Assembly.

DAPAAN

But the Hizb under Burhan also used the visual signature of global Islamist outfits, the researcher observes—military fatigues instead of Kashmiri *pherans*, forefinger pointed to the sky, a symbol of *tawheed*, the oneness of God, which for outfits such as Al-Qaeda also implies the rejection of earthly legislatures. When Burhan asked Kashmiri men to fight, he invoked *shariat*. In some videos, he also spoke of *khilafat*. Some young men in Tral see no contradiction between fighting the Indian state in Kashmir and longing for *khilafat*—'you know India is oppressing you, but what do you die for?'

* * *

In the end, political futures, the mysteries of this world and that, were overshadowed by a story of personal loss. PK remembers a video where Burhan addresses soldiers directly. Come and meet me face to face, don't bother my family, the militant says. It didn't work.

Sometime in April 2015, Burhan's older brother, Khalid Wani, left home with some packed food to meet friends. They were heading to the forests near Shikargah, once the hunting retreat of kings and the subject of *bhands*. When the kings left, the forests became a place of public leisure. Older women in South Kashmir remember going for picnics in school buses. But the forests changed again with the *haalaat*. For about two decades, the road to Shikargah was strewn with security camps so people stayed away.[14] Even when the camps were removed and the area opened up again in 2011, there were few tourists. Instead, the forests became a refuge for militants. Khalid left home saying they were going on a picnic, but they were really going to meet Burhan.

It is said, they reached a spring believed to have healing powers. They had parked their bikes and started climbing the hill above it when gunshots rang out. The army had found out about the meeting in the woods. Burhan and other militants are said to have fled but Younis Ganie, a Hizb militant, was later found dead at the spot. The army said Khalid was killed in the crossfire.

But Muzaffar Wani said his eldest son was not shot dead. His skull was smashed in by rifle butts and he did not have a single tooth left.[15] Pictures of his funeral show his head swathed in bandages. The grieving father and most of Tral believe Khalid was tortured and killed in custody.

In many ways, Khalid's story casts a shadow over Burhan's. Both brothers were taunted by soldiers in 2010, the humiliation that is said to have driven Burhan to the Hizb. In some tellings, only Khalid was beaten up that day and not Burhan. Khalid was calm while Burhan was *tez*, fiery. Khalid listened to reason even after soldiers beat him up, while Burhan brooded over the injury. Khalid's body bore the marks of *zulm*. Burhan pledged to fight *zulm*.

Annealed by grief after Khalid's death, Burhan was beyond question. He now embodied loss itself. It was a loss that many Kashmiris had borne, their sons and brothers dragged away at night or summoned to camps and never seen again. 'A lot of people would say Burhan was an Indian agent, that he had a girlfriend,' says QA. 'After Khalid's death, the comments stopped. That made Burhan Wani Burhan Wani.'

But for GB, a thirty-year-old in Srinagar, the apotheosis of Burhan Wani started with his death. Until then, GB had been suspicious. The social media posts struck him as showboating, Burhan's long life as a militant impossible unless he was backed by agencies. But all suspicion disappeared after Burhan was killed. 'I started loving him when he died.'

* * *

RK was still a child when it happened, but she remembers it was the third day after Eid. They had gone to Badamwari, a park full of almond trees in Srinagar. Many accounts of 8 July 2016 start the same way. It was just after Eid; everyone had gone out. Then, suddenly, a change in the air.

As they made their way back to their home in downtown Srinagar, RK and her family saw clouds of tear gas. News had travelled fast on Facebook and WhatsApp. A cousin who was plugged into social networks told them Burhan was trapped in Kokernag; an informer had tipped off the forces. The next few hours, everyone waited with bated breath. Some women started crying even before the news of Burhan's death was confirmed.

And then it was chaos. RK's uncle left for the hospital to see his pregnant wife but was hit by pellets on the way and forced to turn back. They had to prise out the pellets with a knife, because going to a hospital with pellet wounds meant risking a police case. All pellet injuries were being treated as suspicious, proof that someone had been out in the streets protesting. Police officers were haunting the hospitals. Many of the boys taken in with serious pellet injuries gave the same name to the hospital authorities, 'Burhan Wani'. In the weeks that followed, road junctions across Kashmir were renamed 'Burhan *chowk*'.

RK saw her mother and grandmother crying for Burhan as if he were their own son. She herself had long admired him. When she met her friends in the local park, they copied the chants they heard on the streets. *'Tera bhai, mera bhai, Burhan bhai, Burhan bhai.'* Your brother, my brother, brother Burhan, brother Burhan. Since she was too young to own a mobile phone, she pleaded with adults to show her the videos and pictures they always talked about. Now she wished she was a boy so that she could join the street protests. But she also had the feeling that it was all over, now that Burhan Wani was dead.

For GB, a new era of the *tehreek* was beginning. He read up about the famous militant, how he had lost his brother, how he had chosen to stand up to indignity. 'Burhan represents me,' GB thought. As he saw it, nothing was lost with his death—much

MELANCHOLIA

was gained. Hundreds of boys were taking up arms now. Burhan's death had clarified a few things.

GB sorted through the tangle of new thoughts in his mind. Kashmiris were always pulled this way and that; they wanted *azadi* but they also wanted government jobs. There was no halfway for Burhan. He could have been anything he wanted—a doctor, a lawyer, an engineer, the dream jobs middle-class parents want for their children. But in the end, GB felt, what is your life worth? Burhan had kept his honour. GB did not think he had it in him to make the same choice, but he became a fan.

* * *

To the generation that came of age in 2016, the boy from Tral has become a name for freedom. '*Burhan waala azadi*,' says RK—that Burhan sort of freedom. For her, this is the object of the *tehreek*, the reason so many marched in the streets.

Like everything else in his life and death, it is an idea filled with contradictions. All definitions are bent to the persona of Burhan Wani. He was part of the pro-Pakistan Hizbul Mujahideen but the *azadi* he wanted had nothing to do with Pakistan, RK explains. The *khilafat* he spoke of has two meanings for her. It is rooted in the idea of a caliphate but traditionally such an Islamic state does not recognise geographical borders as it expands continually. Burhan's *khilafat*, as RK understood it, would be geographically bound to Kashmir. To be *khilaf*, in Urdu, means to oppose or resist. So, to RK, *khilafat* also means political resistance.

Not everyone agrees on the wisdom of Burhan Wani. '*Nizam-e-Mustafa* is not a strategy, it is anti-strategy,' says an elderly history writer in Srinagar. According to him, Burhan did not have a sustainable politics; he only had *junoon*, passion. He is sceptical of Burhan's legacy, the cult of martyrdom that he helped create, where young men took up arms and died in a battle they could not win. But this much he will concede: Burhan had been able to mobilise a very Kashmiri militancy, which drew its lifeblood from the Valley. The militancy of the nineties, according to the history writer, had been driven by Pakistan.

But AB thinks it is Pakistan who made Burhan Wani a 'poster boy' of the *tehreek*. The jaded former militant joined the Hizb twice in the nineties. He was arrested, did jail time and finally abandoned militancy, feeling betrayed by Pakistan. But he had survived. Fighting to die is just not practical, AB feels. In the nineties there had been thousands of militants. In the Burhan Wani years, there were a few hundred at most. 'They had the wrong idea,' AB says. 'We older militants would say it's no use. Only when everyone rises will Kashmir be free.'

A faint note of bitterness has entered his voice. His generation of militants had operated in the real world. Many had made difficult choices in order to live and return to their families, spending the rest of their lives as private people forgotten by the public. The Burhan Wani generation had chosen an early death, and a long public afterlife. The only reason Burhan Wani is famous, says AB, is because he knew how to use social media.

But the online traces Burhan Wani left behind have also grown faint. Eight years after his death, teenagers no longer carry his pictures or videos on their phones. Social media posts have been taken down and WhatsApp groups have wound up because they could get you arrested. Phones are checked and profiles are watched closely in Kashmir. So photographs of dead militants have been replaced by pictures of the Indian flag and other symbols of Indian nationalism, images that would be unimpeachable should you be stopped at a checkpoint or summoned to a police station. It is, GB says, a form of digital burial.

Many of the videos released by Burhan Wani are now unsearchable online. They reappear as fragments, in YouTube clips of programmes on Indian news channels. They are framed by tickers screaming 'terrorist' and soap opera music. The viral

MELANCHOLIA

picture in the orchards, a poster for militancy, also became a hit list for armed forces and sections of the national media. Each time one of the cohort was killed, his face would be circled in red as the picture was flashed on TV screens or published in the papers. The 'Burhan Wani group', as many in the media called them, has long been wiped out.

It has been a while since RK has seen the Burhan videos that punctuated her childhood. But when she closes her eyes, she still has a 'clear vision'—Burhan Wani in battle fatigues warning the police to stay away from the families of militants. Driven underground by the government crackdown, the videos no longer need to be seen to be remembered. Burhan videos have gone offline, becoming part of public memory in Kashmir, forming a deep vein of loss that has changed it irrevocably.

PART IV

BLOOD MAPS

11

THE TRIALS OF MAJNUN

Majnun, the crazed prince, can move seamlessly between worlds. His father is a king of the earthly realm. When Majnun is born, the king is told the infant prince will survive only if he is suckled by a *peri* from Peristan, a fairy from the land of the fairies. So Shahperi, the youngest of seven *peri* princesses, is brought to the court through a mix of trickery and force. But she does not seem to be bound by the laws of the court. She can fly across realms without causing a diplomatic incident. She can ascend to the skies and rain down hailstones if needed. In spite of initial plans to escape the court, she grows to love Majnun, who is then raised on the milk of other worlds.

As he grows up, Majnun falls in love with Laila, a princess. But of course it will not do, their fathers being implacable foes. On being parted from Laila, Majnun falls into a fever dream. He roams deserts howling with desolation. He gives up his earthly body and wanders off into the icy mountains of Djinn Mulk, the kingdom of the *djinns*, only to get caught up in an insurrection against the tyrannical king of the *djinns*. It turns out his arrival had been prophesied there. Many travails later, Majnun is persuaded to return to his father's kingdom.

DAPAAN

The two kings arrive at a truce and a wedding is arranged—Laila and Majnun's. But even the wedding parties of the earthly realm are a kind of delirium. Thousands of guests and thousands of attendants for each of the guests, and thousands of horses for each of the guests and for each of the attendants of each of the guests, endless multiplication like reflections in a gallery of infinity mirrors. The wedding procession weaves such a slow path that several dramatic conflicts rise and fall along the way. Then Majnun sees Laila's puppy and showers such affection on the creature that he is taken for insane, and the ceremony is hastily called off.

Death too is delirium. After Laila dies of a broken heart, her father sets her grave among twelve thousand other graves so that Majnun cannot find her. In the end, when both Laila and Majnun are dead and buried together, the grave splits open to let in Laila's grieving father. He finds them in a garden, whole and beautiful as in life. They tell him to stay but he says he must return to his kingdom. When he leaves the grave after a few minutes, hundreds of years have passed in the earthly realm and his kingdom is gone.

Majnun, whose name means 'possessed by *djinns*' in Arabic, experiences love as madness. He becomes *deewana*, a state of ecstasy beyond reason. He has severed ties with the earthly realm and is free of all natural laws because he is *deewana*. It is as if the story is driven by Majnun's fugue state, travelling through the crevasses and hellfires of his mind, arriving at last in a paradise where there is no more desire, only a love annealed by suffering.

There are many forms of possession. The *haalaat* arrived in Kashmir as their own kind of fever dream, turning everyone into Majnun. Everyone was now *deewana*, ecstatic, with the fear of death and with visions of *azadi*, which had taken on the features of a different dimension, not just an altered political state. Stories of the *haalaat* also move through many worlds.

* * *

THE TRIALS OF MAJNUN

The story of Laila–Majnun was told to me by Abdul Rashid Mir, who might have gone travelling with his romantic hero himself. He was sitting in his house in Mujgund, a village on the outskirts of Srinagar, surrounded by the noise of family: a grandchild crawling in, his wife bringing tea and cakes. But his voice was filled with quiet despair as he recounted the trials of Majnun.

Abdul Rashid was telling me the short version, only two hours long. When he was a young boy, he played Laila. It was a smash hit. He did not sleep for three months. He was on tour with his father, Mohammad Ismail Mir, a legendary *dastaangoh*, a teller of tall tales.

It is said, when Ismail Mir was about eighteen, he met a *pir baba*, a Sufi mystic, who told him to sing stories. Ismail said he did not know any stories. So the *pir baba* hugged him and suddenly Ismail was singing stories day and night.

Sometimes Ismail would also say he learnt the art from his father-in-law. But this is a story about stories. So let it be said, his powers of storytelling came from the other world. Suddenly, Ismail was singing stories day and night. Although mostly at night.

He was summoned to homes on winter nights, when people stayed up to shovel the heavy snow that fell on the eaves and the *kahwa*, green tea boiled with saffron and other spices, was not enough to keep them awake. He was summoned on wedding nights, when everyone kept vigil for the bridal couple before they got married.

At first, it was just in his village. Then it was in three or four nearby villages. Then he was on the radio, and his voice could be heard across Kashmir. Finally, he was on Doordarshan, a face to go with the voice. By the time he died in 2016 at the age of eighty-five, Ismail Mir had become a name in Kashmir.

As he grew famous, Ismail acquired a chorus of musicians. A few lines of song set to the sarangi and the rabab, then a few lines of story, with the chorus exclaiming at every plot twist, then a few lines of song again. His sons, Ghulam Hassan and Abdul Rashid, started travelling with him. Sometimes, they played the characters in the story. Abdul Rashid, who had thick hair that covered his ears and an oval face, often played women.

They told stories that came from the lakes and springs of Kashmir. Himal–Nagrai, star-crossed lovers. Akanandun, the beloved son who must be sacrificed. They also told stories that had travelled a long way, across the deserts and gardens of West Asia, over the mountain ranges of Central Asia. More stories about doomed lovers. Laila–Majnun. Yousef–Zulaikha. Farhad–Shireen. And Gulrez, a favourite, where the lovers are not quite so doomed. To lettered elites, they probably arrived as Persian *masnavi*, narrative poems, which were later adapted in Kashmiri— Gulrez by Maqbool Shah Kralwari, Laila–Majnun and other tales by Mahmud Gāmi. But Ismail's stories came from elsewhere. Not for him the orderly progress of Gāmi's *masnavi*, written in tight little couplets, with a beginning, a middle and an end.[1] According to his son, Abdul Rashid, Ismail went from house to house, speaking to village elders who remembered the stories. Tell me, what have you heard? And the elders would tell him what they had heard from their grandparents. Ismail listened to different versions of the same story. Then he laid one version upon another upon another.

Narrative minimalism was not the way of the *dastaangoh*. Laila–Majnun could go on for nine hours, Himal–Nagrai for six or seven hours, minimum. Listeners could doze off in one story and wake up in a completely different story but then find themselves back in the first one. There were stories coiled within stories coiled within stories. Or stories colliding mid-air, making new stories. Characters from the main plot could disappear, dreamlike, into a subplot and stay there for a while. Sudden conflicts could crop up and then be put to rest. Things could

THE TRIALS OF MAJNUN

happen for no apparent reason. Fahad was fooled by the words of a wandering old woman. Majnun was distracted by a puppy. Masoom Shah in Gulrez was undone by a bird. Maybe it was fate or maybe it was the string of random incidents that add up to life. Either way, the stories of the *dastaangoh* became the stories Kashmiris knew themselves by.

For instance, love was hard. You were bound to fall for someone who could not be yours. Then you set yourself an impossible quest to find them. On the way, you lost your mind. Sometimes you died.

Death was not final. You could turn into a parrot or a snake and then back into a human prince. You could sleep for a hundred years, then wake up and carry on. You could be dismembered and cooked and then be put back together, good as new, much to the relief of your mother and father. Or you could die and live your best life in the other world.

Because the cartographies of the *dastaangoh* are not restricted to the earthly realm. The worlds of Majnun contain Quranic geographies carried by the *dastaans* as they travelled through Arabia, Persia and Central Asia. In death, Laila and he seem to have reached Jannat, or paradise, imagined as a garden filled with fruit trees, where four rivers flow. It is located above Jahannam, or hell, an underworld of abysses and fires. Then there is Duniya, the world we know in our daylight minds, which does not feel quite as real as the other worlds. Time works differently in each world, Abdul Rashid explains. Hundreds of earthly years can pass in a second in Jannat. A second can feel like hundreds of years in Jahannam.

But these are moral universes into which people are sorted after *qayamat*, end times. Majnun also travels to other worlds that are not Jannat or Jahannam, but not quite Duniya either.

He is transported to Djinn Mulk in an instant because he is *deewana*. According to Abdul Rashid, the kingdom of the *djinns* is part of the earthly realm but so far away that it would take ordinary humans more than a lifetime to walk there. Peristan is not in Duniya. But it is everywhere, just below the skin of the daylight world. The portal to Peristan lies in Shuniye, or wildernesses where no humans go. To snare a *peri* who could suckle Majnun, Abdul Rashid tells me, Aklah Wazir, a minister from his father's court, must lie in wait near a lake high up in the mountains. *Peris* are known to bathe there but such reprieve is always short, for they are bound to return to Peristan. No man or woman can enter this world unless the *peris* take them. But it is also said that you can reach *peris* through years of prayer, severing all ties to the world, becoming *deewana*.

Duniya sometimes dissolves into these realms, at least in Kashmir. Zutshi argues that Persian retellings of pre-Islamic myths helped work Islam into the Kashmiri landscape. Sufi mystics are described travelling across the land, visiting groves and springs that contain miracles which belong to older sacred geographies, absorbing them into new mythologies.[2] At the same time, Persian hagiographies inscribe Kashmir into the landscapes of an Islamic imaginary, refashioned as a garden of unearthly beauty.[3] Such stories imbued places with meaning and often stood in for a historical understanding of the past. The *dastaan-goh*'s repertoire also contained myths of various traditions which lived together with no apparent disjunctions.[4] So *peris* shared space with *nagas*, creatures who belong to myths about ancient Kashmir. Tal Patal, the realm of the *nagas*, existed along with Peristan. The portal to both was water. But Peristan was everywhere. Tal Patal was below.

Walk down the narrow path between the willows and step into that deep blue spring and you enter Tal Patal. Its element is water and the *nagas* who populate it are half serpent, half human. It is said, they were the original inhabitants of the Valley, from the time it was filled with water. Later, the Valley was drained and inhabited by humans. In some written histories, this was done by the intercession of the sage Kashyapa.[5] In others, by *djinns* acting on the behest of Prophet Solomon.[6] Some say it was both.[7] Either way, the *nagas* retreated to lakes and springs, and the new inhabitants of the Valley paid tributes to keep the peace.

This braiding of narrative traditions is suggested in myths about the Sufi shrine on a mountain above Akingam. Two brothers, Kauser Reshi and Gauhar Reshi, both Sufi saints, lie buried in a green shrine with a pagoda roof. The saints are strict vegetarians. A board outside the shrine warns visitors not to enter if they have eaten meat, fish or eggs. It is said, not far from the shrine is a small spring whose waters can work miracles. It is said, should visitors try to enter the shrine after having eaten non-vegetarian food, a snake who lives in the spring will come charging towards them. For the spring is sister to the saints and protector of their shrine. Echoes of the *naga* myth linger in this story about Sufi saints. The spring is a portal where the myths of one religious tradition travel into another.

Apart from precise earthly locations, unearthly realms also have well-defined political arrangements. Tal Patal, Abdul Rashid explains, has its own kings and courts. For instance, Nagrai was a prince from Tal Patal who fell in love with Himal, a princess of the earthly realm. The spring where the two first met was in Himal's garden. Himal's father's kingdom, Abdul Rashid says, was around the villages of Balpora and Batpora in Shopian district. Now, you have the prime minister of India or the governor of Jammu and Kashmir, he explains, but back then there was a king for every eight or ten villages.

The story is one of transformations, Nagrai turning from serpent to human to enter Himal's world. It is about crossing worlds for love, Nagrai being dragged down to Tal Patal and Himal following him, only to come to grief in the *naga* court. It is about death and rebirth and the gods interceding before the lovers can be together. In some written versions the lovers never end up together. In other versions it is a less metaphysical conflict—

DAPAAN

Nagrai is a Muslim who pretends to be a Hindu Brahmin so that he can marry Himal.[8] Maybe Himal–Nagrai is also a story about longing for political worlds that are out of reach.

* * *

Ismail Mir was the last of the great storytellers. Like other traditional entertainments, *dastaangoh* was being edged out of Kashmiri villages even before the *haalaat* arrived. In the recollections of JD, a resident of South Kashmir's Kulgam district, the old tradition of storytelling has become a form of lost intimacy. In village homes, he says, cows and sheep lived on the ground floor and humans above them, all under a roof of hay. On winter nights, as heat rising from animal bodies warmed the upper floor, everyone drew close together and listened to the stories of the *dastaangoh*.

As the *haalaat* spread, the Kashmiri night that had held their stories also changed. Sarangis were burnt in Pulwama, Abdul Rashid says. Musicians and storytellers were warned of *khatra*, danger. That is all he will say about it, leaving unsaid that some of the more purist militant groups had decided the arts of the *dastaangoh* went against Islam. Besides, the night held more than one kind of *khatra*. Steel *daens* wandering the streets. Knocks on the door. Eyes at windows. Old streets and trees twisted into new shapes. Old stories too.

Sufi myths and *dastaangoh* were not the only stories where Duniya was permeated by other realms. The existence of different worlds had become a belief that filtered into stories about the everyday. Some of these are hearsay—I have it on good authority; this happened to my uncle; that happened to someone in my grandfather's village. Others recount personal experiences—yes, I woke up to a crushing weight on my chest and knew it was a *djinn*; I once attended a wedding where *peris* mingled with the guests.

THE TRIALS OF MAJNUN

JM's father, who is interested in the occult, offers to take willing travellers to Peristan; you must first go to a forest high up in the mountains. JM himself knows of a man who went to plough his fields, which were near the edge of a ravine in a desolate part of Budgam district. He set his cows to the plough and thought he would take a nap while they worked. It was around four in the afternoon. When the farmer woke up, it was late at night. He could hear wedding music floating up from the bottom of the ravine. It was a *djinn* wedding. Someone brought him a copper plate full of food and told him not to speak of what he had seen. The farmer quietly polished off the excellent *wazwan* and went home. But as he could not keep the story to himself, he had a nosebleed for seven years. His daughter was also ill for a long time. A *djinn* appeared in a dream and informed him it was punishment for telling.

Djinns, in these stories, are both far and near the haunts of man. Once, *djinns* summoned JM's great-grandfather to the old stone bridge that crossed the Sindh river in Ganderbal town. A *djinn's* wife had broken her elbow and JM's great-grandfather was a healer. He fixed her elbow and they gave him a *kangri*, a fire pot, full of coals. When he got home, he threw away half the coals before he slept. A mistake, for when he woke up the coals left in the *kangri* had turned to gold.

There are other stories, more domestic. *Djinns* are drawn to dirt, just as *peris* like cleanliness. Leave a room shut for forty days, let it gather dust, and you will hear *djinns* knocking about. Should *djinns* take a liking to you, or should they be angry, they will possess you. And then you are dragged away into a twilight world of dreams and visions, much like Majnun.

It is not surprising that these shadow worlds too would be drawn into the *haalaat*. If storytelling had once created new sacred geographies, it could now produce other geographies: a relief map of conflict. There were two ways in which this place-making happened.

DAPAAN

First, everyone had their own experience of the *haalaat* which reconfigured their sense of place. Like Majnun, everyone now walked in their own vivid psychoscape. Cities were dissolved and made again in the fever dream of the *haalaat*. There was no more Srinagar, Sopore, Anantnag, Baramulla. There were no more streets, no more towers, no more town squares. There was instead a stretch of road where you had once felt hope, a copse where a boy from your childhood disappeared, a corner that you learnt to avoid because a one-tonne was always parked there. Everyone carried their own map of the Valley, drawn by the mind's wandering, the heart's remembering. These were memory maps, blood maps. Most people I spoke to understood immediately when I asked them to draw their blood map.

Second, as the *haalaat* rolled through the Valley, it created its own paradise, its own hell and other worlds in between. Places of pleasure such as cinema halls were turned into camps. Graveyards filled with the recent dead. The Line of Control became a mystical frontier between two political states, one resisted by the *tehreek* and the other so desired that it pulled in thousands of young men. These places stood for such different registers of experience that it seemed they could not even belong to the same reality. They often appear in stories as different realms. I did not know how much time had passed in the cell; each second was a hundred years. We were so happy in our old home; it feels like a dream now. The earth here is scented; it speaks to us of paradise. Land is not just land any longer but a metaphor for experience.

12

BLOOD TOWNS

Blood maps live in the head. Blood maps contain places that cannot always be named, places of love and death and pain and shame. Blood maps show their lineaments in the quiet of one's own thoughts. There is no past or future in such a map, only a present that is continually happening. Everyone walks in their own blood map until they reach a node, a place of happening that is shared by many. A market set alight in Sopore. A patch of street in Hawal, Srinagar, where protesters are shot. The narrow triangle of a park in Bijbehara which still bears the names of the dead. Or maybe it is a square known for public protests; a school turned into a camp.

 The Valley has been redrawn in a delicate tracery of veins, hers and his and his and theirs. Only those who have lived through the *haalaat* can read a blood map. Others can be shown but cannot read it themselves.

 Take a vein. It flows into a classroom filled with morning light. DB is here, one of the twelve-year-old boys straining to listen to the sounds outside. DB's age, and the name of the school printed neatly in exercise books, tells you it is Sopore,

DAPAAN

1990. Their school is living on borrowed time. It is funded by the Falah-e-Aam trust, which is linked to the Jama'at-e-Islami. The government has banned the Jama'at and the trust for their alleged ties to the new militancy. All schools supported by Falah-e-Aam are to be shut down, their teachers and students transferred to government schools. Only a few teachers have refused, staving off the demise of the school in Sopore. But these are nervous days.

This morning, CRPF men have chased militants down the street outside the school and one of the students has drawn a gun on the black board. When their teacher enters class and sees the drawing, he is furious. They cannot afford to show support for the militancy right now. Who has drawn the gun, he demands. But such is the solidarity worked by the *haalaat* that no one gives him a name. All right, then everyone will get a beating, the teacher announces. One by one, the boys walk up to take their beating. Then it is the turn of the last boy, who has watched, with growing dread, his classmates staggering back to their seats. Finally, he cracks. He blurts out the name to the teacher. Very well, the teacher says, twice the beating for you. But why, the boy protests, for he has given him the name. First, for staying silent when I asked you, the teacher replies, then, for not staying silent now.

DB flinches as he watches wood come down on flesh; his own flesh is still on fire, a splotch of purple spreading under his skin. A blinding flash of pain and his body is hurled up in the air, landing in a narrow stream. It is two years later; he has joined a new school in Sopore and he is hiding from gunfire. The stream flows into the Jhelum river at a right angle. It runs by a street that leads up to the Chan Khan bridge, one of the two bridges spanning the Jhelum at Sopore. This bridge, with a military check post at either end, is a popular target for militants. The gunfire is coming from the bridge.

BLOOD TOWNS

This morning, militants told schools in Sopore to shut early—they were planning something. Militant attacks in Sopore in the early nineties are so bureaucratic they might as well be announced by gazetted notices. Since they don't want civilian deaths that would cost them public support, militants usually give warning. Stay home after dinner tonight—we are planning something. Everyone visiting relatives or out in the market hurries home. The whole town knows and holds its breath. But the principal at DB's new school chose to ignore the warnings today. Halfway through the school day, it became clear the attacks had started. Classes were dismissed, and DB and a few of the older boys were put in charge of taking the nursery children home. They took the road by the stream.

They reached the Chan Khan bridge, which lies on their way home. Just then, a military cavalcade passing through it came under fire from militants across the river. Soldiers from the opposite end of the bridge returned fire. The schoolboys were caught in the middle. DB and the older boys swept the nursery children with them as they dashed into the stream, ducking bullets. They will hide out here for a while before stealing into one of the side alleys. They must make their way home through the other bridge, close to the Sopore Jamia Masjid down the river. This too has military bunkers at both ends. They will crawl through this bridge, not taking any chances.

The battle for Sopore is a battle for the bridges. In December 1992, militants blow up the bridge by the Jamia Masjid; the checkpoints had been making it difficult to cross the river. With the bridge and its checkpoints gone, they could take boats in peace. This plan backfires. Forces announce that boats may only be taken from one point on the riverbank, heavily manned by soldiers. So militants are forced to cross the Jhelum farther up the river, away from the main town.

The old, wooden Chan Khan bridge, which now has to bear the whole city's traffic, starts to look worse for wear. The administration decides to build a grand state-of-the-art bridge, a symbol of New Kashmir, just a token of the government largesse that may be had if Kashmiris give up this *tehreek* nonsense. KV Krishna Rao, former army chief and now governor of Jammu and Kashmir, is to inaugurate the new bridge at a ceremony in the Sopore government college. A big ceremony needs a big crowd so the military declares a crackdown and orders everyone to gather at the college grounds. A marquee is set up and the governor arrives. But the crowd, far from being impressed, starts chanting *azadi* slogans and brings down the marquee. After that, the governor declares that such people do not deserve a grand state-of-the-art New Kashmir bridge. Just a bridge will do.

A surge of red wells up around the college campus before irrigating Ganjoo House nearby. Except it isn't Ganjoo House anymore, DB is reminded every time he walks past. The Ganjoos, Kashmiri Pandits, have left the Valley. Tensions between communities had been rising through the eighties—petrol bombs after an India–Pakistan cricket match, a gun brandished by one side, beatings administered by another—so when the *haalaat* came the Pandits of Sopore knew it was time to go. Ganjoo House has become Ganjoo Camp.

Ganjoo camp is one of many that have blossomed across Sopore town, blood flowers held in a mist of concertina wiring. Militants set fire to the Border Security Force camp near the Hatishah mosque. The terrified soldiers who manage to escape the fire take refuge in the mosque. The militants decide to spare them. If they had not, the militants later explain, forces would spend their wrath on ordinary civilians. Sopore is awash with foreign militants. They have come from Pakistan, Afghanistan, Uzbekistan, even Sudan, to fight Kashmir's war. Engineer Masood, a chemical engineer from Sudan. Akbar Bhai, said to be the former bodyguard of Gulbuddin Hekmatyar, the mujahideen leader turned prime minister of Afghanistan. Akbar Bhai is a

BLOOD TOWNS

legend in Sopore. It is said, he jumps from house to house to escape security forces during gunfights, although he will eventually suffer a most undignified death. DB, like every other boy in town, cannot get enough of Akbar Bhai stories.

Which is why a filament of red attaches itself to an outhouse bathroom in Sopore. Akbar Bhai is killed here on 7 August 1993. Word has spread that new foreign militants are on their way to Sopore. The rookie militants have gone and embroiled themselves in a gunfight immediately upon arrival. They are holed up in a house in Sopore, surrounded by soldiers. Akbar Bhai rushes to their rescue, no doubt jumping from one roof to another to save time. All seems quiet when he gets there; the soldiers appear to have retreated. There is really nothing left to do but take position in a convenient outhouse and wait. A BSF soldier has also had the same idea. He has not retreated with his colleagues. When Akbar Bhai enters the bathroom, the soldier shoots him point blank.

Fifteen-year-old DB is swept up in the mourning that follows, which is why he is here now, in a procession that has gathered at the Sopore Jamia Masjid three days after Akbar Bhai's death. As the procession snakes past a BSF check post, a soldier points his gun at them. Immediately, dozens of guns go up in the air from the crowd. The BSF man backs away. Only in Sopore in 1993 could this happen. The town is considered a liberated zone, controlled by militants. Pakistani flags fly from buildings. *Azadi* is just a day away. But the mourners do not know that Akbar Bhai's death is a turning point in the fight. It allows the military to make a concerted push to take Sopore. Militants ramp up defences. They take refuge in nearby villages and blow up a couple of roads connecting them to Sopore town. It is no use. By November 1993, the army is in control of the town.

The sound of bullets never stops chasing DB in these years. It has chased him down here, in front of the army camp set up at the

DAPAAN

Industrial Training Institute. He is crouching while bullets scream overhead. To think he had just stepped out to do some quick shopping for his sister's wedding. On his way to the market, he was stopped by a soldier posted at the camp gates, who gave him some money and asked him to get cigarettes. On his way back, everything had changed. The camp was under attack. The soldier told him and a couple of other civilians to squat on the footpath before the camp gates. DB offered up the cigarettes, hoping they would make a special case for him and let him go. The cigarettes were waved away, so here he is, sitting with the others.

A man who had been asked to fetch milk for the soldiers is squatting next to him. He has bad news. The camp has been surrounded by militants since morning; this attack has been in the works for a while. They will later learn there was no such elaborate plan, just a couple of militants shooting at the camp from the river. But for now, DB believes it is all over, that this will be his last day. After a while, his uncle is stopped as he is passing by the camp, and now he too is one of the squatters. DB decides to try his luck one more time. His sister is getting married, he tells the soldiers; he really needs to get back home. In his innocence, he thinks the soldiers will listen to reason. His uncle barks at him to keep quiet. They keep sitting in silence while soldiers and militants exchange fire. Then a passing bus is flagged down. The passengers, about thirty of them, are made to get off and squat in front of the camp. DB is just thinking what a relief this is, for there is safety in numbers, when a bullet whizzes past his ear and buries itself in the bunker behind him. It later occurs to him they might have been used as human shields. We have civilians here, the forces seemed to be telling the militants—shoot if you dare.

In spite of the bullets, it doesn't feel real. It feels like a game of cops and robbers. When does that change? Maybe a few years later, when a BSF man raises his hand threatening to slap him and DB is suddenly conscious of feeling humiliated. Or maybe when they jail his brother for a month and beat him until his wounds fill with pus and start itching madly but he cannot scratch them because his hands are bound. When his brother asks for a drink of water, they bring a stick down on his wounds. This is a relief, for the wounds burst, letting out the pus. Or maybe it is when DB is sitting with some other boys in his class around a favourite *chinar* tree and he realises that his friend will never sit with them again. There was a shootout in their locality and all the young boys ran away. His friend's mother told her son to stay home and not panic. He stayed home, along with his cousin. Both boys were shot dead.

It does not feel real on 6 January 1993, when DB spends a quiet day pottering about at home. He has heard a few blasts, seen a few columns of smoke rising in the distance, but that has become routine. He turns on the radio and Deutsche Welle says, 'Thirty-three people killed in Kashmir.' He still thinks they are talking about other parts of the Valley—the death toll is often in double digits these days. Then a neighbour turns up at their door in a state. He has heard at least one hundred people have been killed in Sopore. After that, DB's brother, who had gone out, sends word that he is alive, safe, staying at a relative's house. Suddenly, the columns of smoke are rearranged, leaping higher into the sky as they speak of something big, something out-of-the-ordinary terrible.

For two days, there is a curfew. On the third day, DB goes down to the market near the old Sopore bus stand. Entire rows of shops have been burnt. Smoke is still rising from the ruins. It is deep winter but the heat is so intense that even glass bottles have melted. This is no ordinary fire. BSF men, angered by the killing of a colleague, have gone on a rampage, burning and shooting whomever and whatever they could find. Fifty-seven civilians have been killed and the old bus stand market has become a node, pulsing with memory, where the veins of DB's map meet GP's map and the maps of many, many others.

GP's map enters the old bus stand market through Shaheen Studios, whose owner is a friend of his uncle. The owner has a relative who helps him out at the shop, a teenager who is little more than a child. When the BSF storms into the market that morning in 1993, the owner pulls down his shutters and hopes to sit out the attack. They find the charred bodies of the owner and his assistant afterwards, still clinging to each other.

A trail of dried blood travels up the road from Shaheen Studios to enter a building in Muslim Peer *mohalla*. It is January again, nearly a decade after the big fire, and GP has assembled with his friends at a tuition centre. Soldiers invade the hall before coaching lessons can start. GP knows they have come for him. Walking to the centre that morning, his friend and he were summoned by soldiers at a check post. The two boys had their arms tucked inside their *pherans*, letting the sleeves hang loose. They were carrying books which bulged underneath the woollen cloth. Maybe the soldiers thought the books were guns. His friend wanted to obey the summons and started towards the check post but GP refused to stop. So he knows they have come looking for him at the centre. He is picked out of the assembly and beaten up right there. He is shaken but not so much. He has been beaten many times before. The girls gathered in the hall are screaming.

Rods land on his head, punches in his stomach, releasing red corpuscles that travel back down the Sopore market road, past the *chowk*, or junction, near the police station that is a favourite spot for grenade attacks and shootouts, past New Light Hotel, which caught fire twice, mysteriously, past the camp near the old State Bank building, which was occupied first by the BSF then the CRPF, past the graveyard where a section is reserved for those considered martyrs—militants who died fighting forces, as well as civilians who died at the hands of forces—before pooling into the grounds of the Government Boys' Higher Secondary School. His school. The wide road in front is another staging ground for gunfights and bombs. Whenever the schoolboys hear blasts, they climb over the wall into Government Degree College, Sopore. This is where GP is in the autumn of 2003, throwing stones at forces posted outside. They respond with tear gas shells.

Protests have broken out in Sopore because a boy has been killed in the forests near Tujar Sharief, a former student of the government college who had been married a few hours before he was taken from his home by forces. Days later, forces say he is dead, killed in an explosion as he was leading them to a militant hideout. His family says no, he died because he was tortured and then his body was strapped with bombs and blown up in the forest. So protests have broken out. Someone from the college authorities has the idea of extending the height of the campus walls with tin sheets so that no stones can fly out and no tear gas shells can fly in. But when large processions march down the road, GP and his friends leave their college fortress to walk and chant with them as they pool into the nearby junction.

He does not know yet that less than a decade later he will be here again, walking up the road, not down, walking up till he has passed his old school, passed the government college, and reached the building euphemistically known as Town Hall. Every other person in Sopore has been tortured at Town Hall. It houses the police superintendent's office and a special operations group camp. The complex of grim buildings has also quartered various military and paramilitary camps throughout the course of the *haalaat*. It is said, all counterinsurgency operations in North Kashmir are planned and coordinated here.

It is the winter of 2012 now. GP has reached the SOG camp and is standing outside in the December cold. He is here because his father is inside. They took him in for questioning, and when

DAPAAN

GP called he answered, trying to sound casual, saying he was fine. But he had forgotten to cut the call and GP could hear the blows landing on him. His father has been taken in because the police think he is sending money to his uncle, the militant commander across the Line of Control. They think he uses his apple trading business to send the money. GP's father says they can check his account books—he has nothing to hide. So they confiscate the account books. This is the worst time to take the books because apple traders settle accounts in December.

After the first night, they let GP's father go home. But he has to return the next morning and submit himself for questioning all day. This continues for about four days. On one of the days, the routine is different; he has to report to a nearby army camp and then to the SOG camp. Each day, GP stands outside the SOG camp in the December cold, waiting for his father to come out. The day they tell his father he is in the clear, he may go, they leave Town Hall and go straight to a new restaurant called River's Edge, on the banks of the Jhelum, and eat a hot *wazwan* meal.

But GP does not know that yet as he chants slogans with the crowd in 2003, walking down the road, not up, down to the *chowk* that has become a regular scene of protest.

The Sopore protests do not spread across Kashmir as protests will in years to come, but already there are angry veins surging south, plunging down the apple orchards, into the highway, through the avenue of poplars that starred in many Hindi movies and will one day disappear to make way for New Kashmir, until they meet a quickening, a gravitational force that comes from a great roaring of blood contained in the dense network of veins that is Srinagar. And here is a room in the thickest part of the city, white cloth spread out on the carpet. Here is the quiet boy, holding a paintbrush dipped in blue.

Here it is 2008, and he has been sent to spend the summer with family friends in Nowhatta, a ring of chaos around the vast calm of the Jamia Masjid. The quiet boy does not know what to do with himself here. Far away, they have heard, Israel is bombing Gaza. Downtown Srinagar is seething. Kashmir will not be silent if Palestine burns. The family friends' son, a young man in his twenties, has decided to protest that day. He will paint an Israeli flag and set it on fire. The quiet boy watches as the man tries to draw the blue star of the flag, badly, the paint straying out of the lines. Finally, the quiet boy can't take it anymore. He takes the brush and gets to work on the flag himself. When it is done to his satisfaction, they walk out into the streets, holding the flag high between them so that the paint can dry. People dart curious glances their way. In five minutes, the flag will burn.

They walk down to the *chowk* in front of Srinagar's Jamia Masjid. This is the oldest and grandest of Jamia Masjids in Kashmir. The Mirwaiz who preaches from its pulpit also leads a faction of the Hurriyat. Three roads meet in front of the mosque, creating a stage where protesters gather to throw stones, demand *azadi*, decry the horrors visited on the Muslim world by powerful states. The quiet boy hangs back in the crowd and watches the flag burn from a distance. He feels detached but cannot take his eyes away.

He will come to know this *chowk* well. It is on the road that leads up to the mosque. Over the years, a careful choreography of protest has been devised between forces and protesters. With the Jamia Masjid as a backdrop, boys at the *chowk* will throw stones at forces posted further down the road. There is a buffer zone, marked by a Bata shoe shop, possibly because the shop stands at the mouth of an alley that sometimes spouts forces out into the main road. Boys do not go further down the road from the Bata shop and forces generally do not come up. Friday afternoons are for protesting. This has become a ritual after the congregational prayers every Friday so there are two armoured CRPF vehicles parked outside the mosque, fatigued men watching stones fly as

DAPAAN

they sit behind wire mesh and bulletproof glass. This may go on for several hours. Then the forces down the road from Bata will breach the buffer zone and break up the protests. The unspoken deadline is six in the evening. On winter evenings, this deadline is advanced to half past five. Afterwards, injured protesters retreat into the mosque compound to cool their burning eyes, prise out the pellets that forces have buried in their flesh.

If the choreography breaks down, even more blood will flow. It breaks down one Friday afternoon in the summer of 2018. A CRPF van drives straight into a protesting crowd and runs over twenty-one-year-old Kaiser Amin. Forces later say that they had lost their way trying to flee from the angry crowd. Protesters say no, they ran over Kaiser on purpose. A video of his death goes viral in Kashmir. The quiet boy has watched the video many times. So when he walks through that Nowhatta street, Kaiser is always there, being crushed under the wheels again and again.

The quiet boy is not in the protests of 2018 but here he is at the Nowhatta *chowk* in 2008. All of Kashmir is up in arms because the government has decided to parcel out forest land to the Amarnath Shrine Board, which manages a Hindu pilgrimage into the Valley every year. Here he is again in 2010. This time the Valley is angry because three men have been killed and passed off as foreign militants. When protests break out in downtown Srinagar, it is seventeen-year-old Tufail Mattoo, returning home from tuition one evening, who dies after a tear gas shell pierces his skull. The protests spread to other parts of the city. When the quiet boy tries to enter Lal Chowk he finds it quarantined, all exits from the main square sealed by metal sheets, as if this will protect it from the contagion of downtown protests. That year, the quiet boy sees another boy in front of him crumple as he is hit by a bullet. As he is taken away to the hospital where he will die, the injured boy looks straight into the quiet boy's eyes for a moment. The quiet boy thinks the bullet was meant for him. He never protests again. That is all he will say about that.

A stone hits him on the head at the Eidgah, large open grounds not far from Jamia Masjid. It is 2013; everyone is marching for the customary Eid protest, and he is here not to protest but to watch, camera in hand. CRPF men in the armoured vehicle that is posted outside the Eidgah are most solicitous. They take him inside to dress his wounds. The stone, thrown at him, who once threw stones himself, marks him out as a witness, no longer part of the crowd.

Maybe RM sees him from where she is sitting, high up at a window that looks out over an intersection on a road that runs past the Eidgah. It is a window in her grandmother's house. In 2023, the road below is just a calm drone of traffic. But when RM enters the room, she sees the street as the street has been. It is 2008, the year of the shrine board protests; 2009, when Asiya and Neelofar are found dead in a stream in Shopian district; 2010, when Tufail Mattoo collapses; 2016, when Burhan Wani is shot; and all the years in between.

RM has traced a pattern of protest around the Eidgah. Boys throwing stones will emerge from the alley behind her and spill out into the road that runs past the prayer grounds. Further up the road, forces will emerge from a bunker set in front of the wooden Ali Masjid. Boys and forces will meet at a bus stop midway, stones versus pellets, slogans versus teargas. Sometimes, bullets. Once, she sees protesters ferrying a boy who was shot at the nearby Kawdara market. They are taking him to a hospital, but midway, someone realises he is already dead.

RM watches from the window as she is not allowed to go out into the streets for the major protests. Her own memory of protesting starts at the women's college on MA Road in 2014. It is not for Kashmir but for Palestine, which is being bombed by Israel again. Their principal warns them not to assemble but all the girls gather in the college field and go out anyway. They make it to the clock tower at Lal Chowk, a route that is paved with tiles in 2023. Tourists dance victory dances on these tiles; they are invited to take selfies here by hashtag signs. It has become, for RM, a route of immurement, where the furies of previous years are buried.

So what explains the feeling that the Eidgah intersection is still humming with protests from the past? Maybe it is the 'Mazar-e-Shuhada', the martyrs' graveyard, at one corner of the Eidgah, where the air sings in many voices. The roses are brighter here, the narcissi more fragrant. Maybe this explains the pull of the Eidgah, where so many protests are bound and so many blood maps meet.

NA can still hear the slogans from the 'Eidgah *chalo*' march in 2008. Faced with protests, the government has reversed the land grant to the Amarnath Shrine Board. This has outraged Hindus in Jammu, who have blocked the highway leading into the Kashmir Valley, disrupting the flow of food and other supplies. So now the Hurriyat has called for counter protests in Kashmir, blockbuster rallies where rousing slogans are chanted. '*Maaro ya mar jaawo.*' Kill or be killed. '*Deen ke aage duniya kya hai?*' What is this world compared to our faith? Busloads of people are brought in for the march. Everyone is on a *hartal*, strike. Shops are shut all day except during the windows of *dheel*, relaxation, permitted by the Hurriyat leadership. In the villages, they manage fine. Most people have a kitchen garden where they grow enough to eat: a few rows of collard greens, plump Kashmiri chillies, turnips, aubergines, some beets. In downtown Srinagar, there are no gardens; supplies are running low. So the busload of protesters brings vegetables. There is a sense that something huge is about to happen. NA hears her father and uncles joking that everyone is standing with their vessels ready, as if someone has asked them, '*Kisko kisme azadi chahiye?*' In what would you like to receive your *azadi*? As though it is something tangible, like vegetables.

BLOOD TOWNS

They are still waiting, a decade later, when someone asks NA for the pins she uses to fasten her hijab. They need it to tease pellets out of their flesh. She is in Zadibal, a Shia neighbourhood on the edges of downtown Srinagar. It is 2019; the state of Jammu and Kashmir has just been carved up into two Union Territories and stripped of autonomy. There is a curfew and an information blackout to contain protests. But an Ashura rally for the sacred month of Muharram has turned into a march for *azadi*. She has heard one of the banners carried by the Muharram procession does not speak of the martyrdom of the Prophet Muhammad's grandson Hussain. Instead, it features a picture of Burhan Wani. Forces respond with the usual tear gas and pellets. As usual, protesters are avoiding hospitals for fear of the police. So rooms in Zadibal turn into operating theatres and hijab pins must replace scalpels. This will be the last of the anti-government protests for years to come.

What was it all for, NA sometimes wonders. Her whole life has been punctuated by camps and protest sites, places where the pulse quickens, places marked in red. The bunker at Sazgaripora, dismantled for a few years as the militancy waned, but back again after 2019. Jamia Masjid, which she has learnt to avoid on Fridays, even when the ritual protests have stopped. Firdous Cinema, turned into a military camp in the nineties and periodically attacked by grenades so that she has got into the habit of closing the windows every time she hears a loud bang. Even when the camp has been disbanded and Firdous Cinema lies deserted.

Firdous Cinema is another node, humming with the rush of blood. It is still a camp when ZB, the researcher, is a schoolboy. His route on the way home from school is also mapped out in camps and bunkers. Khayam Cinema, which became a camp and then a hospital. Mill Stop, named for a spinning mill, now one of the euphemisms of the *haalaat*. In the early nineties, the mill is taken over by forces; so is the sheep husbandry centre next to

DAPAAN

it, and the United Nations Development Programme office next to that. In years to come, forces will move out of the mill building, which will then be turned into a crafts development institute. Part of the sheep husbandry building will be reclaimed. Only the UN offices will remain fortified, renamed the UN camp. But all three camps are still there as the school bus hurtles towards Mama's restaurant, near which Ashfaq Majeed Wani is always falling, shot dead just as he is about to throw a grenade at Firdous Cinema camp.

The bus tears past Mama's, past Firdous Cinema, and comes to a shrieking halt in the courtyard outside the Zadibal *imambara*, a Shia prayer hall. Ashfaq Wani is long dead. But ZB is here in a line-up of men. His first crackdown. He is about ten years old. He is staying at his grandmother's house when the crackdown is announced. His aunt has just got married and the house is still recovering from the festivities. Gifts and dried fruit are laid out. Red chillies left over from the wedding feast are drying in the kitchen garden. When the soldiers come and ask the men in the house to get out, ZB's father takes him along. The *imambara* is the oldest of the Shia prayer halls in Srinagar, built in 1518 and burnt down at least ten times since then. The prayer hall's history is traced through riots, massacres, arson and sectarian tensions. Shias know it well, this specific current of *zulm* that pulses through generations of their community in Kashmir. Now they are standing in a line-up outside the *imambara*, facing a row of Maruti Gypsies and who knows what next. ZB sees at least two of his neighbours being dragged away.

At his grandmother's house, the women listen as forces barge in with three or four men who have been picked off the line-up. They listen as the captives are hauled off to the courtyard where there is an ancient water tank with no water left in it. They hear cries as the men are stripped to their underwear and made to crouch in the tank while they are beaten up. They hear them being taken into the kitchen garden where there are big drums filled with water for the plants. They hear more screams as the captives' heads are shoved into the drums, where the water has been mixed with red chillies. After some time, the men are dragged off to a camp. ZB and his father return in the evening to find the cheerful wedding mess turned into chaos. The dried fruit is gone. Some money is missing. The tank has become the place where three men in white vests were beaten. He sees it every time he visits his grandmother's place. Just like he hears a phantom grenade every time he walks past the fountain near the Tourist Reception Centre near Lal Chowk. Just as he can still see the bunker near his own house although the bunker is long gone, the mound it stood on levelled and two new houses built on the spot.

Srinagar is a city of ghost bunkers. Here is the bunker outside Kashyapa School in 1993. SK and his friends, all in their early twenties, are frozen in front of it. They have just been visiting the Batamaloo mosque where the preacher makes fiery speeches on the *tehreek*. The way home lies through the road in front of Kashyapa School, turned into a camp after its students, mostly Kashmiri Pandits, left the Valley. Now several things are happening at once. SK and his friends are walking past the camp. A minibus carrying passengers is driving past the camp. Someone is throwing a grenade at the camp.

Soldiers in the bunker guarding the camp assume the grenade comes from the minibus. SK thinks this is very unlikely because public vehicles are not allowed to have their windows down these days. They must also have a wire mesh to reinforce the windows. The soldiers, however, start shooting at the minibus, piercing the flimsy tin of the body, taking out one tyre so that it is just a tangle of metal and rubber. SK and his friends are diagonally across the camp, the minibus in between them and the bunker. Bullets aimed at the minibus also fly towards them. The boys make a flash decision. They jump into the minibus, which

DAPAAN

careens madly down the road before turning into an alley. Three passengers have been hit. But SK lives to make his way home.

The way home is marked with fallen bodies. Here is the cycle repair shop in Nawabazar where they kill Valve Tube, a boy so small they named him after the tiny tube found on bicycle pumps. Valve Tube reigns over Nawabazar, going from house to house expecting to be fed and doted on. That day he is visiting the cycle repair shop. It is early 1989; the *tehreek* has not yet flared up but there is a crackle in the air, a concatenation of ions. Boys from Nawabazar have been protesting on the street all day, throwing stones at policemen posted nearby. Finally, one of the policemen loses patience and fires a shot. It is meant to be a warning shot, not aimed at anyone. But the bullet has entered the cycle repair shop and found its mark in Valve Tube. The shop owner carries the small body out through the door. Valve Tube's tongue is sticking out of his mouth to say life has left his body. SK sees it all from a window opposite the cycle shop.

And here, down the road, is the spot where they shoot Kharbooz Kal a couple of years later. Kharbooz Kal, Watermelon Head, lives with his family on a boat in a canal that peels away from the Jhelum. As children, SK and he had played together.

Should SK not go home, should he instead loop back and walk east through the streets of downtown, he will reach a protest in Daribal in 1993. Maybe it is Valve Tube and Kharbooz Kal who have impelled him to the protest. Another child has died, shot along with his parents by BSF soldiers who barged into their home. When protesters pour out into the streets, they shoot more people. Days later, the *raantas* will be seen in the streets of downtown Srinagar, forcing people back into their homes.

Blood flows into blood flows into blood. Now they are all here, Valve Tube and Kharbooz Kal and the boy from Daribal, crowding over SK's shoulder as he stares at a school bag. It is 2016 and he is in a room in Harwan, a wooded mountain area near Srinagar. Mass protests that started in summer are stretching into autumn. The bag belongs to an eleven-year-old whose body has been found near a reservoir, perforated with pellets. The boy's sister is showing SK the bag and talking about the child who is gone. As she speaks, the years slide from protest to protest, from street to street, until SK finds himself back on the Nawabazar road in 1990 or 1991, holding a banner.

He is marching to Lal Chowk. Processions from different parts of the city are supposed to converge at the clock tower for a grand rally. SK's procession will never make it out of downtown Srinagar. Forces will shoot at them near the Zaldagar bridge, killing three. But for now, SK is still holding the banner. He has made it himself out of a cardboard plank used for storing bolts of cloth. He has written on it the legend: '*Azadi* Soon'.

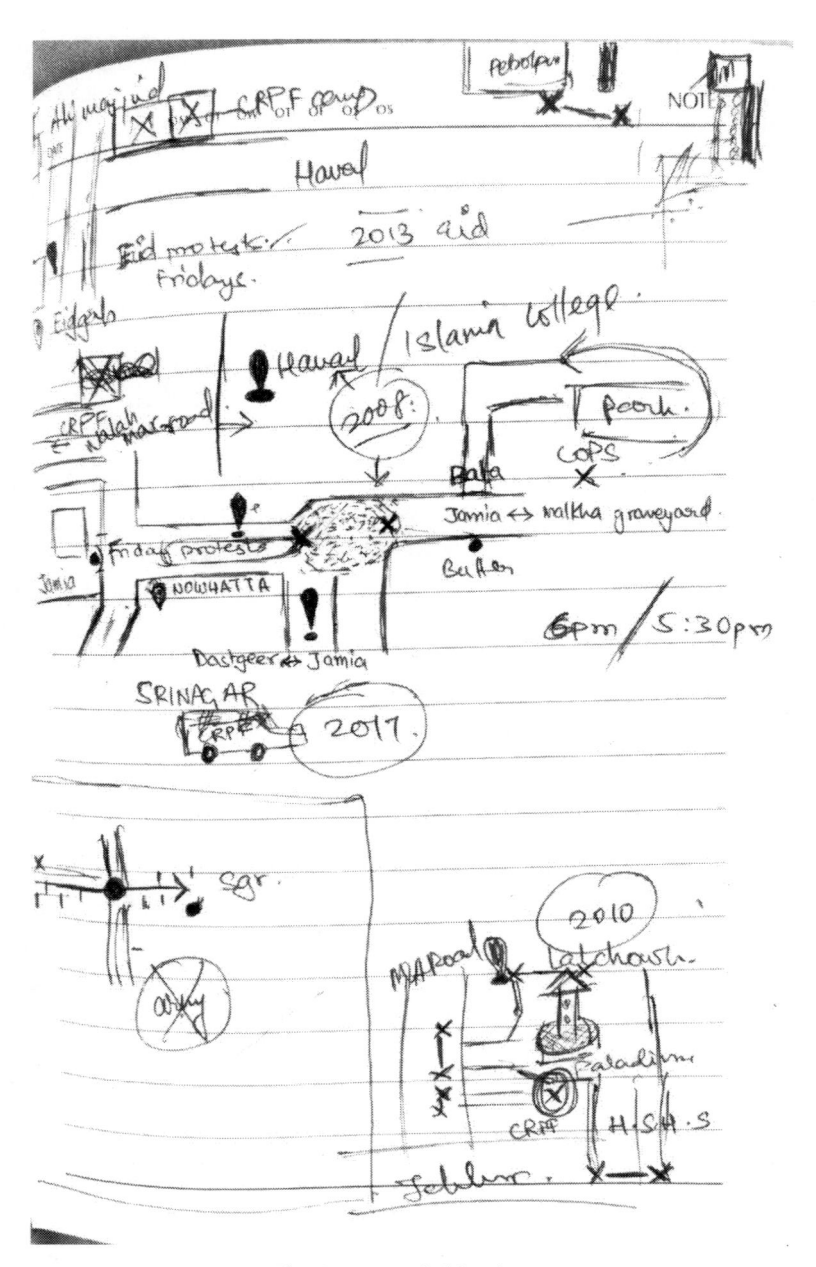

The Quiet Boy's blood map

13

FIRDOUS CINEMA

PP's memory is neatly folded. She spreads it out. There, in the centre, is a grey building laced with concertina wiring and a rusted neon sign that spells out Firdous Cinema. 'Firdous', meaning paradise.

Once, it is said, there was nothing. A bare field girded by a wire fence. Then, her father told her, the government rigged up a shed on the field. Horses and cows that had strayed would be penned up there. Their owners could get them back for a fine. Sometime in the sixties, she has heard, the Kawoosas bought the land from the government and built Firdous Cinema.

The movie theatre is in Hawal, once on the peripheries of downtown Srinagar and now absorbed deep into the dense urban growth. But it is also part of other geographies, some of this world and some not of it.

Firdous Cinema was not the only movie hall in Srinagar to be turned into a camp. It was not the site of the worst massacres—that was Islamia College, also in Hawal, where about seventy people were killed in one day. Nor did it have a name for torture, unlike, say, Kawoosa House in nearby Nowhatta. It was attacked a few times, most notably by Ashfaq Wani just as he was killed in 1990. But such attacks were routine in those days.

Still, Firdous Cinema is curiously lit up in the memory of those who knew it in their youth and saw it change from movie hall to camp. It flickers between dream and nightmare. It lives in both historical time and impossible time, time that belongs to other worlds, but also to a past that no longer feels believable.

PP starts out historical. So, where was she? Yes, a road running past the side of Firdous Cinema connects it to Hari Parbat, travelling through concentric circles of history as it ascends the hill. Hari Parbat is circled by a wall built by the Mughals in the sixteenth century and crowned by a fort finished by the Pathans in the nineteenth century.[1] The wall had three main gates and the gates used to have check posts in Pathan times. PP knows this because her family had lived there since Pathan times. By the time she was growing up, the walls were largely gone, leaving behind the gates, grandiose and lonely. When PP was very small, her grandfather took her to see the fort. They saw guns and heavy, heavy cannonballs still strewn about. That was before Indian soldiers moved into the fort and closed it to the public for decades.

Hari Parbat also lives in mythical time. It is said, the mountain is a rock dropped by a goddess to kill the demon Jalodbhava. It is also called Koh-i-Maran, the mountain of serpents, a Persian name with echoes from Kashmir's ancient past, when *nagas* are said to have lived in the Valley. But PP has no time for these stories. She thinks Koh-i-Maran got its name because the road winds up the hill like a snake. Still, it is sacred ground. On one side of the hill lies the Makhdoom Sahib shrine, the empire of a powerful Sufi saint. On the other, the temple of the Hindu goddess Sharika. PP's childhood home was right below the temple, in an area known as Devi Angan, courtyard of the goddess. From wall to fort, the road once travelled through an orchard of almond trees, Badamwari. People went for picnics there in PP's childhood, drawn by the fresh air that was scented with almond blossoms.

Not everywhere was pleasant. If you walked up the hill from Firdous Cinema and turned left before you reached Devi Angan, you reached the psychiatric hospital originally set up by British missionaries in the nineteenth century. Further up this road, you reached the central jail set up in Dogra times. The almond groves once thickened into forests on this side of the hill, haunted by older places of punishment. The forests were named Bagh-e-Waris Khan, after a bloodthirsty official who liked to hang his victims upside down over a well. When PP was growing up, this corner of the hill was a place of fear that most people avoided.

What else? Oh yes, if you went down the hill, past Firdous Cinema, and kept walking, you would reach a canal that drew water from the Anchar Lake. Her father sometimes went down to the canal to fetch drinking water. It was clean and sweet.

Then the waters grew polluted and the canal disappeared beneath a road. And PP seems to remember a fire in Badamwari. Soon afterwards, in the seventies, the government gave land on one side of the road leading up to the hill from Firdous Cinema to Tibetan refugees. Land on the other side went to downtown families who wanted to move into the relative quiet of Hawal. And that was the end of old Badamwari.

Years later, the forest of Bagh-e-Waris Khan would be cleared to make way for almond trees and a ticketed park calling itself Badamwari. Only Waris Khan's well remains, a wire mesh stretching across the abyss below.

Old Badamwari was gone but some of its enchantments remained for a while. Residents of the area, human and otherwise, continued to rub along. Walking home one evening, PP's brother saw the outline of a gigantic shadow as he passed under a streetlamp. It was a *djinn*. In Devi Angan, PP and her family were close friends with their Pandit neighbours. So much chatter, so much laughter, their lives so entangled that they would run over and borrow supplies from each other without a second thought. When the *haalaat* arrived in 1989, their neighbours would leave Devi Angan. A couple of years later, PP and her family would also leave.

When she thinks about it now, those decades before the *haalaat* feel like a dream, lit by the neon sign of Firdous Cinema. To many in the quiet neighbourhood, the movie theatre brought the shock of the new. PP recalls the hooting and shouting of movie goers after the evening show, not without some disapproval. She only went to Firdous Cinema once. A group of five to ten girls had been dispatched to the cinema with an older cousin in charge. The cousin had omitted to buy dress circle tickets so they had to make do with grubby stall seats. *Izzat* (Honour), a full-blooded Dharmendra movie about revenge, oppression and sex appeal, was playing at the time. Half the girls slept through the film.

For others, movie halls like Firdous Cinema promised slightly contraband freedoms. KB went to the movies with gusto. He caught the night show, seven to ten o'clock, three times a week—two days to get away from power cuts scheduled for that time in the evening, and then on Fridays, which were holidays. Broadway and Regal were the posh cinemas: no black-market sales, people forming orderly queues for their tickets. Shiraz and Firdous, both in in the old city, offered more facilities. For instance, you could smoke in these halls.

Firdous Cinema, close to KB's home in Rajourikadal, was a favourite. For a rupee and a half, you got stall tickets right in front. The rows behind that were two and a half rupees. Dress circle tickets were five rupees and balcony seats seven rupees. If you went with a girl, especially if that girl was your future wife, you bought balcony seats. If you went with friends, you sat in the stalls. For five rupees, you got tea and cake. Five rupees also got

FIRDOUS CINEMA

you four skewers of kebab made from head meat. Cigarettes were lit, and when the film reached a particularly tense moment everyone had their head in a cloud.

KB was so addicted to movies that he once stayed over at his aunt's house just to catch a late show of *Muqaddar ka Sikandar* (Conqueror of Destiny) at Broadway. Returning home the next morning, he ran into a couple of friends who were on their way to the cinema, so he turned around and watched the movie again. Yet going to the movies was becoming increasingly dangerous. One day, he was going home after a show at Broadway when someone said, hadn't he heard, there had been a shooting in Rajourikadal. KB said no, he had not, he had been at the movies. When he went home he found his neighbour, a compounder, had been killed. Another day he was at Regal to watch a movie, he thinks it was *Jaws 2*, when there was a blast at the cinema. That was the last movie he ever went to see in a theatre.

In Hawal, too, intimations of the *haalaat* appeared around Firdous Cinema. CP remembers a gun went off one morning at the *chowk* right in front of the movie hall. That, he says, is when they knew the age of militancy had started. It was a warning shot fired in the air, as if to say, cinema halls will no longer be permitted. Certain militant groups did not approve of cinemas, just as they did not approve of *bhand paether* and *dastaangoh*.

Firdous Cinema had been an escape for CP since his childhood. When he was very small, his father took him to the cinema. After he turned twelve, he would go with a group of friends. Time was marked by movies watched at Firdous Cinema. *Bobby*, young love, 1973. *Sholay* (Embers), friendship and revenge served cold, 1975. Amitabh Bachchan, angry and rebellious in those years, was his favourite. They went to the pictures with open hearts, willing to be moved and changed. No policemen to stop them on the way, no tension. It was time stolen away from time.

When the *haalaat* arrived, they forgot all about the movies. Few people wanted the cinema halls closed at first. Besides, CP says, local thugs had built lucrative businesses around the cinema and they were not going to give those up in a hurry. But then the orders came. Some militant groups wrote an open letter saying cinema halls should be shut down. There was a blast at the nearby Shiraz Cinema, followed by the firing at the *chowk*. By the end of 1989, it was curtains for Firdous Cinema.

Forces moved in—first the CRPF, then the BSF and then the CRPF again. Turns out a movie theatre makes an excellent security camp. It is designed to keep the world out. The walls are windowless so no one can see inside. The walls are soundproof so no screams are heard outside. Firdous Cinema became Firdous Cinema Camp, a darkness enclosed by mesh wiring and one-tonnes. You never walked past it at night.

Crackdowns started in Hawal. Everyone stood outside shivering while their homes were searched. It seemed to CP that forces came from all directions. They had to catch militants, he says, but they caught civilians instead. They took away boys as young as ten or twelve. If you were rounded up after a crackdown, Firdous Cinema could be your first pit stop. According to ZB, the researcher, there was always a golden hour for release. If your family got to you while you were still at the local camp, it was well and good. If not, you were likely to be transferred a day later to bigger camps and it would be harder to get you out. If you were actually suspected of militancy and not just caught up in the dragnet, you could disappear into the bowels of the security system, maybe ending up at Hari Niwas or Papa 2, the top-notch interrogation centres. And then you could disappear altogether.

Firdous Cinema Camp acquired a force field. Over the next two decades, it became a magnet for militant attacks, starting with Ishfaq Wani's doomed attempt. Militants storming the camp in 2005 killed three CRPF men before being killed themselves. It was here that CP learnt the menace of large crowds. In the daytime, the current of people eddying around the camp offered

FIRDOUS CINEMA

anonymity. Should the person next to you reach into his pocket and pull out a grenade, what could you do? And should he hurl that grenade at Firdous Cinema Camp, and should that grenade ricochet off the mesh wiring and fly back into the crowd, what could you do? To CP it seemed there were fires everywhere.

The *haalaat* spread across downtown Srinagar like shockwaves from a blast, the epicentre at Nowhatta, with waves of decreasing intensity travelling to the peripheries. As it travelled to Hawal, it met the force field of Firdous Cinema, which had rippled through the neighbourhood. While some were moving into Hawal from the hotter parts of downtown Srinagar, others were leaving.

PP was home one May afternoon in 1990 when she heard *khatarnak*, deadly, firing. By then, they had become used to the sound of gunfire, but this was something else. It was as if the ground had split open. And then the screams. They were coming from the direction of the Islamia College, which had also been occupied by a camp. Forces had opened fire on a funeral procession for the Mirwaiz of the Jamia Masjid, assassinated earlier that day. It was a completely peaceful procession, PP says, making its way to the Eidgah graveyard.[2] Later, they would hear that over seventy people had been killed.[3] That the road outside Islamia College was slick with blood, boot upon boot, slipper upon slipper, all slick with blood. They knew then that their days at Devi Angan had come to an end.

As for CP, he found work outside the Valley that took him to Jammu, Punjab and other states. His old home near Firdous Cinema was not safe for young men anymore. How to describe the change that came over his life there? CP searches for the words. For the first twenty years of his life, he says, it was Jannat. Then it was Jahannam.

14

LIGHT AND DARK

In this cell, close to the road, MK can hear noises from outside. Big laughter, people talking, the horns of passing cars. Only a wall separates him but he feels he is not of that world, the world of everyday comings and goings, the daylight world.

Here, it is dark; he cannot tell if it is day or night. There is a gap the size of a brick through which food and water are pushed in. There is a cot to lie on, a tin pot to piss and shit in, another pot filled with water to clean himself with. On the third day, he is given clothes. Or what he thinks is the third day. He has lost track of time here. Each minute feels like a whole day. It is hell time, not the time of the daylight world.

His jailers are mostly Kashmiri. They beat him on his privates, push burning cigarette butts into his skin, hook him up with electric wires. The inside of his thigh has swelled up so much that he cannot bend it. We are only doing our duty, they tell him. When they are drunk, he knows it will be worse for him. The blows will fall harder and faster.

It is 2016 in the SOG camp in Awantipora, about thirty kilometres south of Srinagar. A few days earlier, MK was driving from his village in Kulgam district to the University of Kashmir in Srinagar. The police stopped the car and picked him up. MK will later say he was not sure why he was picked for detention. Yes, he had been protesting that summer, but so had all the boys he knew. And yes, one of his childhood friends had become a militant, but he had not heard from him since he went underground.

When the police brought him to the Awantipora camp, they put him in a cell with seven or eight others. They were stripped and beaten. One boy, Bilal, was beaten worse than the others. Seven years later, he would still be in jail, probably somewhere in Agra in the plains of North India. After a couple of days, MK was shifted to the cell with the brick-sized gap.

Here, in complete solitude, there is not much he can do but pray. And smoke. He is a chain smoker and allowed a continuous supply of cigarettes, although his family pays for them. Later, he will be told he spent eleven days at the SOG camp. From there, he will be shifted to a regular police lock-up in Awantipora. After two months in lock-up, he will find himself in a Srinagar jail.

Nine months after he was first picked up, he will be allowed to go back home. But how do you return to that world when you have known a darkness that is different from the earth's turning away from the sun, that is not simply a lack of light? He will never be free of this cell. His skin will be imprinted with cigarette burns and the tattoo of electrodes. Pain will shoot up his body every time he tries to urinate. He will keep to himself and drop out of college. Why bother when you will never get a proper job because there is a first information report to your name?

The FIR filed by the police four weeks after MK was first detained charges him with unlawful activities. It will keep him tethered to a routine of court appearances and police station visits. Every time anything happens—a new government order likely to cause public anger or a tourism summit for G20 dignitaries—he will be picked up and thrown into police lock-up for a few days.

There, he will meet others like him, men and boys who have done time at detention centres and camps. They will exchange notes about their time there, these former denizens of Jahannam, Narak, Hell, every underworld that any religion could think of.

* * *

What of the people outside, those who talked and laughed and drove past—what did they make of these places?

When the *haalaat* first broke upon the Valley, there was a great rush to find space for new torture centres, sorry, interrogation centres, sorry, detention centres. New camps were coming up, but regular camps alone would not be enough anymore. Space was found in abandoned cinema halls and hotels, of course, but also in government buildings. The famous Papa 2 had been a guest house for bureaucrats before it was turned into an interrogation centre. Space was found in schools.

These accommodations released a sudden darkness into the daylight world of classes, exams, sports days. The students of the Jawahar Navodaya Vidyalaya, Aishmuqam, got used to screams from the block of toilets behind the school buildings. They learnt to ignore the women waiting at the gates, begging for news of sons held captive in the same complex.

The Jawahar Navodaya Vidyalaya was the best school in the area, says PM, a student from one of the early batches; only the cream sat the entrance examination. Established in 1986 in Aishmuqam, a village in the hills of Anantnag district, it was a boys' school starting from sixth grade. Classes were initially held in someone's home, PM remembers. It became a boarding school after they shifted to a large complex shared with the department of mining and geology. As the militancy picked up, the mining department moved out and never returned. The home department allocated its empty offices to forces. As PM remembers, it was first the army, then the BSF, then the CRPF.

The school was now in a warzone, surrounded by bunkers. Forces stood guard at the gates and frisked the staff. Over time, they became friendly with the schoolboys. But this could change very quickly, remembers JB, another former student. If they got back from an operation where they had lost men, they would take it out on the students.

Past the gates, the two worlds within the complex rarely met. Students would see men being taken into the other half of the complex. Some were militants and some, PM realised as he grew older, were ordinary civilians suspected of a vague array of offences. In makeshift camps such as these, people could be held for months without judicial remand. They could, in other words, disappear without a trace.

At night, they were all penned in together, student and prisoner, teacher and jailer. During the daytime, the boys would pretend not to see the prisoners, not to hear the screams. But nobody taught them how to shut off that low thrum of fear, how to shake off that melancholy which settles on the shoulders and gathers weight.

One night, the camp entered the school. Militants had thrown a grenade at the complex and forces had returned fire. Sleeping students woke up to find light beams blading through the dark of the dormitory, casting about for the attackers. They crouched under the beds but there was nowhere to hide. The ground was flooded with light. PM thought that would be his last day.

Now a father of teenagers, he knows this much: a camp and a school cannot coexist.

* * *

As militant numbers dropped after a massive state offensive in the early 2000s, many of the camps started winding up. The

LIGHT AND DARK

buildings they had occupied started being restored to their original character. But you cannot shut down an underworld. It howls under the skin of the light, straining to break through.

The joint interrogation centre at Khanabal, on the edges of Anantnag town, had spilled over into surrounding buildings. It had taken over the Gujjar and Bakerwal Boys' Hostel across the road and the grounds around it. For several years, men were seen disappearing into the hostel. Some never returned.

After some years, Chief Minister Mufti Muhammad Sayeed began administering a 'healing touch' to the Valley, which seemed to entail tucking away the military where it would not offend. By 2005, the forces had moved out of the hostel building. Shortly afterwards, the Government Boys' Higher Secondary School moved in.

It was a *khaufnak manzar*, a terrifying scene, says FN, who was part of the school staff in those years. The old hostel premises were set amid a cluster of government buildings including the District Institute of Education and Training and the Government Degree College for Boys, Anantnag. But these respectable buildings stood around a compound with a square tank dug into the ground, used for unnamed purposes. One of the rooms on the ground floor of the hostel building still had wires attached to it. FN had heard that prisoners used to be interrogated here.

The ground-floor rooms were always dark in those early days. Students peering into them picked out the outline of blood stains on the walls and the shape of bones and nails—whether animal or human, they could not tell. It is said, when a new school wing was being constructed behind the original hostel building, the earth turned up skeletons.

The walls of the ground floor were whitewashed and fitted with lights. But school staff who spent time in the rooms reported headaches, fainting spells, a sudden increase in heart rate. These afflictions disappeared as soon as they left the building. Nobody wanted to stay on once the rooms were deserted after school hours.

Once, FN stayed back late as she was on examination duty. It was four in the evening; the students had left and she was saying her evening *namaaz*. A voice from one of the rooms cried out, 'Mummy!' But the building was empty, save for the sweeper cleaning up after the boys. He too had heard something—a voice crying, 'Baba!'

It must be psychological, reasoned PG, a former student of the school; a place of death will always be associated with death. The air remembers. The light, sliced open, may reveal a room within a room where every minute feels like a whole day.

Nearly two decades after the forces moved out, the government school is also gone and the building is a Gujjar hostel once more. Do underworlds ever close up and disappear? Or does a reconfiguration of bricks and air put an end to the disturbances they cause? How long does it take?

After a while in the new school premises, FN says, everything seemed fine. It was as if nothing had ever been there.

15

THE AFTERLIVES OF LAND

Land is political in Kashmir. Almost every family owns a patch of it. This may be enough for a small house and a strip of kitchen garden or acres and acres of orchards. If someone rents a house, they are regarded with pity. Such an unfortunate has no marriage prospects.

Most angry tirades against Sheikh Abdullah will end with a grudging nod to his land reforms. Yes, after he did away with big estates and distributed land to tillers, life got better for many people in Kashmir. Apart from the reforms, protections under Article 35A ensured that land in Jammu and Kashmir stayed with its people. In towns and villages, people grew familiar with the different kinds of land under this legal regime.

There is state land, owned by the government. There is *shamilat* land, village commons, which was not meant to be touched without the consent of the community. There is *milkiyat* land, private property. Almost every village and town has an Eidgah, open grounds used for congregational prayers that are also at the heart of community life. The Eidgah in Srinagar is owned by the Auqaf, the administrative body in charge of a number of Islamic institutions, including a range of mosques, shrines and schools. But in most villages, the Eidgah is held by the local mosque committee, or it is private land donated for public use.

The legislative changes of 2019 threatened to undo the Sheikh's reforms and did away with Article 35A. This was felt to be the worst blow—the erosion of the legal framework that had rescued Kashmiris from the tyranny of the Dogra regime. Land is central to a Kashmiri political identity. But it is not just the legal life of land that makes it important. Stories told about land give it another life beyond its material existence.

In these stories, there is no more *milkiyat*, no more *shamilat*, no more state land. Land is narrated into mythic realms where it cannot not be measured, valued and slotted into legal categories. These afterlives of land are also central to Kashmiri political identity.

* * *

It is said, Asadullah Parray was born in Hajin in North Kashmir's Bandipora district. He travelled down to Wanipora in Ganderbal district and stayed on, probably because he had family there. In his lifetime, Parray worked miracles and made a name as a *pir*. People from faraway villages came to visit him hoping to be healed or at least soothed.

Parray abjured the earthly realm in 1912, leaving behind strict instructions for his descendants. Clean my grave every day. Clean your house, which is next to my grave, every day. All visitors to Wanipora must be sheltered and fed, offered tea or sherbet.

For over a century, Parray has lain in the quiet graveyard in Wanipora, tended by his family. A *chinar* overhead catches the rays of the setting sun and directs them to his gravestone. There was a time when hundreds of his disciples would gather at the grave. It is consecrated land imbued with the same miraculous powers that Parray once possessed. It is said, the pir's protection still hangs over Wanipora. But more on that later.

THE AFTERLIVES OF LAND

Parray's grave lies along the main village road in Wanipora. On the other side of the road is a scrap yard owned by the water department and a government school. No traces left of the army camp that once sprawled across the land where the scrap yard and the school stand now. According to residents of Wanipora, the camp was built in 1997. Around 1998, they seem to recall, a new army battalion moved in. Anyway, that's when the visitations started. More on that later.

The army camp had skirted another graveyard that lies behind the school today. This, residents say, was built on *shamilat* land when militants started dying in Kashmir. The militant leadership of the time told the people of Wanipora to build a graveyard here and so they did. *Shamilat* land became a 'martyrs' graveyard'. It is said, the very soil is fragrant here.

Till the mid-nineties, it was mainly filled with foreign militants who arrived in legions to fight in Kashmir. When the army camp was built, the burials stopped for a few years. After the camp wound up, the burials started again. Mostly local militants but also other bodies. More on that later.

Three squares of land, three realms. Strange phenomena were observed when they rubbed up against one another.

Sometime in 1998, people living in Wanipora and surrounding villages noticed a new disturbance at night. Around ten or eleven o'clock, they would hear gunfire at the army camp. Soldiers said they were shooting at a figure who came charging at the camp from the direction of the pir's grave. The figure rode a white horse and brandished a sword. They opened fire but bullets did not seem to stop him. Residents of Wanipora did not see the figure. How could they? After dark, everyone was indoors, turning off the lights at the slightest sound.

Everyone except JP, who rose very early in the morning, before the sun was out, and went to an outhouse for his ablutions. JP was the pir's descendant and lived in the house next to his grave.

DAPAAN

He worked a government job but also had mystical leanings himself. He was a faith healer, with a range of amulets for various ailments and ointments which he would rub on boils and scars, chanting incantations.

One night, the soldiers cornered JP as he made for the outhouse, suspecting that he was behind the visitations. He protested that he had nothing to do with them. But he had a suggestion.

The soldiers had set up a latrine in the camp that lay directly across the road from the pir's grave. Such impurities would naturally anger so squeamish a pir as Asadullah Parray. The soldiers agreed to remove the latrine and the figure stopped charging towards the camp. JP sometimes saw him wandering through the trees when he went to the outhouse early in the morning. But they didn't bother each other.

Residents say the camp never quite settled in Wanipora. In a couple of years, it shifted out of the village road to the highway that passes by Wanipora. After that, it receded further. It would seem the wrath of the generally hospitable pir had left the soldiers in no doubt—some guests were not welcome in Wanipora.

The historian Dean Accardi writes that Sufi saints in Kashmir often represent an 'alternative bureaucratic order'.[1] Each saint has a sphere of influence, a jurisdiction centred on their shrines or graves. They preside over otherworldly kingdoms where healing and justice may be sought when earthly courts fail. This was powerfully felt after 1989, as thousands were killed or disappeared while courts and legislatures did nothing.

Accardi points out that two forces were at work at the same time. While ordinary people took refuge in saints, the government also found use for them. In early hagiographies, local pre-Islamic cultures are linked to mediaeval Sufi saints spreading their faith in Kashmir.[2] Sufi mystics of the Reshi order, such as Lal Ded and Sheikh Noor-ud-din Noorani, also known as Nund Reshi, are claimed by both Islamic and Hindu religious traditions.

THE AFTERLIVES OF LAND

Such mystics, the government decided, stood for '*Kashmiriyat*', an essential syncretism that foreshadowed Kashmir's natural union with a secular India. As avowedly secular governments gave way to Hindu nationalist governments in Delhi, the Hindu antecedents of Lal Ded and Nund Reshi were emphasised.[3] Either way, in the stories told by the government, the Sufi tradition was pitted against other forms of Islam that were rejected as alien and un-Kashmiri.

These appropriations, Accardi argues, were meant to weaken cultural links with saints and icons which were so essential to a Kashmiri sense of self. If the public could be made to abandon their saints to the state, they would also lose the independent cultural identity that resisted the state.[4] But he also suggests another possibility. What if, instead of surrendering to the state, Sufi saints and pirs became a 'geography of resistance'?[5] What if the state's reliance on such figures for cultural control of the Valley was amplified and used against it?

In Wanipora, ordinary residents were untroubled by the visitations. They recall, with faint amusement, how it was the army that was haunted by the spectre of the Sufi pir, who eventually drove them out of the village he was meant to protect. But the skirmishes were not just one-way. By the time it left, the army had also made incursions into the pir's kingdom.

SF, who grew up in Wanipora, remembers how the camp spread fear across the village. Suddenly, everyone was watched. Visitors had to register their presence at the camp. Over time, the soldiers grew friendly with residents but even these exchanges were guarded. Be seen talking to the soldiers too often and you could be labelled a *mukhbir*. Both sides were watching.

Not many boys from Wanipora joined the militancy but the village lay right next to Saloora, known to be a shelter for militants. Saloora was a large village surrounded by paddy fields and patches of woodland that came in handy when fleeing soldiers.

SF thinks it was to breach the militant stronghold at Saloora that the army set up camp in their village. The camp's new regime also choked off the flow of disciples to Parray's grave, striking a mortal blow to his kingdom.

Yet his disciples had been dwindling for decades, SF explains. While famous saints like Sheikh Noor-ud-din, Hamza Makhdoom and Mir Sayyid Ali Hamadani still held an important place in Kashmiri public life, more local mystics had started fading. Many considered the veneration of saints and shrines '*shirk*', idolatry that went against the principles of Islam. At best, the feeling went, these were superstitions that had worked for a poor, unlettered populace but did not sit well with a more modern understanding of Islam. Besides, SF recalls, there were militant commanders who were loved and admired who did not encourage the veneration of saints.

In Wanipora, there was new hallowed ground, the *shahid malguzar*, or 'martyrs' graveyard', where militants were buried. In the public vocabulary, militants are described as martyrs because they have sacrificed their lives for the *tehreek*. It is widely believed that to die a militant's death is to be assured a place in Jannat. According to Islamic beliefs, most people go to Jannat or Jahannam after their good deeds are weighed against the bad, but martyrdom wipes such accounts clean. The martyr reaches the gates of Jannat as pristine as the day he was born. Such martyrdom, it is said, leaves its mark in the very soil in which he is buried. The *haalaat* laid *shahid malguzar* across Kashmir, places where the soil was perfumed and the grass was greener, speaking of another world.

In 2006, Nazir Ahmad Deka was buried in the Wanipora 'martyrs' graveyard'.[6] He wasn't a militant. He was a perfume seller from Kokernag, killed and passed off as a Pakistani militant by the police.[7] Four such graves were discovered in Ganderbal district in early 2007, those of civilians killed by forces and buried

THE AFTERLIVES OF LAND

as militants. The usually quiet Ganderbal erupted in protest. Innocent lives had been extinguished by the state. So far as the public was concerned, they were also martyrs.

SF had been a teenager when they brought Deka to Wanipora; residents of the village had been pressed into service for the burial. He remembers seeing wounds on the body. He also remembers the police confiscated a few of Deka's belongings before he was buried—such belongings as a perfume seller who sold his wares on the streets of Srinagar might have on him. Some money and two bottles of attar. When Deka's body was exhumed a year later, SF was not allowed to see his face. But he remembers the fragrance of his body.

* * *

Kashmir is filled with such bodies. JM's father has heard of a militant who was buried in Anantnag district. He had died young, when his children were very small. Fifteen to twenty years later, they dug up his grave and found he had not changed. His body was whole and healthy as in life, not much older than his children were now. Not for him the mortal processes of decay and returning to dust.

So powerful is the martyrdom of militants that even the land will tell you they are in paradise, says JM. He thinks of the soil in which they are buried as *Jannat ke zameen*, the land of paradise.

In 1990, as the *tehreek* was gaining ground, people living near the Eidgah in Srinagar put up a sign on a new graveyard that said, 'Bihisht-e-Shuhada,' paradise of martyrs.[8] Some believe that as Islam spread in the Valley, Hamadani bought the Eidgah land and donated it to the public so that they had a place to pray. By the twentieth century it was owned by the Auqaf, but the public still felt it belonged to them. Even in 2022, when the Auqaf planned a cancer hospital on the Eidgah grounds, there were protests. The hospital was seen as a planned incursion into a space that was important to the *tehreek*.

DAPAAN

The vast open grounds of the Eidgah had always been central to public life in Srinagar. Apart from the big Eid prayers, major political rallies had always been held here. On most days, there were at least five games of cricket going on at the Eidgah. So when the *tehreek* started, it made sense to make room for the dead here, or at least, the public dead who were mourned by the community.[9] Residents of downtown Srinagar decided a square of the Eidgah land should be reserved for a graveyard. It was thought that all the people who died in the *tehreek* would be buried here but it soon became clear that one graveyard would not be enough. According to residents in the area, the Eidgah graveyard was expanded at least once but the last time they wanted to do so they were denied permission. Sectioned off by iron fencing, the Bihisht-e-Shuhada was no longer ordinary land that fit the language of deeds and transactions.

Mohamad Junaid describes a 'martyrs' graveyard' as not just a place but 'place-time', which holds bodies but also thoughts and memories.[10] The epitaphs in the Eidgah graveyard, with their names and dates, tell the story of the *tehreek* through the years. An empty grave waits for Maqbool Bhat, the JKLF militant hanged in Delhi's Tihar Jail in 1984. Ashfaq Majeed Wani, killed in March 1990, is buried here. Mirwaiz Mohammad Farooq, assassinated a few months later, has a raised grave at the back. From 1994, a man shot dead as he went to get milk. From 1995, Mushtaq Ali, the photojournalist killed when someone left a parcel packed with a bomb at an office in Srinagar. From 1996, three militants who had gone to surrender in a park in downtown Srinagar but were shot instead. From 2008, a Hurriyat leader who fell to bullets during a protest march called 'Muzaffarabad *chalo*', which was to cross the Line of Control to reach the town of Muzaffarabad on the other side. The last three militant graves date back to 2018. The last person to be buried there is a sixty-five-year-old man killed in 2020 as he was driving to Kupwara with his three-year-old grandson. Pictures that went viral online show the child still sitting on his grandfather's body while forces and militants exchange fire.[11] After that, says one resident of the Eidgah locality, no more burials have been allowed.

The graveyard itself embodies a history of defiance, all under the gaze of bunkers that surround the Eidgah. As researcher Umer Jan points out, death in the *tehreek* is imbued with the sacred. So the lands in which militants are buried are also considered sacred spaces, separate from the lands of the ordinary dead.[12] A custodian of the graves who died a few years ago was frequently interviewed by journalists. He reported a heavenly fragrance rising from militant bodies as well as the soil.[13] Residents of the Eidgah neighbourhood corroborate this—rotting bodies buried in the graveyard were healed and fragrant months later. RM grew up near the Eidgah and has heard stories about the graveyard all her life. How at night people heard the sound of women singing and boys playing cricket, just as they would have in life. How visitors to the graveyard were conscious of an unearthly calm. It is said that martyrs never die; they surround the living even if they have passed into the other world, explains RM. In such stories, the land enacts, again and again, the martyrdom of those buried there.

Such is the talismanic power of the Eidgah graveyard that burials there invoke otherworldly geographies. RM speaks of a woman whose brother was killed and buried there. She was still in deep anguish when, a few weeks after his death, she was admitted to a hospital for surgery. There, in an ether dream, she saw her brother, looking happy and well. He took her by the hand to show her the place he inhabited after death. Mirwaiz Mohammad Farooq was there, still reading the sermons that had been cut short. The woman claimed she saw paradise that day. Towards the end of the dream, her brother told her not to grieve as that was painful to him. It helped her make peace with his

DAPAAN

death, she said. Even the memory of the dream spreads calm years later.

* * *

In Kalaroos Khas, there is a shelf of land with young trees. Up close the trees are revealed to be standing on quiet mounds. Only a few have headstones. One says that a militant who lived in Sopore and was killed in 2016 is buried here. Another speaks of a militant killed in Kalaroos in 2006. One mound is a woman killed by a stray bullet in 1991, but she has no headstone.

The '*shaheed ma/guzar*' has almost melted back into the land. On a cold November day in 2023, a cow chews grass phlegmatically in the field below. The torn head of a toy rabbit lies in the mud. Women dry clothes on balconies overlooking the graves. It is easy to walk past the graveyard and not notice it is there.

Yet, in 2010, it was this graveyard that put Kalaroos in the newspapers and started a summer of protest. The bodies of three men, their faces disfigured, were dug up here.

It is a long drive north from Srinagar to Kalaroos, a bright green basin in Kupwara district. You must drive until you enter the Lolab Valley. If you could keep driving north, you would reach the Neelam Valley. But you cannot keep driving much further north. Before you reach the Neelam Valley, you will hit the Line of Control, which replaced the old ceasefire line in 1972. As soldiers took position in check posts along the LoC, Indian and Pakistani, eyeball to eyeball, it became one of the most militarised frontiers in the world. And the Lolab Valley became part of this frontier region, the edge of the navigable world in Indian-administered Kashmir. Kalaroos lies in the Lolab Valley, several kilometres from the LoC, but close enough.

Anthropologist Aditi Saraf locates Kashmir in a long frontier that stretches across the highlands of Central and South Asia.[14] This frontier, created by trans-Himalayan trade routes and the blurred edges of empires, enabled ebbs and flows, solidarities and rebellions that subverted national identities and enabled expressions of autonomy when the *tehreek* started.[15] The LoC, cutting across this frontier, tried to establish the logic of territorial control by a state. But what it really did was create a frontier within a frontier and new mythic geographies. Pakistan-administered Kashmir became Azad Kashmir in the lexicon of the *tehreek*, a region with such a powerful imaginative pull that thousands crossed the LoC for arms training. Foreign fighters, meanwhile, crossed over to fight in the storied Valley of Kashmir.

In the hinterlands of the Kashmir Valley, forces and militants were locked in an intimate battle. At the LoC, the fighting took a different form. Militants crossed over and militants crossed back in while the Pakistan Army allegedly provided cover fire and the Indian Army retaliated. News columns in Delhi and Srinagar filled up with reports of 'ceasefire violations' as the army foiled yet another 'infiltration bid'. But these battles took place far away from the news-producing capitals, often unwitnessed by civilian eyes. The official version of skirmishes, encounters and foiled infiltration bids would have to do.

The shadow area of the LoC, the frontier within a frontier, is a region at the edge of imagination for both Delhi and Srinagar: a place of improbable geographies where anything might happen. The natural laws of time and space might be suspended. So might the laws made by governments.

For instance, it is said the frontier along the LoC is dotted with graveyards where no laws apply. In 2008, the Association of Parents of Disappeared People published a survey of unmarked graves in the Uri area, which lies along the LoC in North Kashmir's Baramulla district.[16] Over eight thousand people had disappeared in Kashmir since 1989, the report said. They were summoned to camps and taken at crackdowns, or they just left for work one day and never returned. Many of them lay in these graveyards, the report suggested, buried as foreign militants.

DAPAAN

Residents of the frontier have their own improbable geographies, which compete with those of the state.

Before the three bodies were dug up, Kalaroos's only claim to a wider public imagination lay in the caves. The green basin holds a cluster of villages. At one end lies Kalaroos Khas, with its *'shaheed malguzar'*. At the other end is the hamlet of Lashtiyal. On a mountain above Lashtiyal is Satbaran, a row of seven stone doorways that lead nowhere, or so it seems. Behind the doors lies more stone. Nobody knows who carved out the Satbaran rocks and when. The mountain staggers up, shouldering forests of pine and deodar, until, about a mile above, the rock parts, first here, then here, and then further up, here again. It is said, the caves created by the parting of the rocks once led to Russia. That's why the name: Kalaroos, or Quila-e-Roos, Russian fort.

The hamlet of Lashtiyal clings sadly to the slope below. Most of its residents are poor and don't have much time to think about the past. Still, the caves and the Satbaran rocks looming over the village for generations have left their imprint on memory. Some people have heard that the stone doors were built by the Pandavas, the mythical princes from the Mahabharata, that it was a place for religious rituals. In these stories, the tunnels behind the caves are always impenetrable. It is said, the Pandavas went up the tunnels to see where they led. They sent a man up ahead with a drum. He was to beat the drum when he saw light at the other end of the tunnel. Except he fell asleep a little way in and the drum clattered to the floor. The Pandavas turned back at the noise, thinking he had seen light. Nobody explains why they did not follow him further into the tunnel.

The Russia myth is more recent. An elderly resident of Kalaroos Khas thinks it dates back to British times. MS, his grandson, thinks it goes back to the eighties. The old trans-Himalayan frontier running along the edge of empires appears briefly in these stories. Since the early nineteenth century, the

THE AFTERLIVES OF LAND

colonial government had entertained lively fears of a Russian invasion into British India. By the turn of the twentieth century, the British and Russian empires were locked in a Great Game for influence in Central Asia. The Dogra state of Jammu and Kashmir became vital to the British. It was to be a buffer against a possible Russian invasion of India. As the northern Himalayas heaved with spies and colonial expeditions, could stories about a secret tunnel have spread among the public?

Russia floated into the Kashmiri public sphere once more as it invaded Afghanistan in 1979, only to be driven out by the mujahideen, who were backed by Western powers. This development was watched with some interest in Kashmir. Before this, nobody had thought it possible that a superpower could be defeated by bands of mountain fighters. The war was covered in such detail by certain newspapers that some of the Afghan mujahideen became household names.[17] *Rambo 3*, in which a sweatband-wearing Sylvester Stallone helps the mujahideen fight Soviet forces, was a great hit in Kashmir.

In 2018, a team of American explorers went up the caves and said they didn't lead to Russia. But people in Kalaroos could have told you that much earlier.

'Where is Russia and where are we?' asks GS, who went up one of the tunnels in 1975. 'How many streams, how many mountains lie between here and Russia?'

Men from Kalaroos had journeyed up the caves for decades. So had their fathers before them. No one made it more than a few kilometres in. Their lanterns ran out of oil just as they heard sounds of water. Always, the rumours of water.

Once, it is said, the government had big plans for Kalaroos. Older men remember government officials prospecting for copper in the sixties and seventies. One of the caves is called Tramkheani, copper mine, but the mountain was never mined very much. Someone had seen survey reports for a dam, but that was decades ago and the dam was never built, either. It is said, the mountain is hollow and filled with water. If you break the Satbaran rocks, the whole area will drown. MS once put his ear to the rocks and heard the sound of water.

These geological rumours have lingered, blurring the difference between water and land, between this place and that. Teachers taking middle-school students on excursions to the Kalaroos caves will tell them firmly that the tunnels do not lead to Russia but then allow themselves to grow dreamy. Maybe the tunnels were part of the Silk Route once, an underground passage safe from storms and snow, linking Kashmir to Kabul, Kashgar and other places farther west.[18]

New wars bred new stories. Some residents of Lashtiyal recall that the army blasted one of the tunnels in the nineties because they suspected militants were hiding out there. Who knows where the tunnels might have led. If not Russia then maybe somewhere else. In Kalaroos Khas, many are of the opinion that the tunnels do not lead anywhere at all; they merely circle back into the mountain and open out at the army camp a few kilometres away.

It was this war, which laid army camps across the mountains and led to the traffic of men across the LoC, that gave rise to the plot with young trees. It was once *milkiyat* land meant for a mosque. But when the bodies started coming in from the LoC, the people of Kalaroos Khas decided to turn it into a graveyard. Most of the graves belonged to foreign militants. Or so they were told.

As a place for unmarked graves, Kalaroos had much to recommend it. It was not a long drive from the LoC. It was quiet. It was far from the noisy towns of Sopore, Baramulla and Srinagar, with reporters nosing around and this body or that body always asking questions and going on *hartal*.

The army would bring down bodies from the LoC and hand them over to the police, who would then instruct the local volunteer committee to bury them. They would arrange for shrouds and planks of wood to place in the graves. JH grew used to bodies, most of them in bad shape, their faces disfigured but still showing remnants of a seven-day-old stubble. Evidence, he thought, of a long trek through the mountains.

Nothing could shake him after what he saw in 1990, when he was about twelve years old. This was before land for the mosque was set aside for the graveyard. For two days, there had been shooting in the woods above the village. When it stopped, JH tagged along with a group of men into the woods. They saw Gujjar huts, burnt. Then they found a leg, then a head. He counted seventeen body parts in all. They dug three graves, buried the parts and left quickly. There was an army cordon still in place; nobody was supposed to be wandering about.

At first, JH says, they didn't want to bury strange bodies brought to them by the police. But when forces gave orders, what could you do? In those days, JH explains, people were pinned between two guns. When militants turned up and demanded shelter, you could not refuse. Then the forces arrived, tailing the militants. According to JH, there was not a single house in Kalaroos where someone had not been detained or 'interrogated', which, in Kashmir, means something more than being questioned.

JH himself was interrogated once, around 1992. Soldiers picked him up at night and took him to a nearby army camp. They put him in a room in complete darkness. As his interrogators flashed torches in his face, he could make out the shape of two or three beds. Then the interrogation started. Where were the militants, they asked as they filled him up with water. He knew where they were and he should give them up, they said as they attached wires to his knees and passed an electric current through them. They let him go the next morning. To this day, his right knee is always cold, even in summer.

DAPAAN

So in the spring of 2010, when the police called men from the village and asked them to bury three bodies, they could not refuse. The unidentified militants had apparently been killed in a shootout at Machil on the LoC. But JH remembers thinking those who crossed the border looked like they had not shaved in a week. These men looked as if they had not shaved in two or three days. A few local reporters took pictures of the bodies before they were buried.

For about a month, all was quiet. A distant shootout on the LoC was of little interest to most people in Kashmir, and in Kalaroos it had become routine. Then, suddenly, Kalaroos was everywhere, talked about in Srinagar, Delhi and who knows what other cities. The three graves were going to be dug up.

It rained the day they dug up the graves. People from faraway towns and villages had poured into Kalaroos Khas. MS was in the flood of umbrellas making for the graveyard at eight in the morning. Water everywhere, as though the mountains were finally giving up their secrets. When they opened the graves, it seemed to him the bodies were floating in water.

The graves belonged to twenty-year-old Riyaz Lone, twenty-seven-year-old Shahzad Ahmed Khan and nineteen-year-old Mohammed Shafi Lone.[19] They were all from Nadihal village in Baramulla district. Shahzad pushed a cart in Baramulla town, Shafi was a labourer and Riyaz worked as a mechanic. Money was always short so when they were offered jobs as army porters on the LoC, they went. Turned out the job had been to get shot and passed off as foreign militants.

A lot had happened in the month since the bodies were buried in the Kalaroos graveyard. The families of the three youths had held protests on a highway in Baramulla district and complained to the police that their sons had gone missing. The police had started investigating. Public interest in the disappearances had started growing across the Valley. Then, on 28 May 2010, an

THE AFTERLIVES OF LAND

article on the three bodies buried in Kalaroos appeared in *Kashmir Uzma*, an Urdu daily. The families recognised their boys from the pictures, and most of Nadihal drove up to Kalaroos for the exhumation.

A lot would happen in the months afterwards. Protests would start in downtown Srinagar. On 11 June 2010, a tear gas canister aimed at the protesters would hit seventeen-year-old Tufail Mattoo. The protests would turn into an uprising that would claim over a hundred lives and make national headlines. Briefly, the worlds of the frontier and the centre would meet.

For a moment, it seemed the Machil killings and the protests would bring up the bodies. In 2011, the police wing of the Jammu and Kashmir State Human Rights Commission found 2,730 bodies in unmarked graves in Kashmir.[20] Over five hundred were identified as local Kashmiris, not foreign militants. Investigators visited Kalaroos too and collected testimonies. Plans were made to collect DNA and identify the bodies so that they could be returned to their homes.

In 2014, when a military court handed out life sentences to five army men for their involvement in the staged encounter, Kalaroos shimmered into view in Delhi—if only at the edge of vision, if only as a place of graves. But then in 2017, the armed forces tribunal in Delhi, the military court of appeal, suspended the life sentences. The worlds of the centre and the frontier separated once more.

The other unmarked graves of Kalaroos kept their secrets. In 2019, when the Indian Parliament turned Kashmir into a Union Territory, the state human rights commission ceased to exist. There would be no more talk of disappearances.

In a land composed of so many stories, what difference do a few more make? A frontier is a good place to hide a story among other stories. So let it be said that Riyaz, Shahzad and Shafi were not poor workers from Nadihal but armed fighters trying to slip through the fence at the Machil sector of the LoC. Let it be said that, upon being told to stop, they opened fire and the army retaliated. Let it be said, that's how they died, in a skirmish, not killed in cold blood. And let it be said they were in 'Pathan suits' and not shirts and trousers when they were shot dead.

Nothing left to challenge this story but the plot with young trees, still considered sacred ground by the people of Kalaroos Khas. Prayers are offered there on Eid and other occasions. Each year, the trees reach closer to the sky.

Among the many stories told in Kalaroos Khas is a story of silence. It is said, a man from a nearby village once chanced upon a pir meditating at the Satbaran rocks. Do not tell anyone you saw me here, the pir warned him. But the man would not stay silent. He told others of what he saw and, soon afterwards, went mute.

CONCLUSION

DISMEMBERMENT

Now the lights have dimmed again at Tagore Hall. No security guards today. The hall is half filled as the sound of the *swarnai* pierces the dark. Maybe others, like me, have come because they were intrigued by the poster quietly passed around on WhatsApp. A beetle-browed godman with a trident. This was not how I had pictured the story of Akanandun, a folktale told to children in Kashmir. The *bhands* have chosen Akanandun for today's show.

Once again, the *maskharas*, bright in floral caps and shirts, wheedling the audience with their jokes. They usher in a *fakir*, who starts telling a story. Once there was a king and queen. Enter king and queen. They had seven daughters but no son. Enter seven daughters, all unfortunately named—Pride, Lust, Rage. The king and queen still pined for a son.

Then one day, a *sadhu*, a godman. Enter godman, his followers trailing behind him, for such a man is not just one man but a crowd. This entrance is an event. The godman carries a trident that towers above his head. He bangs it on the juddering ground and bellows, '*Jai Nirankari!*' Oh, Formless One!

He offers a deal. The king and queen will have their son but after twelve years he must be returned. The king and queen will take anything at this point. A son is born. They name him Akanandun: the only one, the beloved one. His seven sisters dance with joy and twelve years pass.

The godman returns. *Jai Nirankari*, it is time to keep your pledge. Not only must Akanandun be returned—he must be killed, dismembered and cooked. The mother weeps and pleads, the male actor's voice suddenly adding heavy notes of tragedy. It is no use. Trembling, she receives the hatchet with which she must kill.

The murder takes place at the back of the stage, behind a screen of white. The queen emerges with a pot of something, the flesh of her son, whom she has just killed and cooked. She walks to the front of the stage, beyond the proscenium, and lets it crash into the auditorium.

Now the godman returns to tell her she must lay eleven places at the table—one for him, one each for her seven daughters, the king and herself, and finally one for Akanandun. For Akanandun? The mother is speechless now, shock upon shock, grief upon grief. She has just killed him with her own hands.

And then Akanandun returns, alive and whole once again. It had been a test, says the godman, suddenly all munificence. The seven daughters were seven weaknesses who had to be transcended before Akanandun could be reached. Akanandun, the only brother of seven sisters, who was pure soul, *mana*. The old folktale made no bones about patriarchy.

The audience blink as the lights are turned up in Tagore Hall, their heads still ringing with the rap of the trident on wood. They have grown up with the story of Akanandun. The name has become a term of endearment for sons who are excessively loved. But now this claim to divine justice does not convince. The young boy returning pales beside the figure of the *sadhu* making terrible demands in the name of some inscrutable god.

This is Kashmir four years after 5 August 2019. Maybe they are thinking of another powerful man who invokes his god as he

CONCLUSION

promises jobs, economic development and peace while he takes away their sons. Or maybe they are thinking of how even the king and queen, local rulers both, must bow to this distant godman. This is the *phir kath* of our times, says Arshad Mushtaq, the director. A silent exchange between the players and the audience to say that all is not well, has not been well since 2019, even if the gods of development have descended on the Valley.

It is for the good of the people, the *markaz* had said as it struck down autonomy under Article 370, locked up former chief ministers and *azadi* leaders and moved its bureaucrats into Srinagar. It is for their good, the *markaz* had said, as it tore up Article 35A. It is for the people, as it dismembered the state of Jammu and Kashmir and declared its constitution a piece of fiction.

Maybe, as they stream out of Tagore Hall, the audience are thinking of the mother bending over her child's torn body. Ahad Zargar, a Sufi poet who wrote the story of Akanandun in Kashmiri verse, made much of the dismemberment. The poem left a powerful impression on Mushtaq. Every part of the body served up to the godman is described in detail. Here are the eyes and ears, portals to the outside world; here the limbs. The heart must also be served in the end. In Sufi poetry, Mushtaq explains, the heart is not blood and muscle but a form of consciousness. Every attachment to the world, every part of the known self, must be given up to reach the heart.

Maybe the audience are thinking of other mothers bending over other bodies, unable to grieve. There are mothers who pressed Kalashnikovs into their sons' hands and sent them to their death. This was a sacrifice to which they had agreed. Then there are mothers who had not agreed, whose sons were taken into custody and suddenly died of heart failure. The *haalaat* filled Kashmir with people who had died in custody. Cause of death: the heart stopping.

There are mothers who wonder what sacrifice it will take to bring back their sons. For years, in the mountains of Ganderbal,

DAPAAN

JM's grandmother would invite the imam for dinner on the day her oldest son disappeared. It happened sometime in the late nineties. A soldier posted in their village had said something about her daughter, JM's mother, as she returned from classes at the local seminary. Something that made her brother's blood boil. He picked a fight with the soldier and beat him up. Twenty days later he disappeared. They tried looking for him in camps and police stations but soldiers would visit their home and beat up everyone in return. They stopped looking for him. Two years later, JM's mother was to get married. All the guests were inside the wedding tent and her father was outside, making final arrangements for the feast, so nobody saw the gunmen as they walked up and put sixteen bullets in him. They know this because they have kept the sweater he wore that night, white, with sixteen bullet holes in it.

So every year, JM's grandmother would make *wegre*, rice porridge flavoured with cumin seeds, to mark the day she last saw her son. They call it the *vaharwaer*, the anniversary, not of his birth or his death but of his disappearance, which was something of both. During the day, before the imam came to dinner, women and children would pour in to eat *wegre*, sing songs and talk about JM's uncle. At night, when everyone had left, JM would hear his grandmother humming quietly. He caught snatches of Habba Khatoon songs. Come, my lover of flowers. Let us go gather basil, my friend, he wounds my heart with an axe.

But when they moved away from the old village, the gatherings stopped. The web of friends and relatives who knew JM's uncle and mourned him was lost in this new place. And a gathering of strangers could not be trusted. What if there were informers? It could be considered seditious to even grieve sons who disappeared. So the gatherings stopped. But JM's grandmother still made *wegre*, hoping it would bring her son back.

And every month in Srinagar, a group of ageing men and women would go to Pratap Singh Park, named after the third

CONCLUSION

Dogra king, a cool length of green opposite the newspaper offices of Press Colony, surrounded by the noise of Lal Chowk. This was the Association of Parents of Disappeared People, a group formed by Parveena Ahangar after her son was taken one night in 1990 and never seen again. The parents in the park carried fading pictures of young men, taken twelve, fifteen, seventeen years ago, each month the time lengthening a little, every year the shops around them changing. First, shops selling embroidered *pherans* and shawls, the old Pandit sweet shop and Ahdoos, the hotel rumoured to make an excellent *gushtaba*, a dish of meatballs in a rich yoghurt gravy, favoured by tourists and agencies. Then, mobile phone stores, a new gelato place, a cafe downstairs from Ahdoos. And still they sat in Pratap Park every month with their ageing posters.

At first, the journalists in Press Colony took note and there were stories; Ahangar's picture in the papers; pictures of pictures of the disappeared. Other parents and wives became known through their stories. Mugli, the single mother from Habbakadal who wouldn't stop asking where they took her son until the day she died.[1] A village near the LoC named Dardpora, 'the place of pain', where so many men disappeared that it became a village of half-widows, women who were not fully widowed because their husbands could not be declared dead.[2] Stories spread through protests, newspapers and reports by human rights groups, held in the pool of common talk. Calendars published by the APDP and the Jammu and Kashmir Coalition of Civil Society, a federation of human rights organisations, carried pictures of the disappeared. Pratap Singh Park became a public square and the faces of the disappeared rose to the surface like reflections in a pool. Not life or death, but something in between that would have to do.

After August 2019, the monthly protests disappeared. All protests disappeared at the park. A group of women holding placards that said 'Release All Detainees' and 'Resist to Exist' were hastily bundled into a van and taken to a police station. The police chief announced no protests would be allowed until the situation improved, as if the situation—the arrests, the lockdown and the communications blackout—had nothing to do with the government.

Pratap Singh Park was soon claimed for the Balidan Stambh, Martyrs' Memorial, a colonnaded pavilion whose name echoed the Sanskritic Hindi of the plains. The home minister, who flew in to unveil the foundation stone, clarified which martyrs were being commemorated—the martyrs of the Jammu and Kashmir Police, to encourage patriotism among Kashmiri youth. By the time bulldozers entered Pratap Singh Park to gouge out trenches in the green, members of the APDP and the JKCCS had been raided or arrested. Terror funding, said agencies. By the time selfie points were laid in the streets around Lal Chowk, slogans wiped off the walls and murals painted instead, Press Colony had almost been emptied out, the throng of journalists replaced by one-tonnes to guard a newly formed anti-terror wing of the police. Srinagar is going to be a Smart City, said the officials of the *markaz*, just like Delhi, Pune, Ahmedabad, cities downloaded straight from the internet, so full of modern conveniences there would be no place for silly politics.[3] Lal Chowk, Rajbagh, Zero Bridge, the Jhelum riverbank, all lit up one by one in patriotic tri-coloured lights, glittering so brightly no one would notice the drones blinking above in the skies, watching.

Jammu and Kashmir is to be reorganised, the *markaz* had announced in 2019, taken apart and put back together, new and improved. To reorganise a place, it is not enough to take down its government and rewrite its laws, to tear down buildings, dig up roads and change the physical shape of things. It is not even enough to rename government offices and stadiums so that there is no memory of what has been. To reorganise a place, it is necessary to kill its stories. It is necessary to take apart the public

CONCLUSION

sphere that held these stories—walls, parks, marketplaces, news pages, web pages.

Most local newspapers got the memo. In the first half of 2024, all the news is health and wellness, drug busts, inaugurations, flyovers. If there is a gunfight or a skirmish, only the official account is published, dutifully copied from the press release sent out by forces or agencies. Meanwhile, online platforms are suddenly flooded with news videos which tell lurid tales of thefts, stabbings and sexual crimes. At official functions, it is forbidden to refer to the *haalaat* because all is now well. Slogans painted in marketplaces have gone through a mysterious rewrite. Walls which once said, 'Go India, Go Back,' now carry the cryptic message, 'Good India, Good Back'. One shutter in downtown Srinagar said, 'We Want Freedom,' to which someone has thoughtfully added, 'From Stonepelters'. At the morning bakeries, conversations have turned cautious. The *haalaat* have become a rumour, carried by the winds, hanging low in the clouds.

On 29 April 2024, three days of incessant rain threaten floods. The rivers are swollen and angry, rising until they meet *chinar* branches drooping along the banks. The mountains are spitting stones and shaking down earth on passing cars. Already, in Sonamarg, the waters have pulled a van into their depths, taking five tourists. In Jammu's Reasi district, they have claimed two women trying to cross a stream on their way to a wedding; in Doda district, a thirteen-year-old boy. In South Kashmir's Qazigund, they have eaten a hole into a bridge. In Srinagar, the waters are seeping into mounds of earth disgorged for flyovers, swirling in the craters left behind, filling up the sunken track of a new joggers' park. Panic is rising because no one has forgotten the floods of 2014, just a decade ago. Two-storeyed houses were filled with rain back then and nothing seems to have changed. Smart city, everyone is muttering, weighing the words like bombs.

The waters of the Jhelum near Lal Chowk are almost high enough to declare a flood. As I walk along the river a day later, the waters are still tugging silently at the banks. It seems to me they carry shredded newspapers from Press Colony and the vanished reels of Doordarshan Srinagar along with the refuse of hotels. Further downstream, they will gather chicken feathers; the remnants of a *wazwan* meal; the discarded coals of a *kangri*; the lid of a copper samovar, finely carved. Further still, the lines of a Friday sermon, never delivered; the *pheran* of a young man, never found; spit that was spat out at Zainakadal, rich with rumours. I see the river has pulled down the cheek of a houseboat, as if to say what cannot be said. Brown waters roping higher and higher along the banks are speaking in many voices. Young men, old men, young women, all speaking in voices of water, telling many stories that are really one story.

'We had a warm winter. It did not snow. So now we have to bear the rain and cold in April. Nature must find its level. If for five years snow does not fall and the sun does not shine as it should, there will be a big flood. This place is like a baby laid bare to the elements in the middle of a storm. This place is like a naked *fakir* at the mercy of the elements; all he can ask for is a loaf of bread. Losing Article 370 felt like being stripped. After 2019, people are worried about their future. We tried everything, from politics to militancy, but nothing changed. Snakes have two kinds of venom: one heats the blood, one freezes it. There are two kinds of *zulm*. One is short view; you see it in clashes on the street. The other is long view, what is happening now. Calm on the surface but repression underneath. We cannot say anything—hundreds in jail. This silence is birthing future agitations. This silence is a bomb.

'There have been periods of silence before, followed by periods of turmoil. In the eighties, there was anger about the 1975 accord. It was followed by militancy. From 2002 till 2008, all was quiet. We forgot what militancy was. Then the 2008 Amarnath uprising happened. After that there was a decade of turmoil until

CONCLUSION

2019. Someday, this too will change. After 2019, everyone is ready to take up arms for Article 370; they've forgotten *azadi* for now. There's a shortage of guns, otherwise everyone would join. Two things you cannot take away from Kashmiris: their love for Pakistan and their demand for *azadi*. The commander who got me into the Hizb said we are living like slaves under *zulm* because those who rule us are not Muslims; we need to be free. If we knew in 1995 that Pakistan would betray us, I would not have done it. In 1990, I told the leaders of the *tehreek*, sheathe your swords, we'll fight a political battle. We would have lost fewer lives and got somewhere. This is a religious fight, a civilisational fight, not a political fight. There are forty-eight countries like us, Muslim countries. It is another matter that the Indian government politicises everything.

'Time stretches and contracts. Sometimes, when people say thirty years of conflict, it feels absurd. Have thirty years really gone by? But then, when you think of dates, Gawkadal and Bijbehara [massacres in the early nineties, when protesting civilians were shot down by government forces], the uprisings of 2008, 2010, 2016, it does feel like a lot of water has flowed under the bridge. And during crackdowns, when they searched room after room, the minutes seemed to pass very slowly. All suffering is slow. The first dead body I ever saw was down the road from my house. A boy had been killed as a policeman's gun went off. He had been playing when the bullet entered his stomach. When a bullet enters the body, it makes a small hole, but when it leaves, it makes a ghastly wound. They took my father and grandfather for three days, gave them no food, made them clean a house they had blown up, made them take out the bodies. This was *begaar*. One militant's body had a torn jaw. My father was a tailor. They gave him a piece of leather and told him to sew it on. After that, every time he sat at his sewing machine, he would think of that body. In 2005, five Gujjars were used as human shields and killed in the mountains of Bandipora district. Then their bodies were dragged across the snow to be buried. One young man had mehndi on his hands because he was going to be married soon. His mother told us this, sitting over the body. She said it quite clinically. They arranged hot water for his final ablutions, a luxury he could not afford in life. During the 2016 protests, I remember photographing a boy from Sopore brought into a hospital with bullet injuries. Blood flowed from the stretcher and down the ramp. I stared until someone pushed me.

'Militants also killed. Women were killed for being army informers. If you were seen close to army camps, talking to army people, you were under suspicion. You could be killed on perception. One man, a supporter of the National Conference, lived near the house of Ali Mohammad Sagar [long-time National Conference legislator from downtown Srinagar]. One day, CRPF men asked him where they could find meat. He guided them to a shop. For that, militants shot him and banned people from attending his funeral. Later, when they investigated further and found he was not a *mukhbir*, they offered to have him buried in the Eidgah martyrs' graveyard. But his family said no, he was fine where he was. It was Eid. I was collecting donations outside our mosque. I was giving this man a ticket when the bullet went through him and got lodged in my arm. He was said to be a *mukhbir*. There had been many attempts on his life. In one attack, his wife was killed and his children injured. After that, he went underground and his brother joined Al Jihad. There was a civil war between the Hizb and Al Jihad in the early nineties. That Eid was the first time the *mukhbir* came out of hiding to visit home. Hizb militants killed him. Militants used to squeeze my father for money because he was in the National Conference. Militants and Ikhwan used to squeeze my father for money because he was in the police. The Ikhwan came to our house and asked for Eidhi [cash gifted by older relatives or family friends on

CONCLUSION

Eid]. My father said he had five hundred rupees to give. They got angry and threatened to open fire on the house if he did not give them five thousand rupees. He did not. But they did not either. Another time, militants came asking for money. My father looked at one of them, a local boy, and said, get lost, till yesterday, you were stealing chickens. They got lost.

'If we could get back all the time we gave to the *tehreek*, what would we do with it? My classmate became a militant. He used to carry a gun in school. A lot of kids did in those days. It was a style statement. In the nineties, when we were teenage boys, we wouldn't sleep at home, we would spend the night in the fields. '*Shaal tsaelith, baithan lohri.*' The jackal has left, we're still waving sticks. We used to say this after crackdowns. They [the militants] had fled but civilians were still being beaten up. In Habbakadal, I had two Pandit teachers, Sita and Gita. One day they were gone. Even now, sometimes, people will jump when crackers are burst at weddings. It reminds them of gunfire. In Anantnag town there was a militant called Raju. We nicknamed him Rajiv Gandhi. When he was killed, even the policeman involved in the encounter did a salute, such a deadly militant was he. In 2005, I was walking on the road in Anantnag, past an auto rickshaw that had been rigged with a mine. The deputy inspector general's cavalcade was also passing through and there was a blast. The police started firing at me first, thinking I was a militant. Afterwards, I spread word that there should not be mine blasts in crowded areas, and then there was a check on such blasts by militants. Dogs did not bark for militants; they only barked when the military came to villages at night. The army came to our house and beat up my brother, my father, my uncle, everyone. We found my uncle's glasses in the drain outside. When they were leaving, the special task force men who were with the army took my brother's watch. It was a new watch, with a train to mark the minutes. The army would take wood from our mill.

DAPAAN

They always paid. But when the Wandhama massacre happened, twenty-three Pandits killed in one day, they broke into our mill and took firewood to cremate the bodies. They didn't pay that day. When I was small, I would go to our neighbour's house and play, and they would come to ours, even after dark. But then, the walls we built in our hearts.

'In Kashmir, the economy is seventeen percent agriculture, twenty-five percent industry, eight percent horticulture, fifty percent trade, thirteen percent conflict. Sheikh Noor-ud-din called this place *'soan Pampore'*, golden Pampore [an area in Pulwama district known for saffron cultivation]. He prophesied that if saffron was cultivated elsewhere, it would disappear from Pampore. And that is happening. The government is trying to grow saffron in other districts and saffron is disappearing from Pampore. Now the shopkeepers of Zainakadal sit mum at their shops, with folded arms. In Kashmir, only people who have approval of the *markaz* can come to power. They have no self-respect, so why should others respect them? I was the National Conference's *mohalla* president in the 2000s. After August 2019, they were looking for my son and me. I was ready to join the Bharatiya Janata Party [the ruling party in India since 2014] to save my son.

'People tell their children, *kar tsoppe*, be quiet. But this is a deliberate silence, an understanding among the masses—do not reveal yourself yet. When Burhan died, we thought it was over. I think it is not over yet. My younger brother and sister don't care about the *tehreek* anymore. They say it held them back, both sides held them back. They want to get ahead. But there are many who have fathers and brothers in jail. They cannot forget. This is not peace. This is a pretend calm. Everyone gets up and goes to work pretending they're okay. I was a journalist, I was a storyteller, but now I work in pharmaceuticals, of which I know nothing.

'When we were growing up, there was so much *zulm* in the present, there was no time to think of *zulm* in the past, in

CONCLUSION

Mughal, Pathan, Sikh, Dogra times. Our folktales had monsters. Things that were talked about in secret—we turned them into stories and put them out. The Indians turned themselves into these monsters; they became the *raantas*, throwing stones at night, cutting off women's braids. Kashmiri women became the *raantas* in the coloniser's fantasies. Sometimes, they were beautiful and desirable; reversing Article 370 would mean Indian men could marry them. At other times they were ugly, unwashed, demonic like the *raantas*. You can't draw a map of Djinn Mulk or Peristan. People would often visit the 'martyrs' graveyard'. Not just relatives of militants buried there but the public. Now they've stopped going because of the *haalaat*.

'Our sufferings would fill a book. When this is over, it will become written history. The Dogra, Sikh, Afghan eras, their histories were written afterwards. Kashmir has five and a half thousand years of written history. Even the Nilamata Purana [a sixth-to-eighth-century epic text on Kashmir] talks about insiders and outsiders, an identity defined by the sense of being a different race living in the mountains. I love Agha Shahid Ali. I really wanted to study his poems but they took him off our syllabus. This is how forgetting starts, with the textbooks. Till 2008, I felt Indian, I thought Gandhi was my leader—I grew up reading NCERT textbooks [published by the National Council of Education, Research and Training, and prescribed for school students in India]. Then the Amarnath protests happened and everything changed. The tri-colour [of India] everywhere and other symbols of occupation—people are silent about them. That is also a sign of the times. But you never know when it will change. A bomb is forming. It is accumulating slowly.'

After two days of threatening floods, the waters recede and the Jhelum loses its intimacy with houseboats and low-hanging *chinars*. Absurd to think, in the bright-blue sunshine of late spring, that the river spoke in voices, because of course rivers do

DAPAAN

not speak. Anyway, someone is grumbling, the waters would not have gone up so much if the government had not insisted on building a raised railway line smack bang in the middle of the Jhelum flood bowl. As it stands, the river will carry its sad refuse to the Wular, where it will sink to the bottom of the lake or be tugged onwards into lands further west.

But something must have stirred in the rain-awakened earth, for roses have bloomed overnight. Who knows what else has been coaxed out of the ground—wild flowers, summer grasses, the last golden burst of mustard. In the mountains, pine sap is oozing out of bark, sharp and sweet. And in one mountain above Akingam, maybe the rain has drawn out a snake that lives in a spring next to the shrine of two vegetarian Sufi saints. It is said, the spring is sister to the two saints. Their father, also a saint, is buried at the bottom of the mountain, by the highway. His seven children are scattered all over the Anantnag mountains. The siblings are whimsical. They have planted upside-down trees in parts of the forest.

Once, the *bhands* of Akingam and Mohripora would have danced at their shrines, praying for rain, crops, miraculous cures. Once, the tears of Gannak would have fallen with the rain. Few people in Akingam know where the gardens of Gannak are anymore. And if you ask, they look worried. What do you want with open land—you want to buy it? They look worried too when asked for directions to the Akingam Cultural Centre, gathering dust down the highway. What is this, some sort of government survey?

Once, the snake would have hissed at meat-eating pilgrims but few pilgrims go to the shrine now. Maybe something else has drawn the snake out of her spring today. Maybe she is swaying her head from side to side because she hears snatches of song and laughter. The *bhands* are performing again. They are doing a play they have never done before. Something to do with soldiers cir-

CONCLUSION

cling a neighbourhood and disappearing boys. Something about a *raantas* dragging women off by the hair. Now the players break into a wedding song and the story gets confusing. Anyway, this cannot be happening because *bhands* hardly ever perform at the shrine anymore.

Still the snake sways her head, keeping time to a silent tune. The light catches the outline of robed figures with pointed caps, the glint of a *swarnai*. Then it dissolves. Now a shaft of light slants through the trees, catching the outline further up the mountain. Then it dissolves once more into sunshine and leaves. But there it is again, dancing on the crest of the mountain one last time before it disappears. As if to say, it is said, it is said, everything happened. Nothing happened. Everything happened.

ACKNOWLEDGEMENTS

It took a Valley to write this book. There are many people who have been essential to the words and stories in this book whom I cannot thank by name. I hope someday, in better times, I will be able to do so. For now, I name those I can.

This book would not have been possible without the strength, courage and patience of Safwat 'Dada' Zargar, who always knows a guy but despairs of my shoe choices and my Urdu, and of Naveed Iqbal, Kashmir's top purveyor of cookies. It would not have been possible without the care and friendship of Muneeb-ul-Islam and Sameer Mushtaq, who always know a good place to go for a kebab; without the thoughtfulness of Peerzada Arshad Hamid and Mehraj D Lone, who always know what to say to a journalist in a panic. It would not have been possible without Iliyas Rizvi, the original collector of stories and walker of cities, and Rayan Naqash, stringent critic and active listener. It would not have been possible without Hilal Shah, who will not only climb every mountain but also help you up, and the brave Shafia Bhat, who went with me on many long walks to protect me from leopards.

For impromptu Kashmiri lessons, I thank Asif Tariq Bhat; for impromptu trips to the police station and much more, I thank Zaid Bin Shabir. For their courage to tell the story and sheer

ACKNOWLEDGEMENTS

gusto, I thank Shafat Farooq, Khalid Bashir Gura, Junaid Manzoor Dar and Faizaan Bhat.

There are people whose sense of a place is so vivid, so intensely imagined, it becomes a life force that makes the place real to others. Kashmir was real to me long before I visited, thanks to my colleague Muzamil Jaleel. It became a fully realised place through conversations with Parvaiz Bukhari, Hilal Mir and Basharat Masood.

All of this started because Naresh Fernandes and Supriya Sharma, my editors at *Scroll.in*, took a chance on a new reporter, sent her to Kashmir and encouraged her to follow her interests. Pure madness, and for me, pure luck. I am deeply grateful for them and for my other colleagues at *Scroll*, especially Arunava Sinha, Shoaib Daniyal, Sruthisagar Yamunan and Arunabh Saikia.

Friends in Delhi, Kolkata and other cities also made sure the book got written. Christine Franciska gave me a pen with which to write the book before I knew I was going to write it. Ruth Scobie and Parnisha Sarkar kept up a flow of Buster Keaton gifs and thoughtful comments. Anisha Sharma, Meghna Choudhary, Niloshree Bhattacharya and Madhuri Karak were early sounding boards. Indranee Ghosh opened up her own rich store of folktales. Anumeha Yadav, Samit Basu, Priyanka Kotamraju, Devika Shankar and Bini Ghosh put up with far too many hours of agonising. Meghna Nayak and Dhvani Mehta intervened with well-timed revels. Warisha Farasat and Shudarshana Gupta chipped in with valuable inputs. I am also very lucky to have a collection of fiery aunts who took such a keen interest in my work that this felt like a book worth writing.

I cannot thank my agent, Kanishka Gupta, enough for making this happen and my fabulous editors at Hurst, Lara Weisweiller-Wu and Farhaana Arefin, for turning a manuscript into a book.

Finally, my long-suffering family—my grandmother, Sunanda Datta; my parents, Rahul Chakravarty and Suchandra Chakravarty;

ACKNOWLEDGEMENTS

my sister, Amrita Chakravarty—through some superhuman strength only known to them, put up with me as I grew increasingly batty these past two years. Their strictures, their trenchant critique and their misplaced conviction that I'm the cat's whiskers are what held me together as I wrote this book. All my love to them.

GLOSSARY & ABBREVIATIONS

Kashmiri, a language of Dardic origins, has picked up Arabic, Persian and Sanskrit influences over time. Many of the words in this glossary are used across Kashmiri, Urdu and Hindi today.

Azadi	Freedom. The word is often used as a shorthand for Kashmiri political aspirations.
Bhand paether	Folk theatre.
Bhoot	Ghost.
Chalo	Literally, the word is a verb meaning 'let us go', but in the political vocabulary of South Asia, it has almost become a noun, standing for a march or procession.
Chowk	A town square usually surrounded by markets. It can also be a road junction or roundabout.
Daen	A witch or a demonic woman who often crops up in folk tales told in many parts of South Asia. In most of Jammu and Kashmir, *daen* may be used interchangeably with *raantas*. In some pockets, there are subtle differences between the two—a *daen* could be

DAPAAN

Dapaan	an ordinary woman with supernatural powers while a *raantas* is a supernatural being. 'It is said.' Kashmiri stories often begin with *dapaan*, the equivalent of saying 'once upon a time'.
Dastaangoh	A traditional form of storytelling. The word applies to the art form as well as the storytellers.
Fakir	Traditionally, a travelling religious ascetic who lives on alms.
Haalaat	Conditions. In Kashmir, the term is often used to refer to political conditions and life in the armed conflict that spread after 1989.
Hartal	Strike. Shops and offices are closed and work is suspended as a form of political protest.
Khilafat	Usually translated as 'caliphate' in English, it broadly refers to the Islamic state that existed in the centuries after the death of Prophet Muhammad. In South Asia, the word has other political resonances. The Khilafat movement of the early twentieth century was an anti-colonial mobilisation where Indian Muslims sought to rally around the Ottoman caliph as they agitated against the British empire.
Ladi shah	A satirical poem recited in a sing-song manner by travelling minstrels. Both the singer and the song are called *ladi shah*.
Magun	A word used to describe an exceptionally talented *bhand*, or folk artiste. He can direct performances, act, sing, dance and play many musical instruments.

GLOSSARY & ABBREVIATIONS

Markaz	Power centre. In Kashmir, it usually refers to the Indian capital of Delhi.
Markaz ki chaal	The ploys of the powers that be. *Markaz ki chaal* is at the heart of many conspiracy theories in Kashmir.
Maskhara	Jester.
Milkiyat	Land that is privately owned.
Mohalla	Neighbourhood.
Mukhbir	An informer working for the government or security agencies.
Naga	Mythical inhabitants of Kashmir, half serpent and half human.
Nebrim	Outsider.
Nizam-e-Mustafa	Order of the Prophet, part of a slogan made popular by the Jama'at-e-Islami.
Peri	A fairy in Persian mythology.
Pheran	Loose robes worn by both men and women in Kashmir.
Phir kath	Literally translated, it means 'upside-down words'. The phrase refers to a coded language used by performers in *bhand paether*.
Raantas	See *daen*.
Sarkari	Related to the government.
Shahid	Martyr.
Shamilat	Village commons.
Swarnai	A wind instrument similar to an oboe.
Tehreek	Movement. In Kashmir, it refers to the movement for self-determination, starting with political assertions of Kashmiri identity that gained pace in the 1930s.

GLOSSARY & ABBREVIATIONS

Van moenu	A hirsute forest monster similar to a yeti.
Wanvun	Songs sung by women at Kashmiri weddings, with a specific beat and tune. Often, they are tweaked and improvised according to the context.
Wazir	Minister or important political advisor.
Zulm	Oppression.

List of abbreviations

BSF	Border Security Force
CRPF	Central Reserve Police Force
JKP	Jammu and Kashmir Police
RR	Rashtriya Rifles
SOG	Special Operations Group, often used interchangeably with the Special Task Force
SSB	Sashastra Seema Bal, which literally translates to Armed Border Force
STF	Special Task Force
TA	Territorial Army

NOTES

INTRODUCTION: THE STORYTELLER'S TALE

1. Walter Benjamin, 'The Storyteller: Reflections on the Work of Nikolai Leskov', 1937. Available at: https://arl.human.cornell.edu/linked%20docs/Walter%20Benjamin%20Storyteller.pdf, accessed on 29 October 2024.
2. Hakim Sameer Hamdani, *Shi'ism in Kashmir: A History of Sunni-Shi'i Rivalry and Reconciliation*, London: IB Tauris, 2023.
3. Ibid.
4. Benjamin, 'The Storyteller'.
5. Mohamad Junaid, 'Tehreek History Writers of Kashmir: Reconstructing Memory at the Margins of Post-Colonial Empire', in Mona Bhan, Haley Duschinski, and Deepti Misri (eds), *Routledge Handbook of Critical Kashmir Studies*, Abingdon & New York, NY: Taylor and Francis, 2022, pp. 252–267, p. 256.
6. Amir Sultan Lone, 'British Relations with The Princely State of Jammu and Kashmir', *Proceedings of the Indian History Congress*, Vol. 77, 2016, pp. 348–357, p. 349.
7. Khalid Bashir Ahmad, *Kashmir: Exposing the Myth Behind the Narrative*, New Delhi & Thousand Oaks, CA: Sage, 2017, pp. 75–87.
8. Junaid, 'Tehreek History Writers', p. 258.
9. Ibid.
10. Ibid.
11. Ibid.
12. Ibid., p. 259.
13. Ibid.

14. Ahmad, *Kashmir*, pp. 225–244.
15. Junaid, 'Tehreek History Writers', p. 259.
16. 'Fatalities in Terrorist Violence in Jammu and Kashmir (J&K): 1988–2019 (UMHA)', South Asia Terrorism Portal, https://www.satp.org/datasheet-terrorist-attack/india-jammukashmir/Fatalities-in-Terrorist-Violence-in-jammu-and-Kashmir-1988%E2%80%932019, accessed on 29 October 2024.
17. Association of Parents of Disappeared Persons, 'Facts Under Ground: A Fact-Finding Mission on Nameless Graves and Mass Graves in Uri Area', 2008, https://jkccs.wordpress.com/wp-content/uploads/2017/05/facts-under-ground-first-report-on-mass-graves-in-kashmir.pdf, accessed on 29 October 2024.
18. Srishti Choudhary and Elizabeth Roche, 'IMD lists Gilgit-Baltistan, Muzaffarabad under J&K meteorological sub-division', *Mint*, 7 May 2020, https://www.livemint.com/news/india/imd-lists-gilgit-baltistan-muzaffar-abad-under-j-k-meteorological-sub-division-11588854018288.html, accessed on 29 October 2024.
19. A. G. Noorani, *Article 370: A Constitutional History of Jammu and Kashmir*, New Delhi: Oxford University Press, 2011, p. 2.
20. Noorani, *Article 370*, p. 9.
21. B. K. Nehru, *Nice Guys Finish Second*, New Delhi: Viking Books, 1997, pp. 614–615, cited in Noorani, *Article 370*, p. 12.
22. Ranajit Guha, 'The Small Voice of History', *The Small Voice of History: Collected Essays*, edited by Partha Chatterjee, Delhi: Permanent Black, 2009, pp. 304–317, p. 304.
23. Ibid.
24. Guha, 'The Small Voice of History', p. 316.
25. Nira Wickramsinghe, 'History Outside The Nation', *Economic and Political Weekly*, Vol. 30, No. 26, 1995, pp. 1570–1572, cited in Amit Kumar and Fayaz A. Dar, 'Marginality and Historiography: The Case of Kashmir's History', *Economic and Political Weekly*, Vol. 39, 26 September 2015, pp. 37–44, p. 42.
26. Benjamin, 'The Storyteller'.
27. Masood Hussain, 'Rumour Republic', *Kashmir Life*, 25 January 2016, https://kashmirlife.net/rumour-republic-issue-45-vol-07-94981, accessed on 29 October 2024.

28. Walter Roper Lawrence, *The Valley of Kashmir*, London: Henry Frowde, 1895, p. 8, cited in Hussain, 'Rumour Republic'.
29. Hussain, 'Rumour Republic'.
30. Chitralekha Zutshi, *Kashmir's Contested Pasts: Narratives, Sacred Geographies and the Historical Imagination*, Delhi: Oxford University Press, 2014, p. 21.
31. Ibid., p. 274.
32. Lawrence, *The Valley of Kashmir*, p. 179, cited in Zutshi, *Kashmir's Contested Pasts*, p. 285.
33. Farooq Fayaz, *Kashmir Folklore: A Study in Historical Perspective*, Srinagar: Gulshan Books, 2008, pp. 51–52.
34. Ibid.
35. Ibid., p. 52.
36. Junaid, 'Tehreek History Writers', p. 255.
37. Safwat Zargar, 'Seven Kashmiri students arrested after row over celebrating India's World Cup loss', *Scroll.in*, 27 November 2023, https://scroll.in/latest/1059698/seven-kashmiri-students-arrested-after-row-over-celebrating-indias-world-cup-loss, accessed on 29 October 2024.
38. Safwat Zargar, '"For anything and everything": UAPA cases are rising in Kashmir', *Scroll.in*, 9 April 2021, https://scroll.in/article/991077/for-anything-and-everything-uapa-cases-are-rising-in-kashmir, accessed on 29 October 2024.

1. *ZULM*

1. J. Hinton Knowles, *A Dictionary of Kashmiri Proverbs and Sayings* (1885), Srinagar: Gulshan Books, 2005, p. 60.
2. Farooq Fayaz, *Kashmir Folklore: A Study in Historical Perspective*, Srinagar: Gulshan Books, 2008, p. 57.
3. Shabir Ahmad Mir, 'Ladi Shah', *Kashmir Life*, 17 February 2017, https://kashmirlife.net/ladi-shah-132787, accessed on 29 October 2024.
4. Fayaz, *Kashmir Folklore*, p. 49.
5. Ibid., p. 53.
6. Ibid., pp. 61–62.
7. Ghulam Nabi Aatish, 'Sanyan Luk Kathan Manz Soun Tawarikh' (Our History in our Folk Tales), *Son Adab, Kasher Luk Beth* (Kashmiri Folk Songs), Vol. 11, Srinagar: Jammu and Kashmir Academy of Art, Culture and Languages, 2007, pp. 90–106, cited in Chitralekha Zutshi, *Kashmir's*

Contested Pasts: Narratives, Sacred Geographies and the Historical Imagination, Delhi: Oxford University Press, 2014, p. 301.
8. Ghulam Ahmad Mahjoor. Translated from Kashmiri by Zareef Ahmad Zareef and the author.
9. Walter Roper Lawrence, *The Valley of Kashmir*, London: Henry Frowde, 1895, p. 2.
10. Knowles, *A Dictionary of Kashmiri Proverbs*, p. 17.
11. Hakim Sameer Hamdani, *Shi'ism in Kashmir: A History of Sunni-Shi'i Rivalry and Reconciliation*, London: IB Tauris, 2023, p. 28.
12. Ibid., p. 35.
13. Ibid., p. 34.
14. Ibid., pp. 27–36.
15. Lawrence, *The Valley of Kashmir*, pp. 194–195.
16. Hamdani, *Shi'ism in Kashmir*, p. 28.
17. Ibid., p. 35.
18. Salma Bashir, 'That Reading Room', *Kashmir Life*, 15 March 2017, https://kashmirlife.net/that-reading-room-issue-50-vol-08-134877, accessed on 29 October 2024.
19. Ipsita Chakravarty and Safwat Zargar, 'Comeback of Dogra Rule: With special status gone Kashmiris fear losing hard won land rights once again', *Scroll.in*, 9 September 2019, https://scroll.in/article/936652/comeback-of-dogra-rule-with-special-status-gone-kashmiris-fear-losing-land-rights-once-again, accessed on 29 October 2024.
20. Rayan Naqash, 'Protests after pellet-riddled body of 11-year-old missing boy found near Srinagar's Dachigam', *Scroll.in*, 19 September 2016, https://scroll.in/article/816924/protests-after-pellet-riddled-body-of-a-11-year-old-missing-boy-found-in-srinagars-dachigam, accessed on 29 October 2024.
21. Ipsita Chakravarty, 'Exams are over in Kashmir, but a summer of unrest has left empty seats in classrooms', *Scroll.in*, 8 December 2016, https://scroll.in/article/823550/exams-are-over-in-kashmir-but-a-summer-of-unrest-has-left-empty-seats-in-classrooms, accessed on 29 October 2024.

2. CRACKDOWN *PAETHER*

1. The sketch was recounted by actor Bhawani Bashir Yasir.
2. This is said to be the version of the play recorded in Mohammad Subhan

Bhagat's *Bhand Jashen*, 1984. It was recounted to me by his son, Gul Mohammad Bhagat.
3. R. A. Mir, *Afghan Rule in Kashmir (A Critical Review of Source Material)*, MPhil Dissertation, University of Kashmir, 2011.
4. The story of *Armeen Paether* was told by Arshad Mushtaq, who has adapted the play for the proscenium theatre.
5. Walter Roper Lawrence, *The Valley of Kashmir*, London: Henry Frowde, 1895, p. 88.
6. Hafsa Kanjwal, *Building a New Kashmir: Bakhsi Ghulam Mohammad and the Politics of State-Formation in a Disputed Territory (1953–1963)*, PhD Dissertation, University of Michigan, 2017, pp. 159–204. Available at: https://deepblue.lib.umich.edu/bitstream/handle/2027.42/138699/hafsak_1.pdf?sequence=1&isAllowed=y, accessed on 29 October 2024.
7. Ibid.
8. The Foucauldian idea of a panopticon has been invoked by several Kashmiris describing a surveillance state. Take, for example, this article by Rayan Naqash: 'Panopticon of fear and rumours: Inside Kashmir's media centre during lockdown', *Newslaundry*, 5 February 2020, https://www.newslaundry.com/2020/02/05/a-panopticon-of-fear-and-rumours-inside-kashmirs-media-centre-during-lockdown, accessed on 29 October 2024.
9. Ghulam-Mohi-ud-Din Aajiz, *Folk Theatre of Kashmir*, New Delhi: National Bhand Theatre & Centre for Cultural Resources and Training, 2022, p. 20.

3. YOU MAY BE TURNED INTO A CAT

1. Arif is not his real name. It has been changed to protect his identity as well as SK's.
2. Name changed to protect identities.
3. Prem Mahadevan, 'Counter-Terrorism in the Indian Punjab: Assessing the "Cat" System', *Faultlines*, Vol. 18, January 2007.
4. When he was briefly released in 1958, Sheikh Abdullah himself joined the Plebiscite Front. In 1965, the stub of the old National Conference was merged with the Congress. After Abdullah signed an accord with Delhi in 1975, giving up the demand for self-determination, the Plebiscite Front ceased to exist and the National Conference was revived.
5. After Jammu and Kashmir became a Union Territory in 2019, Radio Kashmir was renamed All India Radio Srinagar.

4. THE BUFFOON KING

1. *Lion of the Desert*, dir. Moustapha Akkad, 1981.
2. Ibid.
3. A famous cricket match between India and Pakistan in 1986. India was on the brink of victory but then Pakistani batsman Javed Miandad scored six runs off the last ball. Pakistan won the match.
4. Jagmohan, *My Frozen Turbulence in Kashmir*, New Delhi: Allied Publishers, 2017, p. 325.
5. Safwat Zargar, 'An assassination, a massacre and the forgotten victims of a Kashmir tragedy', *Scroll.in*, 1 July 2023, https://scroll.in/article/1051761/an-assassination-a-massacre-and-the-forgotten-victims-of-a-kashmir-tragedy, accessed on 29 October 2024.
6. Sushim Mukul, 'When guns got to Kashmir Valley after rigged polls of 1987', *India Today*, 19 April 2024, https://www.indiatoday.in/history-of-it/story/jammu-and-kashmir-1987-assembly-election-pm-modi-lok-sabha-jknc-farooq-abdullah-terrorism-militancy-valley-jklf-2525956-2024-04-19, accessed on 29 October 2024.

5. *RAANTAS*

1. Kim Wale, Pumla Gobodo-Madikizela, and Jeffrey Prager, 'Introduction: Post-Conflict Hauntings', in Wale, Gobodo-Madikizela, and Prager (eds), *Post-Conflict Hauntings: Transforming Memories of Historical Trauma*, London: Palgrave MacMillan, 2020, pp. 1–25.
2. Ibid.
3. Martha Lincoln and Bruce Lincoln, 'Toward a Critical Hauntology: Bare Afterlife and the Ghosts of Ba Chúc', *Comparative Studies in Society and History*, Vol. 57, No. 1, 2015, pp. 191–220.
4. Avery Gordon, *Ghostly Matters: Haunting and the Sociological Imagination*, London & Minneapolis, MN: University of Minnesota Press, 1997, p. xvi.
5. Onaiza Drabu, 'Rantas te Khor', *The Legend of Himal and Nagrai: Greatest Kashmiri Folk Tales*, New Delhi: Speaking Tiger, 2019. Available at: https://onaizad.wordpress.com/2021/01/10/rantas-te-khor, accessed on 29 October 2024.
6. Jacques Derrida, *Specters of Marx: The State of the Debt, the Work of Mourning and the New International*, New York, NY: Routledge, 1994, p. 77, cited in Wale et al., 'Introduction: Post-Conflict Hauntings', p. 6.

6. THE STEEL *DAEN*

1. Sajjad Ahmad, '"Bhoot! Dain!" Will State D.G. Police reveal name of this operation?', *Greater Kashmir*, Srinagar, 20 August 1993.
2. 'The Kashmir Horror Show', *Greater Kashmir*, Srinagar, 19 August 1993.
3. 'Radio Kashmir to relay news from today', *Greater Kashmir*, Srinagar, 11 June 1993.
4. Muzamil Jaleel, 'Daribal killings a challenge to humanity', *Greater Kashmir*, Srinagar, 3 August 1993.
5. '16 killed, 200 injured in violence', *Greater Kashmir*, Srinagar, 4 August 1993.
6. '8 killed in valley: Agitated masses defy curfew', *Greater Kashmir*, Srinagar, 3 August 1993.
7. '"Operation Ghost", A report from J&K Forum for Human Rights and Civil Liberties', *Greater Kashmir*, Srinagar, 20 September 1993.
8. '13 killed, 15 injured in continuing violence', *Greater Kashmir*, Srinagar, 6 September 1993.
9. '"Bhoot" keep people on toes in valley', *Greater Kashmir*, Srinagar, 26 August 1993.
10. Bashar Manzar, '"Bhoot"—the unwanted visitor', *Greater Kashmir*, Srinagar, 30 August 1993.
11. 'Nightmarish experience of civilian locality', *Greater Kashmir*, Srinagar, 6 August 1993.
12. Masood Hussain, '"Ghosts" haunt Srinagar residents', *Kashmir Times*, 8 August 1993.
13. 'Nightmarish experience of civilian locality'.
14. Fayaz Bukhari, 'Changing psyche of Kashmiris', *Greater Kashmir*, Srinagar, 11 September 1993.
15. Abeedullah Zaidi, 'Operation Sarkari Jin: A Grand Flop Show', *Greater Kashmir*, Srinagar, 29 August 1993.
16. Bukhari, 'Changing psyche of Kashmiris'.
17. Zaidi, 'Operation Sarkari Jin'.
18. Gulzar, 'Fatal visits', *Greater Kashmir*, Srinagar, 10 September 1993.
19. Manzar, '"Bhoot"—the unwanted visitor'.
20. Emm Bedar, 'Sopore liberated zone or besieged town?', *Greater Kashmir*, Srinagar, 27 September 1993.

21. Sajjad Ahmad, 'Karen witnesses "enmass" migration', *Greater Kashmir*, Srinagar, 20 September 1993.
22. 'Mass rapes alleged in Budgam villages', *Greater Kashmir*, Srinagar, 31 August 1993.
23. Muzamil Jaleel, 'Bandipora, an orphaned town', *Greater Kashmir*, Srinagar, 2 August 1993.

7. THE BRAID CHOPPERS

1. 'Raat mei logon ki baal kaatne wali 'churail' ka viral sach' (The viral truth about the witch who cuts hair at night), *ABP News*, 23 June 2017, https://web.archive.org/web/20170821122219/http://abpnews.abplive.in/videos/viral-sach-is-there-a-witch-who-chops-off-people-s-hair-while-they-are-asleep-642035, accessed on 29 October 2024.
2. '"Mass hysteria" clue in braid mystery', *The Telegraph Online*, 7 August 2017, https://www.telegraphindia.com/india/mass-hysteria-clue-in-braid-mystery/cid/1521301, accessed on 29 October 2024.
3. Naseer Ganai, '"Ghost" of Braid Chopping in Kashmir: 105 FIRs Filed, Panic in Valley, Police Clueless', *Outlook*, 16 October 2017, https://www.outlookindia.com/amp/story/national/ghost-of-braid-chopping-in-kashmir-105-firs-filed-panic-in-valley-police-clueles-news-303123, accessed on 29 October 2024.
4. 'Braid chopping is an attack on Kashmiri ethos: PDP leader', *Kashmir Life*, 1 October 2017, https://kashmirlife.net/braid-chopping-is-an-attack-on-kashmir-ethos-pdp-leader-152160/, accessed on 29 October 2024.
5. 'National Conference youth wing holds protest against braid-chopping in Srinagar', *Kashmir Life*, 11 October 2017, https://kashmirlife.net/national-conference-youth-wing-holds-protest-against-braid-chopping-in-srinagar-153026, accessed on 29 October 2024.
6. Rayan Naqash, 'Who is chopping women's braids in Kashmir? Depends on whom you ask', *Scroll.in*, 4 October 2017, https://scroll.in/article/852743/who-is-chopping-womens-braids-in-kashmir-depends-on-whom-you-ask, accessed on 29 October 2024.
7. Ganai, '"Ghost" of Braid Chopping in Kashmir'.
8. Ibid.
9. Elke Krasny, 'Hysteria Activism: Feminist Collectives for the Twenty-First

Century', in Johanna Braun (ed.). *Performing Hysteria*, Leuven: Leuven University Press, 2020, pp. 125–146, p 126.
10. C. Tasca, M. Rapetti, M. G. Carta, and B. Fadda, 'Women and hysteria in the history of mental health', *Clinical Practice and Epidemiology in Mental Health*, Vol. 8, 2012, pp. 110–119.
11. Ibid.
12. Essar Batool, Ifra Butt, Samreena Mushtaq, Munaza Rashid, and Natasha Rather, *Do You Remember Kunan Poshpora?*, New Delhi: Zubaan Books, 2016.
13. Siddharth Varadarajan and Manoj Joshi, 'BSF record: Guilty are seldom punished', *The Times of India*, 21 April 2002, https://timesofindia.indiatimes.com/india/bsf-record-guilty-are-seldom-punished/articleshow/7503214.cms, accessed on 29 October 2024.
14. 'Two J&K doctors dismissed for fabricating evidence in 2009 "Shopian rape-murder" case', *The Hindu*, 22 June 2023, https://www.thehindu.com/news/national/other-states/two-jk-doctors-dismissed-for-fabricating-evidence-in-2009-shopian-rape-murder-case/article66997254.ece, accessed on 29 October 2024.
15. G. N. Sagar, 'Kashmiri Women—Soft Target', *Greater Kashmir*, Srinagar, 2 September 1993.
16. Peerzada Arshid Hamid, 'Is our police afraid of *bhoot*?', *Greater Kashmir*, Srinagar, 11 March 2004.
17. Ibid.
18. Arshid Hamid and Malik Abdul Salam, 'Soldier murders girl', *Greater Kashmir*, Srinagar, 15 July 2005.
19. Suhail A. Shah, 'Ghosts of '90's back!', *Kashmir Life*, 28 October 2013, https://kashmirlife.net/ghosts-90s-back-45975, accessed on 29 October 2024.
20. 'That Missing Meem Sahib', *Kashmir Life*, 22 August 2011, https://kashmirlife.net/that-missing-meem-sahab-1691, accessed on 29 October 2024.
21. Ibid.
22. Shaswati Das, 'Modi Independence Day speech: Embracing all Kashmiris can solve Kashmir issue', *Livemint*, 15 August 2017, https://www.livemint.com/Politics/aqhgoWyHOCwRZwpbOOoXSM/Kashmir-problem-cant-be-resolved-through-bullets-or-abuses.html, accessed on 29 October 2024.
23. Elaine Showalter, 'Hystories Revisited: Hysterical Epidemics and Social Media', in Braun (ed.), *Performing Hysteria*, pp. 27–37.

24. 'Six foreign tourist mistaken as "braid choppers" rescued by J-K police', *The Statesmen*, 8 October 2017, https://www.thestatesman.com/india/6-foreign-tourist-mistaken-as-braid-choppers-rescued-by-j-k-police-1502507625.html, accessed on 29 October 2024.
25. Toufiq Rashid, 'Kashmir braid chopping: Vigilantes target tourists, outsiders as police, govt clueless', *Hindustan Times*, 12 October 2017, https://www.hindustantimes.com/india-news/why-the-mehbooba-mufti-government-in-j-k-is-caught-between-a-braid-and-a-hard-place/story-E3oIxgSuhhOwiR0ZeemIIM.html, accessed on 29 October 2024.

8. GHOSTS IN THE GROUND

1. Siddharth Varadarajan, 'Dateline Kashmir: A mother appeals to Mother India for justice', *The Times of India*, 21 August 2000, https://svaradarajan.com/2000/08/21/dateline-kashmir-a-mother-appeals-to-mother-india-for-justice, accessed on 29 October 2024.
2. Mukhtar Ahmad, Basharat Peer, and Onkar Singh, 'I don't need DNA tests to recognise my son', *rediff.com*, 12 March 2002, https://m.rediff.com/news/2002/mar/12spec.htm, accessed on 29 October 2024.
3. Amir Ali Bhat, 'The state aggression that bled the peaceful protest at Brakpora', *Free Press Kashmir*, 3 April 2018, https://freepresskashmir.news/2018/04/03/the-state-aggression-that-bled-the-peaceful-protest-at-brakpora, accessed on 29 October 2024.
4. Jaco Barnard-Naude, 'What Pandora Did: The Spectre of Reparation and Hope in an Irreparable World', in Kim Wale, Pumla Gobodo-Madikizela, and Jeffrey Prager (eds), *Post-Conflict Hauntings: Transforming Memories of Historical Trauma*, London: Palgrave MacMillan, 2020, pp. 67–92.
5. 'Patterns of Impunity: Everyone Lives in Fear', Human Rights Watch, Vol. 18, No. 11 (C), September 2006, p. 60. Available at: https://www.hrw.org/reports/2006/india0906/india0906web.pdf, accessed on 29 October 2024.
6. R. S. Gull, 'Evidently Wrong', *Kashmir Life*, 3 February 2014, https://kashmirlife.net/evidently-wrong4905–53181/, accessed on 29 October 2024.
7. Muzamil Jaleel, 'Why justice eludes the victims of Pathribal fake encounter?', *The Indian Express*, 20 August 2017, https://indianexpress.com/article/india/why-justice-eludes-the-victims-of-pathribal-fake-encounter-4804985, accessed on 29 October 2024; 'Kashmir massacre suspects "innocent"', *BBC News*, 16 July 2002, http://news.bbc.co.uk/1/hi/world/south_asia/2131602.stm, accessed on 29 October 2024.

8. 'Final Report Form (Under Section 173 Cr.P.C.)—In the Court of Chief Judicial Magistrate-cum-Special Magistrate, CBI, Srinagar', CBI chargesheet, 9 May 2006, p. 20. Available at: https://www.scribd.com/document/337493861/CBI-Chargesheet#fullscreen&from_embed, accessed on 29 October 2024.
9. 'Kashmir killings overshadow Clinton visit', *BBC News*, 21 March 2000, http://news.bbc.co.uk/2/hi/south_asia/684632.stm, accessed on 29 October 2024.
10. Sikh News Service, 'Operation Blue Star could have been avoided | Retd Lt Gen KS Gill | PART 1 | SNE', *YouTube*, 5 June 2017, https://www.youtube.com/watch?v=aXivbPvkSzE&t=1832s, accessed on 29 October 2024.
11. Cheryl Lawther, 'Haunting and Transitional Justice: On Lives, Landscapes and Unresolved Pasts in Northern Ireland', in Wale et al. (eds), *Post-Conflict Hauntings*, pp. 153–176.
12. Adrian Levy and Cathy Scott-Clark, *The Meadow: Kashmir 1995—Where the Terror Began*, London: HarperPress, 2012.
13. 'Final Report Form (Under Section 173 Cr.P.C.)', CBI chargesheet, p. 21.
14. *Structures of Violence: The Indian State in Jammu and Kashmir*, International People's Tribunal on Human Rights and Justice in Indian-Administered Jammu and Kashmir (IPTK) and Association of Parents of Disappeared Persons (APDP), September 2015, pp. 20–21.
15. Levy and Scott-Clark, *The Meadow*.
16. J. Robinson, *Transitional Justice and the Politics of Inscription*, Abingdon: Routledge, 2017, p. 26, cited in Lawther, 'Haunting and Transitional Justice', p. 163.
17. Lawther, 'Haunting and Transitional Justice', p. 163.

9. SINGING BODIES

1. Translated from Kashmiri by TK and the author.
2. Ather Zia, *Resisting Disappearance: Military Occupation and Women's Activism in Kashmir*, Seattle, WA: University of Washington Press, 2019, pp. 200–215.
3. Translated from Kashmiri by ZB, the researcher.
4. Suvir Kaul, *Of Gardens and Graves: Kashmir, Poetry, Politics*, Durham, NC: Duke University Press, 2017, pp. 137–140.

5. Translated from Kashmiri by TK and the author.
6. Judith Butler, 'Precariousness and Grievability', *Verso* blog, 16 November 2015, https://www.versobooks.com/en-gb/blogs/news/2339-judith-butler-precariousness-and-grievability?srsltid=AfmBOoqwFwVuF1Egggvjm LnY2Plnpa3zY3iH6NWtP1H_0DQCXL6pNhXx, accessed on 29 October 2024.
7. Judith Butler, 'Violence, Mourning, Politics', *Precarious Life: The Powers of Mourning and Violence*, London & New York, NY: Verso, 2004, pp. 19–49.
8. Translated from Kashmiri by TK and the author.
9. 'First time in decade, number of listed militants crossed 300: Report', *Kashmir Life*, 3 September 2018, https://kashmirlife.net/first-time-in-decade-number-of-listed-militants-crossed-300-report-184974, accessed on 29 October 2024.
10. Translated from Kashmiri by TK and the author.
11. Ghulam Ahmad Mahjoor, 'Arise O Gardener!', *The Best of Mahjoor (Selections From Mahjoor's Kashmiri Poetry)*, translated by Trilokinath Raina, Srinagar: Jammu and Kashmir Academy of Art, Culture and Languages, 1989, p. 103.

10. MELANCHOLIA

1. Sigmund Freud, 'Mourning and Melancholia' (1917), in J. Strachey (ed. and trans.), *The Standard Edition of the Complete Psychological Works of Sigmund Freud*, Vol. 14, London: Hogarth Press, 1953, pp. 243–258.
2. Sigmund Freud, 'The Ego and the Id' (1923), in J. Strachey (ed. and trans.), *The Standard Edition of the Complete Psychological Works of Sigmund Freud*, Vol. 19, London: Hogarth Press, 1961, pp. 12–66, cited in Judith Butler, 'Violence, Mourning, Politics', *Precarious Life: The Powers of Mourning and Violence*, London & New York, NY: Verso, 2004, p. 21.
3. David L. Eng and David Kanijan, 'Introduction: Mourning Remains', in Eng and Kanijan (eds), *Loss: The Politics of Mourning*, Berkeley, CA: University of California Press, 2003, pp. 1–6.
4. Zeynep Tufekci, *Twitter and Tear Gas: The Power and Fragility of Networked Protests*, New Haven, CT: Yale University Press, 2017, p. 6.
5. Ibid.
6. Ibid., pp. 115–131.

7. Ayesha Jalal, *Partisans of Allah: Jihad in South Asia*, Cambridge, MA: Harvard University Press, 2008, pp. 242–264.
8. Ibid.
9. In the legislative assembly elections of 2024, the Jama'at tried to join the fray again, fielding independent candidates as the group has been banned since 2019.
10. Basharat Ali, 'Keeping the Faith', *The Caravan*, 6 April 2019, https://caravanmagazine.in/politics/how-jamaat-e-islami-chronicles-failure-mainstream-politics-kashmir, accessed on 29 October 2024.
11. Safwat Zargar, 'Why a captured militant's family in Kashmir say they'd be better off if their son had been killed', *Scroll.in*, 3 May 2021, https://scroll.in/article/993198/why-a-captured-militants-family-in-kashmir-say-theyd-be-better-off-if-their-son-had-been-killed, accessed on 29 October 2024.
12. Although the Jama'at-e-Islami is believed to have retreated from the armed movement after the nineties, stories from Tral suggest the persistence of certain organic ties with the Hizb.
13. 'Burhan makes news again, this time a video talk', *Kashmir Life*, 26 August 2015, https://kashmirlife.net/burhan-makes-news-again-this-time-a-video-talk-83993, accessed on 29 October 2024.
14. Shams Irfan and Ikhlaq Qadri, 'Shikargah re-opened', *Kashmir Life*, 1 August 2011, https://kashmirlife.net/shikargah-re-opened-1626, accessed on 29 October 2024.
15. Ipsita Chakravarty and Rayan Naqash, 'Valley of "martyrs": Burhan Wani, like others before him, knew he was going to his death', *Scroll.in*, 9 July 2016, https://scroll.in/article/811255/valley-of-martyrs-burhwan-wani-like-others-before-him-knew-he-was-going-to-his-death, accessed on 29 October 2024.

11. THE TRIALS OF MAJNUN

1. See Mahmud Gāmi, *Yusuf's Fragrance*, translated and edited by Mufti Mudasir, India: Penguin Random House, 2022, for English translations of Gāmi's Kashmiri *masnavi*.
2. Chitralekha Zutshi, *Kashmir's Contested Pasts: Narratives, Sacred Geographies and the Historical Imagination*, Delhi: Oxford University Press, 2014, p. 36.
3. Ibid., pp. 52–60.
4. Onaiza Drabu, *The Legend of Himal and Nagrai: Greatest Kashmiri Folk Tales*, New Delhi: Speaking Tiger, 2019, p. 13.

5. Zutshi, *Kashmir's Contested Pasts*, p. 74.
6. Ibid., p. 59.
7. Ibid., p. 169.
8. J. Hinton Knowles, *Folk-Tales of Kashmir* (1893), Delhi: Low Price Publications, 2004, p. 504.

13. FIRDOUS CINEMA

1. In Kashmir, 'Pathan' and 'Afghan' are used interchangeably. This is the same fort completed by Ata Muhammad Khan, the tyrannical Afghan governor governor mentioned in Chapter 1.
2. According to police accounts, they opened fire in retaliation.
3. A local memorial lists sixty-seven names, but residents put the toll at over seventy. See Safwat Zargar, 'An assassination, a massacre and the forgotten victims of a Kashmir tragedy', *Scroll.in*, 1 July 2023, https://scroll.in/article/1051761/an-assassination-a-massacre-and-the-forgotten-victims-of-a-kashmir-tragedy, accessed on 29 October 2024.

15. AFTERLIVES OF LAND

1. Dean Accardi, 'Religious and Political Power in Kashmir', in Mona Bhan, Haley Duschinski and Deepti Misri (eds), *Routledge Handbook of Critical Kashmir Studies*, Abingdon & New York, NY: Taylor and Francis, 2022, pp. 239–251, p. 242.
2. Ibid., p. 241.
3. Ibid., p. 248.
4. Ibid., p. 249.
5. Ibid., p. 250.
6. Mukhtar Ahmed, 'Mystery behind fake encounter case solved', *rediff.com*, 2 February 2007, https://m.rediff.com/news/2007/feb/02fake.htm, accessed on 29 October 2024.
7. Aijaz Hussain, 'Heinous killings and fake encounters in Kashmir, 2007', *India Today*, 11 June 2007, https://www.indiatoday.in/magazine/states/story/20070611-kashmir-fake-enconters-has-perturbed-the-valley2007-748375-2007-06-10, accessed on 29 October 2024.
8. Mohamad Junaid, 'Epitaphs as Counterhistories: Martyrdom, Commemoration, and the Work of Graveyards in Kashmir', in Haley Duschinski, Mona Bhan, Ather Zia, and Cynthia Mahmood (eds), *Resisting Occupation in*

Kashmir, Philadelphia, PA: University of Pennsylvania Press, 2018, pp. 248–277.
9. Ibid.
10. Ibid.
11. Safwat Zargar, 'Was a three-year-old Kashmiri boy the only non-police witness to his grandfather's killing?', *Scroll.in*, 3 July 2020, https://scroll.in/article/966347/was-a-three-year-old-kashmiri-boy-the-only-non-police-witness-to-his-grandfathers-killing, accessed on 29 October 2024.
12. Umer Jan, 'Examining Sacred Necropolitics', in Bhan et al. (eds), *Routledge Handbook of Critical Kashmir Studies*, pp. 308–317.
13. Arif Nazir, 'Habibullah Khan: The "custodian" of "1500 martyrs"', *Free Press Kashmir*, 21 October 2017, https://freepresskashmir.news/2017/10/21/habibullah-khan-the-custodian-of-1500-martyrs, accessed on 29 October 2024.
14. Aditi Saraf, 'Trade, Boundaries and Self-Determination', in Bhan et al. (eds), *Routledge Handbook of Critical Kashmir Studies*, pp. 127–137.
15. Ibid.
16. Association of Parents of Disappeared Persons, 'Facts Under Ground: A Fact-Finding Mission on Nameless Graves and Mass Graves in Uri Area', 2008, https://jkccs.wordpress.com/wp-content/uploads/2017/05/facts-under-ground-first-report-on-mass-graves-in-kashmir.pdf, accessed on 29 October 2024.
17. Khalid Bashir Ahmad, 'The Trendsetter', *Kashmir Life*, 6 December 2009, https://kashmirlife.net/the-trendsetter-2076, accessed on 29 October 2024.
18. According to Aditi Saraf, Kashmir is often imagined in a continuum of '*kaaf*' states—that is, states whose names begin with the Urdu letter '*kaaf*'—along the Silk Route. Saraf, 'Trade, Boundaries and Self-Determination', p. 130.
19. Ipsita Chakravarty, '"They will never get justice": In Kashmir, bitterness about the new turn in the Machil case', *Scroll.in*, 29 July 2017, https://scroll.in/article/845393/they-will-never-get-justice-in-kashmir-bitterness-about-the-new-turn-in-the-machil-case, accessed on 29 October 2024.
20. Shams Irfan, 'SHRC On Unmarked Graves: The Investigation Report', *Kashmir Life*, 26 August 2011, https://kashmirlife.net/full-text-of-the-enquiry-report-of-the-investigation-team-of-jak-shrc-on-unmarked-graves-in-north-kashmir-1702, accessed on 29 October 2024.

CONCLUSION: DISMEMBERMENT

1. Shahnaz Bashir and Safwat Zargar, 'Anatomy of a Disappearance', *Kindle*, 3 June 2016, http://kindlemag.in/anatomy-of-a-disappearance, accessed on 29 October 2024.
2. 'The pain of Dardpora: Kashmiri half-widows living in a state of limbo', *Business Standard*, 6 October 2015, https://www.business-standard.com/article/news-ians/the-pain-of-dardpora-kashmiri-half-widows-living-in-a-state-of-limbo-115100600451_1.html, accessed on 29 October 2024.
3. Launched in 2015, 'Smart Cities Mission' was a much-hyped project of the Narendra Modi government. It started with 100 cities that were picked for infrastructural development and the provision of efficient services.

SELECT BIBLIOGRAPHY

Aajiz, Ghulam Mohi-ud-Din, Folk Theatre of Kashmir, New Delhi: National Bhand Theatre & Centre for Cultural Resources and Training, 2022.

Abdullah, Farooq, My Dismissal, New Delhi: Vikas, 1985.

Abdullah, Sheikh, Flames of the Chinar, translated by Khushwant Singh, New Delhi: Viking, 1993.

Ahmad, Khalid Bashir, Kashmir: Exposing the Myth Behind the Narrative, New Delhi & Thousand Oaks, CA: Sage, 2017.

Atash, Ghulam Nabi, Intangible Cultural Heritage of Kashmir, Srinagar: Jammu and Kashmir Academy of Arts, Culture and Languages, 2018.

Bhan, Mona, Haley Duschinski, and Deepti Misri, editors, Routledge Handbook of Critical Kashmir Studies, Abingdon & New York, NY: Taylor and Francis, 2022.

Bhat, Javaid Iqbal, 'Loss of a Syncretic Theatrical Form', Folklore: Electronic Journal of Folklore, No. 34, 2006. Available at: https://www.folklore.ee/folklore/vol34/bhat.pdf.

Braun, Johanna, editor, Performing Hysteria, Leuven: Leuven University Press, 2020.

Butler, Judith, Precarious Life: The Powers of Mourning and Violence, London & New York, NY: Verso, 2004.

———, Frames of War: When Is Life Grievable?, London & New York, NY: Verso, 2009.

Drabu, Onaiza, The Legend of Himal and Nagrai: Greatest Kashmiri Folk Tales, Delhi: Speaking Tiger, 2019.

SELECT BIBLIOGRAPHY

Eng, David L., and David Kanijan, editors, Loss: The Politics of Mourning, Berkeley, CA: University of California Press, 2003.

Fayaz, Farooq, Kashmir Folklore: A Study in Historical Perspective, Srinagar: Gulshan Books, 2008.

Foucault, Michel, Discipline and Punish: The Birth of the Prison (1975), translated by Alan Sheridan, London: Penguin Classics, 2020.

Gāmi, Mahmud, Yusuf's Fragrance, translated and edited by Mufti Mudasir, India: Penguin Random House, 2022.

Gordon, Avery F., Ghostly Matters: Haunting and the Sociological Imagination, London & Minneapolis, MN: University of Minnesota Press, 1997.

Guha, Ranajit, The Small Voice of History: Collected Essays, edited by Partha Chatterjee, Delhi: Permanent Black, 2009.

Hamadani, Hakim Sameer, Shi'ism in Kashmir: A History of Sunni-Shi'i Rivalry and Reconciliation, London: IB Tauris, 2023.

Jagmohan, My Frozen Turbulence in Kashmir, New Delhi: Allied Publishers, 2017.

Jalal, Ayesha, Partisans of Allah: Jihad in South Asia, Cambridge, MA: Harvard University Press, 2008.

Kanjwal, Hafsa, Building a New Kashmir: Bakhsi Ghulam Mohammad and the Politics of State-Formation in a Disputed Territory (1953–1963), PhD Dissertation, University of Michigan, 2017. Available at: https://deepblue.lib.umich.edu/bitstream/handle/2027.42/138699/hafsak_1.pdf?sequence=1&isAllowed=y.

Kaul, Suvir, Of Gardens and Graves: Kashmir, Poetry, Politics, Durham, NC: Duke University Press, 2017.

Knowles, J. Hinton, A Dictionary of Kashmiri Proverbs and Sayings (1885), Srinagar: Gulshan Books, 2005.

———, Folk-Tales of Kashmir (1893), Delhi: Low Price Publications, 2004.

Lawrence, Walter Roper, The Valley of Kashmir, London: Henry Frowde, 1895.

Levy, Adrian, and Cathy Scott-Clark, The Meadow: Kashmir 1995—Where the Terror Began, London: HarperPress, 2012.

Menon, Jisha, Performance of Nationalism: India, Pakistan and the

SELECT BIBLIOGRAPHY

Memory of Partition, Cambridge & New York, NY: Cambridge University Press, 2013.

Noorani, A. G., Article 370: A Constitutional History of Jammu and Kashmir, New Delhi: Oxford University Press, 2011.

Rai, Mridu, Hindu Rulers, Muslim Subjects: Islam, Rights, and the History of Kashmir, London: Hurst, 2004.

Schofield, Victoria, Kashmir in Conflict: India, Pakistan and the Unending War, London & New York, NY: IB Tauris, 2000.

Tufekci, Zeynep, Twitter and Tear Gas: The Power and Fragility of Networked Protests, New Haven, CT: Yale University Press, 2017.

Wale, Kim, Pumla Gobodo-Madikizela, and Jeffrey Prager, editors, Post-Conflict Hauntings: Transforming Memories of Historical Trauma, London: Palgrave MacMillan, 2020.

Zia, Ather, Resisting Disappearance: Military Occupation and Women's Activism in Kashmir, Seattle, WA: University of Washington Press, 2019.

Zutshi, Chitralekha, Kashmir's Contested Pasts: Narratives, Sacred Geographies, and the Historical Imagination, New Delhi: Oxford University Press, 2014.

INDEX

agencies, 26, 27, 28, 66, 82, 83, 104, 120, 135, 139, 140, 148, 160, 188, 190, 200, 203, 277, 278, 279
Akanandun, 214, 273–275
Akbar-e-Noujawan, 2
Akingam, 54, 59–60, 70–72, 74, 75, 109–110, 217, 286
Angrez Paether, 55, 76
Armeen Paether, 55
Article 370, 92, 275, 280
Awuzan, 72
Azadi, 6, 8, 9, 26, 46, 57, 76, 93, 94, 103, 114, 121, 126, 182, 192, 194, 199, 205, 212, 224, 225, 231, 234, 235, 239, 275, 281, 293
Azad Kashmir, 11, 265

Bangladesh, 10, 127, 128
Beacon, 146
Before I Forget (2024), 17
bhand paether, 52–78, 91, 245, 293, 295

allegorical worlds, 91
at Chadoora Government Degree College, 76
Chakdar Paether rehearsal at Wathora, 76
crackdown jokes, 67
coded language, 22, 56
crackdown circles, 57, 59
dark humour, 22
dying out, 61–64
old story of *zulm*, 53
programmes on state channels, 22
roots of, 54
secrets of language, 56
Shikargah Paether performance near Mohripora, 75
Tagore Hall performance, 77–78
tenuous return, 74
the tyrants of history, stock plays about, 20
bhoot, 115, 119, 120, 127, 128, 131, 151, 162, 165, 293

317

INDEX

blood maps, 24, 220, 221, 234, 240
Border Security Force (BSF), 26, 69–70, 74, 83, 85, 87–88, 123–124, 144, 224–228, 238, 246, 252, 296
Border war of 1947–48, 6, 7, 39, 82
braid choppers, 23, 116, 137–150
Buffoon king, 89–106
Burhan Wani, 23–24, 185–207, 233, 235
    beaten up, 33–34
    death of, 178, 181, 204
    funeral, 179–182
    journey to militancy, 193–195
    militant ranks, 197–200
    networked public, 189–190
    poem for, 183–184
    poster, 196
    protests, 34, 139
    stories, 185–188
    video release, 191, 201, 207
    wedding songs, 171, 172, 179

cats (informers), 79–88
    cat under duress, 82
    KF, 86
    making of, 85
    militants, 83
    on the payrolls of agencies, 82
    security term, 81
Central Reserve Police Force (CRPF), 27, 66, 74, 145, 156, 157–158, 181, 222, 228, 231, 232, 233, 246, 252, 282, 296

Chakdar Paether, 55, 76
The Collaborator (2011), 17
Congress, 7, 45, 91-92, 96, 98, 100, 102, 103
Crackdown *Paether*, 51–78
Curfewed Night (2008), 16

daen 23, 118–136
    anti-militancy operations, 127
    cousin to, 138
    curfews and shootings, 124–125
    curious affinities, 119
    fear psychosis, 120, 129
    features of haunting, 119
    feet turned backwards, 114
    ghostly incursions, 145
    haunting, 126
    in Mehjoor Nagar, 129
    in news reports and editorials, 121–122
    in North Kashmir, 130
    no psyops, 148
    old names for a new terror, 115
    special news-reel, 131
    spring boots, 119
    ZM, 117–119, 133
Darze Paether, 55, 91
dastaangoh, 20, 24, 28, 213–218, 245, 294
dhukar, 37
disappearance, 10, 146, 276, 35, 270-271
disappeared, 64, 109, 114, 146, 157, 174, 258, 265, 276, 277
Dogra forces, 6, 7

INDEX

Dogra rule, 6, 44, 46, 47, 183
Dogra state, 6, 10, 12, 44, 183, 267
Do You Remember Kunan Poshpora? (2016), 17

Eidgah, 102, 180, 181, 233–234, 247, 255–256, 261–263, 282

Farooq Abdullah, 90, 91, 96, 97, 98, 105
Firdous Cinema, 188, 235–236, 241–247

ghosts, 23, 109, 120–121, 123, 125, 128–129, 131–132, 134, 138, 139, 140, 145, 149, 151–167
Ghulam Ahmad Mahjoor, 40, 183
Gilgit-Baltistan, 10, 11
graves, 58, 166, 182, 212, 256, 258, 260, 262–265, 268–271
Gul Shah, 96, 98
Gulrez, 20, 214, 215

Habba Khatoon, 43, 46, 175, 276
Haalaat (time after 1989), 2, 3
    AB, 84
    Anantnag mountains, 162
    argot of conflict, 81
    atmospheric conditions, 2
    bad news men, 42
    bhand paether, 59
    blood map, 24, 221
    communication between public and government, 57
    dissociation from the self, 143

Doordarshan offices, 104
downtown Srinagar, 247
euphemisms of, 235
Firdous Cinema, 244–245
first turned bad, 51
forbidden to refer to, 279
frenzy of hope and death, 115
a ghost story, 109
groups from Pakistan, 198
Haalaat kharaab hua, 2
Hazaar Dastaan, 105
interrogation centres, 251
map of the Valley, 220
markaz ki chaal, 98
massive crackdowns, 74
Maulvi Farooq, 100
new haunting, 118
new terrors, 114
no town or village exempt, 162
Pandit mohalla, 165
Pandits of Sopore, 224
people who had died in custody, 275
possession, 212
press under siege, 121
PSA, 63
Sarangis were burnt, 218
shadow war between agencies, 26
shadow worlds, 219
shahid malguzar, 260
Shikargah, 202
soldiers who did not speak or understand Kashmiri, 67
solidarity worked by, 222

INDEX

special operations groups camps, 229
story of, 3, 4, 28, 109, 212
Subhan Bhagat, 71–72
Tagore Hall, 66
taste of fear, 15–16
two stories about any news event, 17
van moenu, 146
visit the 'martyrs' graveyard, 285, 293
Wathora, 64
wedding songs, 23, 173, 177
women, symptom bearers of, 141
worst days of, 106
Har Ghar Tiranga, 75
Hari Singh, 6, 7
hartal, 9, 26, 174, 234, 268, 294
Hazaar Dastaan, 22, 90–105
Himal-Nagrai, 214, 273, 274–275
Hizbul Mujahideen, 100, 140, 146, 171, 180, 190, 199, 200
Hizb, 84, 87–88, 103, 172, 195–200, 202, 203, 206, 281, 282
AB, 84
arrested some mysterious creatures, 128
Burhan Wani, 23, 33–34, 196, 201, 205
goal of, 179
rude and crude propaganda, 131
sword arm of Jama'at, 195
TK, 172

Hurriyat, 9, 10, 14, 87, 103, 121, 140, 194, 200, 231, 234, 262
hysteria, 142, 147

Ikhwan, 135, 152, 161, 163–164, 172, 282
Indian Constitution
   Article 370, 12, 13
   Article 35A, 12, 13, 255–256
Instrument of Accession in October 1947, 7

Jaish-e-Mohammad, 198
Jama'at-e-Islami, 34, 193–195, 197, 199, 222
Jammu and Kashmir Liberation Front (JKLF), 9, 79, 80, 93, 103, 188, 197, 201, 262
Jammu and Kashmir Public Safety Act (PSA), 14, 25, 36, 63
Jammu and Kashmir Reorganisation Act, 13
Jawaharlal Nehru, 7, 8, 13, 39, 45
joint resistance leadership, 9

khilafat, 199, 200, 202, 205, 294
Khizar Sochta Hai Wular Ke Kinare, 19
khoftan fakir, 82

ladi shah, 20, 22, 36–40, 48–49, 294
Lal Chowk, 7, 25, 86, 93, 200, 232, 234, 237, 239, 277, 278, 279
land
   afterlife, 14, 255

INDEX

Amarnath Shrine Board, 232, 234
Asadullah Parray, 256–261
bhand paether, 53
Dogra, 6, 42, 46, 47
Eidgah, 255–256, 261–263
Firdous Cinema, 241, 243
gardens of Gannak, 286
graveyard, 262–264
haunted by traumatic events, 162
Kalaroos Khas, 266–272
Line of Control, 264–265
metaphor for experience, 220
milkiyat, 255, 268
mourning the militant, 179
Mughals, 44
Pandit mohalla, 164
Paradise, 261
permanent residents, 13, 14
shamilat, 255, 275
state, 255
Sufi mystics, 216
to tillers, 45, 92, 255
Lashkar-e-Taiba, 152, 155, 160, 198, 201
Life in the Clocktower Valley (2021), 17
Line of Control (LoC), 10–11, 12, 16, 25, 84, 99, 103, 162, 175, 193, 199, 220, 230, 262, 264, 265, 268, 270, 277

magun
Ghulam Ali Majboor, 64–65

Subhan Bhagat, 60–62, 70–72
Majnun, 24, 211–213, 214, 215, 216, 219, 220
markaz, 26, 35, 44, 66, 74, 81, 82, 87, 98, 99, 102, 144, 148, 187, 275, 278, 284
melancholia, 184, 185–207
Mirwaiz Mohammad Farooq, 99, 100, 247, 262, 263
Mirwaiz Umar Farooq, 9–10, 103, 231
Mohamad Ismail Mir, legendary dastaangoh, 213, 218
Mughals, 35, 42, 44, 242, 285
mukhbir, 133, 179, 187, 197, 259, 282, 294
Muslim United Front, 102
Muzaffarabad *chalo*, 262
Myean Jigraki Daade Wath, 1

National Conference, 8, 39, 40, 45, 46, 81, 90, 92, 93, 94, 96, 97, 98, 100, 101, 102, 103, 139, 183, 194, 282
nuun draag, 38–40

Of Occupation and Resistance (2013), 16
Operation Bhoot, 131
Operation Catch and Kill, 135, 140
Operation Ghost, 133, 135, 140
Operation Sarkari Jin, 131–132
Operation Swift, 159

Peace Brigade, 82

INDEX

phir kath, 53, 56, 59, 64, 65, 67, 81, 86, 275, 294
pink salt, 38, 40, 41
possession syndrome, 143

raantas, 23, 109–116, 136, 140, 141, 142, 143, 148, 152, 238, 285, 287, 294–295
Raaze Paether, 55
raffal, 68
Rajiv Gandhi, 62, 98, 102, 283
Rashtriya Rifles, 26, 115, 145, 163, 296
Reading Room Party, 44
Rumours of Spring: A Girlhood in Kashmir (2021), 17

Salt, history of, 39
memento of oppression, 41
satirical poet of, 184
shortage, 38
song, 40
Sehlaab Singh, 38
Shabir Ahmed Mir, 35–37, 47–49
Sheikh Abdullah, 7–8, 39, 44–47, 61, 63, 81, 91, 92, 93, 94, 100, 183, 255
Shikargah Paether, 52–53, 55, 63, 67, 75, 77
Smart City, 278, 279
special operations group (SOG), 27, 74, 155, 156, 157, 229, 230, 249, 250
swarnai, 52, 53, 57, 60, 89, 273, 287, 295

Syed Ali Shah Geelani, 9–10, 103, 140, 194, 200, 201
Syed Salahuddin, 103, 146, 199, 201

Tagore Hall, 61, 65, 66, 77, 273–275
tehreek, 6
aim of, 6
Akingam, 70–71
All Parties Hurriyat Conference, 9
anthem, 80, 183
anti-colonial and armed movement, 8
Ashfaq Majeed Wani, 188
Batamaloo mosque, 237
Burhan Wani, 187, 204, 206
cats, 83
Chittisingpora, 153
daytime belongs to, 126
Eidgah, 261, 263
graveyards, 25
Greater Kashmir, 121
history of, 6–7
Jama'at-e-Islami, 194
joined the Jammu and Kashmir Liberation Front, 79
killing of Kashmiri Pandits, 8–9
leaders of, 281
liberated zones, 85
life of, 5
Line of Control, 220, 265
militarisation in Kashmir, 10
Mirwaiz Mohamad Farooq, 100

INDEX

Nawabazar, 238
New Kashmir, 224
new histories, 21
object of, 205
plebiscite, 7
political grief, 179
political leaders of, 7
public vocabulary, 260
serious business, 57
social media, 189–191
Syed Ali Shah Geelani, 140
the time we gave, 283
TK, 184
Tral, 181
words with mythic weight, 26
younger brother and sister, 284
torture specialists, BSF, 85, 87

Viksit Bharat, 75

Walter Roper Lawrence, 19, 41, 56
wanvun, 173, 174, 175, 179, 296
wazir, 89, 95, 91, 92, 98, 216

Yasin Malik, 9–10, 193
Yusuf Shah Chak, 43–44, 46–47

Zainakadal, 18, 19, 280

Zakir Musa, Hizbul Mujahideen militant, 180, 184, 193, 198, 199, 200
Zee Horror Show, 120
zulm, 33–49
  bhand paether, 53, 55, 62, 75
  Burhan Wani, 34, 193, 201, 203
  crackdown circles, 57
  cut across ideological faultlines, 46
  five hundred years, 34, 45, 115
  the heaviest word in Kashmir, 35
  history of, 42
  the Hizb, 281
  horizon of Kashmiri political life, 22
  in the present and in the past, 284
  Insha Malik, 47
  kinds of, 280
  ladi shah, 37, 48
  origin story of, 197
  photographic record, 190
  Shias, 236
  story of, 16
  Tk's brother, 172
  worshippers of tyranny, 41, 49